If These WALLS *Could* TALK

Michigan Football Stories from The Big House

Jon Falk with Dan Ewald

TRIUMPH
BOOKS

This book is available in quantity at special discounts for your group or organization. For further information, contact:

Triumph Books
542 South Dearborn Street
Suite 750
Chicago, Illinois 60605
(312) 939–3330
Fax (312) 663–3557
www.triumphbooks.com

Printed in U.S.A.
ISBN: 978-1-60078-657-0
Design by Amy Carter
Photos courtesy of the authors

No play, no game, no championship season can match the warmth of family love.

For my wife, Cheri, and all her support through the long hours and demands of a job that only she understands. To our children, Joe Winkle, Nicki Pfefferle (and husband Kurt), and Katie. To our 12-year-old grandson, Joey. To Cheri's parents, Ramona and Pete Boychuck, who welcomed me into the family. And to my mother, Jean Falk, and grandmother, Rosella Land. I thank all for the love and support they have contributed to my success.

And a special thanks to all the Michigan players, coaches, staff, and fans over all these years who have given me these stories to share with all.

—Jon Falk

The Falk family. Back row (left to right): Son Joe Winkle, wife Cheri Falk, Jon Falk, son-in-law Kurt Pfefferle, and daughter Nicki Pfefferle. Front row (left to right): Grandson Joey Winkle and daughter Katie Falk.

Contents

Foreword

Everyone knows the equipment manager is responsible for all uniforms and each piece of equipment used by the players and coaches of a football team.

But only the players and coaches truly understand how Jon Falk has redefined the position at the University of Michigan.

Describing all the intangibles he brings to the table is like trying to stuff a hundred rabbits into a single magician's hat. It's all those little things that make him one of the most valuable members of the team.

Michigan football is filled with tradition. And after being at Michigan for what seems like forever, Falk has become a tradition himself.

He's an extra arm to the coaching staff. He's a shoulder to lean on for the players. I can't count how many times I spent with Big Jon as he searched for just the right word to help me make it through a tough time. He never let me down.

Big Jon has a keen mind for history. He knows more about Michigan football than all the books written since the days of Fielding Yost. He's a cheerleader, historian, mentor, counselor, and friend. All players eventually have to leave the University of Michigan. But no one ever leaves Big Jon.

A tribute to his loyalty to Michigan is the fact that he's the only member of the team left to have been hand-picked by Bo. Because of his unique position,

Big Jon is the keeper of stories that have evolved over the last nearly 40 years. They've all become little pieces of tradition. And he's happy to share a few with you. While a handful of people may come close, no one will top Big Jon Falk's loyalty to the University of Michigan.

Thanks for everything, Jon.

—Tom Brady

Preface: Tradition Born

Traditions are less about things than the people who have made them.

Makers leave a legacy for future generations to follow. Thirty-eight years after being hired by Bo Schembechler as equipment manager for Michigan football, Jon Falk's legacy is secure.

Falk's title of equipment manager is grossly understated. Would anyone call Santa Claus merely another toy-maker?

"Totally misleading," former All-American Curtis Greer stated emphatically about the title. "Phony as a pirate's map. Big Jon should be called 'vice president of football operations from 1974 'til whenever he decides to leave.' Nothing happens 'til Big Jon makes it happen."

From Bo to Gary Moeller to Lloyd Carr to Rich Rodriguez, to Brady Hoke, Falk has made it happen as the lone man in the storied Michigan program to enjoy such a run.

In his position, Falk is responsible for all matters pertaining to equipment. From the shoelaces on the cleats of the least-likely-to-play walk-on to the bottles of Future Floor Wax that are used to shine those magnificent maize and blue winged helmets, Falk is in charge.

But his passion for Michigan football has lifted him to another level of friend, mentor, cheerleader, historian, and shoulder to lean on for coaches and players for almost four decades.

One of Falk's primary responsibilities is maintaining the integrity of the locker room. In sports, there is no more sacred sanctuary where coaches teach, players learn, and character is built.

It's there where Falk shines even more than those freshly polished helmets.

It's still dark at 6:00 AM on a crisp September Saturday. Throughout the state, even some of the heartiest tailgaters have yet to rise.

At Schembechler Hall, the nerve center of Michigan football, however, Falk, two of his assistants, and a half-dozen student managers already have gulped their first cup of coffee and are primed for a game at The Big House.

All squeeze into a van for the short ride to Michigan Stadium where another assistant, another half-dozen student workers, and a handful of volunteers are busy preparing for a game still six hours from kickoff.

Eastern Michigan University is not the marquis match that Notre Dame was, which Michigan rallied to defeat the previous week. But it doesn't matter to Falk, who treats each game as if it were the Rose Bowl. It's the only way Falk has operated since Bo hired him as a 22-year-old in 1974.

Most of the preparations were done the day before. But as morning creeps into daylight, so many details still must be addressed. The image of college football's winningest program must always be maintained.

There's a litany of last-minute preparations to complete. Even the tiniest unforeseen glitch must be 100 percent resolved before the first player steps into the locker room.

Herb Frederick is an 83-year-old volunteer who has served his beloved university for 67 years. He, along with his grown grandsons, meticulously polish those distinctive Michigan helmets that are known throughout the country.

Frederick has worked under all coaches beginning with Fritz Crisler. He's tended to all the players from Tom Harmon to Denard Robinson. He feels firsthand how the game has grown and become more complex even for those who work behind the scenes.

And he marvels at the vibrant artistry Falk applies to his role.

"The first thing he did when he came here as a young man was to take all of us out to dinner," Frederick said. "He didn't act like he knew everything. He wanted to learn. He knows how to get along with people. Knows when to talk and when to shut up."

Shortly after arriving at the stadium, Falk crosses the field for the long trek up the 95 rows of seats and into the press box. In a corner booth are all the controls for the 15 headsets worn by the coaching staff.

Electronic communication between all the coaches is a critical aspect of the modern game. Falk needs to claim a wavelength early to ensure uninterrupted clarity between the head coach and all of his assistants.

After meticulously checking each set, he makes the long trek down. This time he decides to double-check a switch just one more time. So he reverses his path for another trip up into the clouds.

Upon reaching the field, he tapes cards to the backs of the player benches indicating where each player is to sit or stand during the game according to position.

Walking across the field toward the locker room, Falk's mind is churning with minute details that must be addressed. He is generally chirping and does his best thinking out loud. He barks each order clearly and precisely so as to leave no doubt how a job must be done.

In the equipment room he dispenses the 12 game balls for student assistants to brush with leather to increase the tack. When finished and inspected by Falk, the footballs are stuffed into bags and transported to the officials' room for inspection.

Yard markers are dispensed to the crew. Then two game officials drop in for small talk and to inquire if there are special instructions for any of the day's proceedings.

Most of them have known Falk for years. Few unexpected problems ever occur at Michigan. If one happens to arise, they are confident Falk can get it resolved.

The previous week an official noticed a Michigan player had stuck his mouth guard inside two bars of his facemask. A couple of plays later, the official discreetly spoke to Falk on the sideline.

"Tell your man the guard goes in the mouth, not the mask," he told Falk between plays.

Falk always asks the officials to look at players' uniforms before the start of the game. "Let me know before the game if anything is wrong," he tells them. "I can fix it easier now than after the game starts."

As players run through pregame practice on the field, Falk stands silently perusing each man for any late adjustments needed to a uniform or piece of equipment.

As if with the graceful flip of a matador's cape, Falk handles myriad details before they're even noticed. And all the while he's greeting select visitors with the guile of a politician 24 hours before voting day.

Before this particular game, one locker-room visitor is Olympic swimming legend Michael Phelps, who formerly trained at the University of Michigan.

"Where's your Michigan shirt?" he asks the storied Olympian.

When Phelps answers he left it at home, Falk goes to a supply in the storeroom and hands him a new one.

There is no room for error in locker-room decorum. And this is where Falk separates himself from the crowd in his position.

As game time draws near, he orders all student managers sitting in the equipment room to "cut the levity." And when he enters the locker room for the pregame talk by the head coach, he's as focused as a sniper protecting the president. When the coach is finished, it's Falk's turn to implore a player's best.

"Play like Michigan," he shouts while smacking players on their shoulder pads. "We are Michigan. Let them know we are Michigan."

Even the young players quickly become accustomed to Falk's precision and peculiarities that became legendary long before they were born.

Perhaps even Bo never anticipated Falk's 38 years. But that's how traditions grow. And Falk will never forget the day it all began.

—Dan Ewald

Section 1

The Future

Chapter **1**

This Is About Tradition

In a corner of the window of his Schembechler Hall office, Jon Falk keeps a poster board sign displayed for all coaches, players, staff members, and visitors to see. Captured in bold black letters is the concise essence of what Michigan Football is all about. It reads:

> *"Tradition is something you can't bottle.*
> *You can't buy it at the corner store. But it is there to sustain you when you need it most. I've called upon it time and time again. And so have countless other Michigan athletes and coaches. There is nothing like it.*
> *I hope it never dies."* —*Fritz Crisler*

Crisler, of course, was one of Michigan's legendary head coaches. He didn't create this sometimes nebulous concept called *tradition*. The tradition of Michigan football is something that has developed and enhanced itself over more than a century.

In fact, no university is as tradition-rich as is the University of Michigan. That's what keeps the spirit so vibrant. That's what makes all loyal Michigan supporters feel so proud.

"The University of Michigan is such a special place," Falk proudly states. "The tradition and reputation of Michigan can get a graduate through almost any door. Now what happens after getting inside is up to the individual. But that Michigan name and Michigan history is a powerful piece of influence."

When it comes to the tradition of Michigan football, there is no one more equipped to appreciate it or willing to share it with others than Falk. He has been part of the history for so long that he's become a tradition of the program himself.

Ask any of the players from Curtis Greer to Desmond Howard to Charles Woodson to Michael Hart to Denard Robinson. Each eagerly confirms that Falk has become as much a piece of the fabric as those inimitable stripes that streak each helmet.

Hired by Bo in 1974, he is the lone member of the football staff to have served, Bo, Gary Moeller, Lloyd Carr, Rich Rodriguez, and now Brady Hoke.

It's only a slice of fantasy that Falk used to pump up the footballs for Fielding Yost.

The myriad traditions of Michigan Football are numerous enough to fill the fabled Big House all by themselves. There are the striking winged helmets. The Little Brown Jug. The in-state rivalry with Michigan State. The annual season-ending game with Ohio State. The Heisman Trophy winners. The Big Ten championships. The National championships.

Under the leadership of Athletic Director Dave Brandon, a new tradition is one of the highlights of the 2011 season: the Big House's first official night game—against Notre Dame—under the new, permanently installed light towers.

Of course, one of the most prestigious traditions of Michigan is the distinction of being the winningest program in Division I football. Michigan entered the 2011 season with 884 victories

Falk, incidentally, has been part of 327 of those victories. With 451 games under his belt, he has participated in 37 percent of all Michigan games ever played.

"Think about that," Falk said. "In the history of college football, no school has more wins than Michigan! That's superiority and longevity. Those are the two most critical measuring sticks for greatness."

Perhaps the most precious single piece of the university's tradition is the essence of the "Michigan Man." Bo understood the concept when he popularized the term decades ago. And it's probably what Crisler had in mind when he wrote those words about tradition more than a half-century ago.

To become a Michigan Man, a player, a coach, or any member of the football staff must not only appreciate all of the history that precedes him, but also accept the responsibility attached to representing a university that sets itself apart from the ordinary.

"Dave Brandon is a true Michigan Man," Falk said. "He played for Bo. He represented the university by serving on the Board of Regents. And he displayed outstanding leadership in the business world after graduating from Michigan."

That's why Falk never felt concerned over who would be named the head coach for the 2011 season after the dismissal of Rodriguez in January 2011.

"I knew Dave would pick the right man," Falk said. "And he did. Now we just have to go out and work hard to get back to where Michigan belongs."

Leading that charge is head coach Brady Hoke, who served as an assistant under Carr for five years before leaving to acquire head-coaching experience at Ball State and San Diego State.

"No question Brady is a Michigan Man," Falk said. "He accepted the responsibilities when he was here as an assistant. He fell in love with Michigan when he was growing up in the Midwest. He's got a work ethic that would make Paul Bunyan look like a slouch. He's an up-front, no-nonsense sort of guy. He also has a sense of humor and can laugh at himself. I think Bo would be proud traveling anywhere in the country and telling everyone he met how comfortable he felt with Brady as the head coach."

With Hoke's return comes the return of another Michigan tradition—the one about defense being the foundation to success in the Big Ten. The Michigan faithful who fill The Big House never did get used to their defense being pushed around the field.

With Denard Robinson at quarterback, an experienced offensive line, and a long list of capable receivers, the offense promises to be explosive. Coupled with some smashmouth defenders looking to unleash a barrel full of pent-up frustrations, Michigan has the opportunity to return to its more familiar place atop the Big Ten standings.

"I was really impressed with the staff that Brady was able to assemble so quickly," Falk said. "They're all going to become Michigan Men quickly...very quickly."

Tradition alone does not win championships. It takes committed coaches. It demands talented and dedicated players. It requires the collective effort of staff, former players, and alumni.

But any Michigan team lacking a sense of tradition is bound to stumble. And Hoke, Brandon, and particularly the Michigan faithful simply refuse to accept that.

"I think we're heading for a very exciting period in Michigan football history," Falk said. "All the pieces are coming together. I see more former players returning to visit the campus. I get a sense of cohesiveness. It may not happen overnight, but it's going to happen quickly and it's going to be exciting. Like Coach Crisler wrote long ago, I hope this tradition never dies."

Chapter **2**

The Penalty of Leadership

In his desk, Jon Falk keeps a copy of a full-page Cadillac Motor Car Company advertisement that appeared in *The Saturday Evening Post* on January 2, 1915.

It's the kind of inspirational material upon which Bo feasted. How he got it, no one knows. Borrowing from the copy, however, Bo developed a theme for one of his classic speeches that he delivered to his teams each August before practice for a new season began.

The headline reads "The Penalty of Leadership" and the ad depicts the pressures that every true leader of any field must endure year after year. The advertisement reads:

"In every field of human endeavor, he that is first must perpetually live in the white light of publicity. Whether the leadership be vested in a man or in a manufactured product, emulation and envy are ever at work. In art, in literature, in music, in industry, the reward and the punishment are always the same. The reward is widespread recognition; the punishment fierce denial and detractions. When a man's work becomes a standard for the whole world, it also becomes the target for the shafts of the envious few. If his work be merely mediocre he will be left severely alone—if he achieves a masterpiece, it will set a million tongues a wagging. Jealousy does not protrude its forked tongue at the artist who produces a commonplace painting. Whatsoever you write or paint or play or sing or build, no one will strive to surpass you or slander you, unless your work be stamped with the seal of genius.

"There's nothing new in this. It is as old as the world, and as old as human passions—envy, fear, greed, ambition, and a desire to pass. And it all avails nothing. If the leader truly leads, he remains—the leader. Master-poet, master-painter, master workman, each in his turn is assailed, and each holds his laurels through the ages. That which is good or great makes itself known, no matter how loud the clamor of denial. That which deserves to live—lives."

Bo loved the simple message so eloquently stated. The message to his teams was equally simple and straight to the heart. The "leaders and the best," as referred to in "The Victors," must always be prepared for the challenge of the "envious few."

"I can hear him talking every time I read that advertisement," Falk said. "His voice gives me goose bumps each time. That advertisement came from 1915! What's changed over all those years? Nothing! When you're the best, you expect to wear a target on your back. That's what we expect at Michigan. That's the way it should be.

"Michigan is a leader. Michigan is the best. You have to be able to handle all the things included in this ad. I think Michigan grads are some of the best in this country because they learn to live with all of this on their shoulders. The football players have to live with this envy and jealousy every day."

Results of the 2008–2010 seasons certainly did not reach those lofty expectations. And those "envious few" pounced upon the Wolverines to extract a pound of flesh.

"What's done is done," Falk said. "But just remember...the pounced can turn into the 'pouncers' pretty quickly. We will be back. And we do have a few scores to settle."

Michigan's string of dominance ran for four consecutive decades. In the modern era of college football where parity has become as common as an extra point, that's only a few years short of eternity.

"Just look at all of the big name programs that slipped into a valley for a few years during the last couple of decades," Falk explained. "Ohio State. USC. Oklahoma. Texas. Nebraska. Alabama. Florida State. Miami. Notre Dame."

With the heightened intensity of media coverage, coupled with an explosion of corporate sponsorship, the essence of major college football has changed dramatically.

"You're not gonna see too many long-time runs like Bo had any more," Falk said. "Head coaches at this level rarely last more than ten years in one place.

"Take a picture of any coach and five years later look at his face. You're gonna see a lot more wrinkles. There'll be wear and tear on his face and body from all the things he has to worry about that the public doesn't realize."

No one is fully responsible and no one is fully exonerated for the most dismal three-year period in Michigan history. A confluence of misfortunes derailed the Rich Rodriguez era before it had a chance to start.

"When a team is struggling, the game will do anything it can to take you down," Falk said. "It's true in sports and true in life."

Falk remains fully focused only on Michigan's inevitable return to glory. And he's confident that under the leadership of Brady Hoke, the restoration of prominence will come much sooner than later.

Falk still treasures the most important lesson Bo gave him on the day he was hired. It goes far beyond uniforms and equipment.

"Bo told me the day I was hired that my most important job was to do all I can to make Michigan football the best in the country," he said. "I've always kept that close to my heart. I did everything I could for Bo, for Mo, for Lloyd, and for Rich Rodriguez. It's the same thing I'm doing for Brady now."

Bo also believed that no coach, no player, no member of the football staff was bigger than the Michigan football program.

On the day before Rodriguez was relieved of his duties, Falk walked into the coach's office. He told him he just wanted him to know he did everything he could to help Michigan football.

"Rich thanked me for that and assured me he couldn't have asked anything more from me," Falk said. "That made me feel good. I can live with that. Rich Rodriguez is a good man. He did everything he could for Michigan football."

Although 2008 and 2009 were abysmal, flickers of redemption were realized in 2010. With one of the most explosive offenses in the country, Michigan finished 7–6 and returned to a New Year's Day bowl game after a two-year lapse.

Falk had charged onto the field through The Tunnel hundreds of times before. But the one for the season opener in 2010 was special.

"When I came through that tunnel and saw those 113,000 people in the seats and the beautiful luxury suites that had just been completed, a whole new feeling ran through my body," he said. "I asked myself how any kid in the country would not want to play in this stadium. It's the most magnificent place to play football on the whole planet."

Coupled with the Al Glick Indoor Football Facility that was recently completed, Michigan does, indeed, enjoy one of the finest and most charming athletic facilities anywhere in the world. Glick is a loyal major donor.

Denard Robinson wasted no time establishing himself as the most dynamic player in the country in 2010. In the season-opening 30–10 victory over Connecticut, he set the single-game school record for rushing yards by a quarterback with 197 and also passed for 186 yards and two touchdowns.

"Denard reminds me so much of Desmond Howard," Falk said. "He's always got a smile on his face. He's always jovial and is the clear leader on the team. He's looked up to by every player on the team."

At Notre Dame the following week, Robinson led a last minute comeback and ran for a touchdown with 27-second left for a 28–24 victory. He became only the ninth quarterback in FBS history to gain more than 200 yards rushing and 200 passing in the same game.

Robinson's 87-yard touchdown run in the second quarter was the longest rushing touchdown in the history of Notre Dame Stadium. It also was a not-so-subtle reminder of the loss that the entire Michigan family suffered earlier in the day when Ron Kramer passed away: "87" was the number Kramer made immortal and is one of only five to have been retired by the University of Michigan.

"[Kramer] was a tremendous player and a tremendous friend," Falk said. "I talked to him the night before he died. He'll always be remembered by Michigan."

Michigan ran its record to 5–0 before finishing the regular season with a 7–5 mark. The sixth victory was one for the record books as Michigan outlasted visiting Illinois 67–65 in triple overtime. The Wolverines were invited to the Gator Bowl to play Mississippi State. Despite losing the bowl game, they finished above .500 for the first time in three years.

Now in his 38th season as equipment manager, Falk is prepared for even more excitement. In fact, the recently infused energy surrounding the program often reminds him of his start in 1974.

And that remains something he never will forget.

Section 2

1970s

Chapter **3**

Welcome to Michigan

N o one forgets the first day of a lifelong career that starts with a heave-ho from the boss' office even before getting a chance to shake his hand. Especially when that boss happens to be Bo Schembechler.

"Hi Coach Schembechler," the young and eager new football equipment manager said as he extended his arm to shake hands. "Jon Falk here, reporting for duty."

Bo looked up without saying a word. As he eyed the new employee from head to toe, the scowl on his face did all the talking.

"What are you doing in my office with a red jacket on?" he finally barked. "Nobody wears a red jacket in my office."

Falk was slightly confused and, needless to say, quite shaken. Falk knew Bo had to recognize the Miami of Ohio varsity jacket. That's where Bo played football. He had been the head football coach there.

"Why, you know, Coach Schembechler," Falk said, still managing to smile. "It's my Miami jacket."

A moment of silence preceded the eruption that reverberated all the way down the hall.

"You get out of here and don't come back until you're wearing a blue jacket that says Michigan Football!" Bo ordered. "I won't talk to you 'til you're wearing a blue Michigan jacket! Now get out!"

There are times when even the rawest rookie knows that a coach is not joking. Falk already had previous experience working for Bo at Miami. He sensed quickly this was definitely one of those times.

Falk raced down to the equipment room and managed to talk his way into being issued a Michigan Football jacket and promptly returned to Bo's office.

"Now that's better," the coach said with a smile while shaking Falk's hand. "Welcome to Michigan."

The year was 1974, and since that time, the welcome remains warm. Falk has served as the equipment manager under Bo, Gary Moeller, Lloyd Carr, Rich Rodriguez, and Brady Hoke. He's worked with thousands of players fortunate enough to have worn the famous winged helmet and the maize and blue of one of the nation's premier football programs and elite educational institutions.

Now he laughs at how he almost returned home to Oxford, Ohio, shortly after starting his job at Michigan.

Falk actually got his first taste of Bo while serving as a student assistant equipment manager at Miami when Schembechler was the head coach. Falk even had the legendary coach as a teacher for a football class he took to fatten his grade point average. He retains an indelible memory from that class that taught him an invaluable lesson.

A freshman football player was sitting near the front of the room as Bo was frantically diagramming plays on the blackboard. The unsuspecting player had obviously fallen asleep. His snoring had stirred some snickers from around the room.

With the quickness of an All-American tailback, Bo spun suddenly and fired an eraser at his dozing athlete.

"You do not sleep in this class!" Bo shouted. "No one sleeps in this class! You sleep again, and you are done here! We'll see how you survive in this university with an F in football!"

Bo then proceeded to lift this 260-pound lineman by the collar and throw him out into the hallway.

"Now...anybody else want to fall asleep in my class?" he asked after returning. "You'll all be treated the same way."

Bo was just as organized teaching in the classroom as he was coaching football on the field. He was stern, but his lessons were delivered clearly and concisely. And every student learned to pay attention.

Apparently, however, Bo didn't realize that one of his students was serving as an assistant equipment manager. Shortly after the semester ended, one of the assistant coaches asked Falk what mark he received in Bo's class.

"I got a B," Falk said.

The assistant looked puzzled and asked if Falk had done all of his work.

"I got an A+++ on my notes and an A on my test," Falk said.

"Let me see what's going on," the assistant said.

After investigating, the assistant informed Falk that Bo didn't know his name and made a mistake on the grade form. The assistant told Falk to visit the coach on the handball court immediately.

Bo was a tremendous handball player and attacked each opponent as if he were leading a charge of players against Ohio State.

"He was a fiery competitor," Falk said. "Unforgiving with his serves. People used to come around just to watch him play. He played by the rules, but he was vicious. He played each game like he'd never play another."

The court was in an area called the "pit."

"The sound reverberated like you were in an echo chamber," Falk said. "If he lost, you could hear the scream halfway across the campus. It wasn't often, but everybody knew when Bo lost in handball."

As Falk approached the pit, Bo looked up at him.

"Hey boy," Bo shouted. "What's your name?"

"Jon Falk, sir."

"What did you get in my football class?"

"I got a B, sir."

Bo paused for a second.

"Better go see my secretary right away and get a change of grade," he said.

Falk immediately dashed to Bo's office to tell the secretary what the coach had said. He got the grade changed to the A it should have been.

That was Falk's first personal encounter with his future boss. And it's one that has stuck with him all of his life.

In the fall of his sophomore year, Falk again worked as an assistant for equipment manager Watson Kruzeski. A week before the season started, the Miami team was shocked by the sudden passing of Kruzeski.

It happened while the team was practicing on the field. Falk heard a strange sound coming from the shower room. It sounded as if Kruzeski was trying to say something but couldn't get the words out of his mouth.

Falk charged into the room.

"What's wrong, Watson?" he anxiously asked.

Kruzeski waved him off and sent him back into the locker room before somehow managing to get to his office. A few moments later, Falk felt something was wrong. He peeked into Kruzeski's office and found him lying on the floor.

Falk darted out of the locker room. He jumped into the first car he spotted and drove out onto the practice field.

"Bo looked startled," Falk said. "I remember him saying, 'What the hell is this kid doing driving a car onto the practice field?'"

Falk grabbed trainer Ken Wolfert and sped him to the locker room. Someone had phoned the police who had already taken Kruzeski to the hospital. Three days later, he was dead.

Just that suddenly, Falk became the acting football equipment manager. He worked with Donnie Miller, another student assistant. Bo called Falk in for their first meeting.

"Now you know Watson's passed away," he said. "You're the only one here who knows what's going on. Now do you think you can handle this job?"

Falk promised himself to make the most of the opportunity. Trying to emulate the coach, he worked tirelessly and put in as many hours as possible after school. The team was preparing to travel to San Francisco to play the University of the Pacific. The week before the game, Bo called Falk into his office.

"Son, have you ever been to San Francisco?" Bo asked.

Falk was tongue-tied.

"No sir," he finally managed. "Never been to San Francisco or anywhere in California. But I have been to the Cincinnati stockyards quite a few times."

Bo laughed.

"Well there won't be much difference," the coach said. "You'll be fine. Ol' Bo is gonna take you to California."

It was on that trip when Falk realized the immeasurable intensity of Bo's loyalty and sense of responsibility to one of his teams.

The flight on the four-engine prop plane from Cincinnati to San Francisco was a grueling nine-hour test of endurance that required a refueling stop in Amarillo, Texas. By the time the team landed in San Francisco, everyone was starving and felt as if they had already played a football doubleheader.

Two busses were waiting at the airport to transport the team to the hotel. Unfortunately, one of them stalled while going across the Bay Bridge. A state trooper stopped and boarded the bus to investigate.

"Hey, we gotta get this bus going," Bo barked at the trooper. "Don't you understand I have players here who haven't eaten in nine hours? They're hungry, tired, and we play a football game here on Saturday."

The trooper looked at Bo and then at the driver.

"Who is this guy?" the trooper asked the driver.

Finally the trooper said he wouldn't let the bus move because it was spitting too much oil. The hotel was only about a mile away at the bottom of three hills.

Bo had an idea.

"Defense," he commanded. "Off the bus and push."

The players, of course, jumped to action and pushed the broken bus to the front of the hotel lobby. Upon arrival, Bo issued another order.

"Listen up, men," he said. "Let's go eat."

As the players headed to the dining room, Falk began to unload travel bags into the lobby. A bellhop sprung from his station crying, "You can't do that."

"Hey, buddy," Bo said. "My guys are tired and haven't eaten. Now we're gonna do what we have to do."

The bellhop was speechless and meekly walked away as Falk continued with his unloading responsibilities.

"That was part of the learning process with Bo," Falk said. "When he put his mind to something, it was gonna get done. He was never afraid to stand up for something when he felt it was right."

Although Miami lost the game by one point, Falk's first trip was memorable and rewarding. He was responsible for everything pertaining to the equipment and locker room. Despite a severe case of nerves, everything worked flawlessly.

In Falk's sophomore year of 1968, it was announced that Bo had been hired as the head coach of the University of Michigan. He was also taking assistants Gary Moeller and Jerry Hanlon with him. Miami has long been known as "the cradle of coaches." It wasn't unusual to see former head coach Ara Parseghian return for a visit to Miami after leaving for Notre Dame. John Pont, who had moved on to coach Indiana, would also visit.

When Bo was busy preparing for his departure to Michigan, Falk visited his office.

"Coach Schembechler, I want to thank you for everything you did for me," Falk said.

Bo stared at him with a puzzled look in his eye.

"I haven't done anything for you," Bo said.

With proper deference, Falk corrected the coach.

"Well, sir, you let me be part of the team," Falk said.

Bo put his hand on Falk's shoulder.

"Always remember, you only get what you deserve," he said.

Bob Purcell was hired as the equipment manager for Miami, and Bill Mallory succeeded Bo as head coach. Mallory later went to Colorado as head coach. He had worked for Woody Hayes as an assistant at Ohio State before taking the job at Miami when Bo went to Michigan.

Falk continued to serve as a student assistant and will never forget that chilling November Saturday in 1969 when Michigan shocked the college football world by upsetting No.1 ranked Ohio State—a team that only the Minnesota Vikings were supposed to be able to beat.

Always remember, you only get what you deserve.

—Bo Schembechler

"When the announcement came over the loud speaker at our game, I thought they got the score wrong," Falk said. "I had always been a big Ohio State and Woody Hayes fan. My big dream in life was to go to the Rose Bowl. And now Woody got beat by Bo. Our Bo. I'll never forget that day. Bo was going to the Rose Bowl."

Graduation from Miami was one of Falk's proudest days. He still carries a copy of his diploma in his wallet. Falk was hired by Miami Athletic Director Dick Shrider to work as Purcell's paid assistant.

Then in early 1974, a strange set of circumstances arose that shaped the rest of his life.

Preston Chappelle was a uniform and equipment salesman who serviced Michigan and Miami. His position allowed him to form a friendship with Bo. Chappelle introduced Falk to Michigan equipment manager Ron Pulliam who was on leave because of illness. A few weeks after the meeting, Pulliam died of cancer.

"I've been watching you at Miami and wonder if you might want to be considered for the job at Michigan," Chappelle asked Falk.

Falk had never dreamed about such an opportunity and initially dismissed the thought.

"I don't know, Chappy," Falk said. "I've got my mother and grandmother to think of here in Oxford."

Chappelle looked more surprised at the answer than Falk was at the question.

"You better take a look at it," he said. "That's the University of Michigan I'm talking about. I'm gonna talk to Bo about you."

About a week passed without Falk giving it another thought. Then Dick Shrider called Falk to say that Bo Schembechler wanted to talk to him.

"What would Bo want with me?" Falk asked. The Miami athletic director merely said, "Bo has something for you."

Falk made the call and immediately detected a tinge of anger in Bo's passionate voice. Falk quickly thought it couldn't have been anything he had said because he hadn't said anything to the coach. Later Falk would discover that even after the passing of seven weeks, Bo was still simmering over the last game of the 1973 season.

Michigan and Ohio State had played to a 10–10 tie. A vote by the Big Ten athletic directors sent the Buckeyes to the Rose Bowl, and obviously Bo's temper had at least a seven-week simmering cycle.

Nevertheless, Bo was congenial with Falk. And true to form, he got right to the point.

"I've got this equipment manager's job open here at Michigan and thought you might be interested," he said.

Despite having discussed the matter with Chappelle, Falk still felt slightly overwhelmed by the situation.

"Coach Schembechler, I'm really honored you would even think about me, but I just don't know," he said.

Bo suggested Falk drive to Ann Arbor to discuss the matter. Bo was never the kind of person to suggest anything mildly.

Falk was treated to lunch with assistant coach Hanlon and some of the other personnel he had known during their tenure at Miami. At the meeting with Bo, the coach detailed all of the benefits and advantages of working for a university with the tradition of Michigan.

"I understand your situation with your mother and grandmother," Bo said. "But this is an opportunity you can't throw away. You've got to grow up and leave Oxford."

On the drive back to Oxford, Falk discussed the meeting with Miami baseball coach Bud Middaugh, who had made the trip with him. Middaugh later became the Michigan baseball coach.

"I kept thinking about leaving home and how comfortable I felt at Miami," Falk said. "And the $8,000 salary Bo offered didn't sound too good."

Falk got home at 2:00 AM and told his mother he was not taking the job. Two hours later, his mother entered his bedroom with tears running down her cheeks.

"It hurts me to tell you this, but in the morning you are going to call Coach Schembechler and tell him you'll take the job," she said. "There's nothing left for you to do here. I know in my heart that Michigan will take care of you. Coach Schembechler will take care of you."

In the morning Falk visited Shrider who told him his mother was right. It was time to leave home.

"We all love you here, but you're going to the University of Michigan," he said. "It's a once in a lifetime opportunity you can't refuse."

Falk finally decided to call Bo.

"I was looking over the salary information and saw that some of the benefits don't kick in 'til you reach $10,000," Falk said.

Bo knew he had his man. He was the master recruiter.

"So you'll come to Michigan for $10,000," he said. "You got it. See you in three days."

Falk was still filled with reservations about leaving home. Nevertheless, he packed two travel bags and filled his red Chevrolet Nova with miscellaneous items and headed for Ann Arbor.

Seventeen Big Ten championships, 34 bowl games, and one National Championship later, Falk certainly appreciates his trip of a lifetime. Without the shadow of a doubt, going to Michigan was the right decision.

Chapter **4**

Home Sweet Home

When spring football practice started a few months after his arrival in Ann Arbor, Falk was still battling homesickness for Oxford, Ohio. Bo noticed that Falk had made several drives home on weekends.

Down deep, however, Falk must have realized the opportunity he'd been given.

He had a fresh start with one of the most colorful jobs in college football. He was working for one of the most dynamic young coaches in the game. He felt privileged to be at one of America's leading academic universities.

And he had a new home just off the 18th green of the prestigious University of Michigan Golf Course. It was right across the street from The Big House and a convenient walk to the football offices and practice facilities.

Well, the place wasn't really new. And it wasn't actually a home. It was a three-room first-floor apartment at the corner of the building that housed the pro shop, a string of offices, and meeting rooms. The second floor featured a long row of empty offices that were converted into rooms for various athletes on athletic scholarships.

Falk's one-bedroom apartment featured a kitchen with just enough space for a designated living area. A full bathroom provided all the comforts of home.

Never to be mistaken for being plush, the apartment was comfortable and convenient enough for Falk to spend his first 15 years in Ann Arbor there.

The apartment had one particularly attractive feature. With Athletic Director Don Canham having designated Falk as the unofficial "guardian" of the golf course once everyone had left the facility for the day, it came totally rent free.

When Falk's mother (Jean Falk), grandmother (Rosella Land), and uncle (Don Falk) drove up from Oxford to visit him for the first time that spring, the family approved of the living conditions except for one matter. Mama Falk addressed the issue with Bo.

"Coach Schembechler," she said. "I know you have a lot of power around here. Can you get those big trash cans outside my son's back door cleaned?"

In his entire coaching career, that was the first time Bo had ever been asked to resolve a custodial situation.

"Yeah…ol' Bo is gonna work on getting those cans cleaned," he said with a laugh.

Falk quickly discovered a variety of benefits from living on campus. When Bo or any of the assistant coaches were on the road recruiting, Falk was usually invited to one of their homes for dinner.

"I used to go over to Bo's house maybe two or three times a week to eat dinner with Millie and the boys," Falk said. "When Bo came home, we'd sit around in the living room watching TV or listen to Bo about who he was recruiting."

Living in the apartment provided Falk with other experiences, such as getting close to new assistant coaches when they were hired.

"Bo would call me up and tell me to take them in for a little while until they got situated," Falk said.

Lloyd Carr spent time in the apartment when he was hired as an assistant. So did Don Nehlen, who moved on to West Virginia as the head coach. He later hired Rich Rodriguez as one of his assistants.

Falk got booted from his apartment for a couple of days in 1976 when a former Michigan player happened to be in town to participate in a charity golf tournament.

"Now Jon," Bo told him, "President [Gerald] Ford is coming to town. We need a place for him to relax near the golf course during the day. We're gonna have him stay at your place."

Needless to say, Falk was surprised.

"Coach Schembechler, what am I supposed to do?" he asked.

Bo looked back as if the question was simple enough for any first grader to answer.

"You're gonna move out," he said.

Simple as that, the matter was settled.

For two weeks leading up to the tournament, Bo asked if the apartment was clean. Falk assured him positively each time.

"The president is coming," Bo would say. "That's the President of the United States of America. He's staying in your apartment, Jon. I want that place cleaner than the Board of Health."

Bo must have felt anxious about the situation because he sent his secretary, Lynn Koch, to inspect the apartment. Upon her return, Bo's message to Falk was simple and clear.

"You're getting out early," Bo informed Falk. "We're sending in a professional cleaner."

Falk had to visit his apartment shortly after the president arrived. After clearing himself with the Secret Service agents, he walked into the living room to discover the president sitting on the couch smoking his pipe and reading a book.

"President Ford, if you play golf with Bo today, will you please tell him that the place is clean?" Falk said. "He's been on me for the last two weeks to have it sparkling for you."

The president scanned the rooms and nodded his approval.

"The place looks fine, Jon," he said. "Everything here looks fine. It's a great place for me to rest during the day."

Falk thanked the president, and the two shared a few words.

"If you ever come to town again and need a place to stay, you're always welcome here, Mr. President," Falk finished.

The president smiled.

"Well if I do, Jon, I'll give you two weeks notice so you can get it cleaned up for me," he cracked.

Seasons slipped by quickly for Falk, who spent his first 15 years in that apartment. He then purchased his first home in Ann Arbor and began to date his eventual wife, Cheri Boychuck-Winkle. A year later, Bo made the appropriate wedding toast.

Now the last member from that staff still in the program, Falk has obviously made his own imprint on the most tradition-rich college football program in the country.

Chapter **5**
1974: The Rookie Arrives

I t was perhaps hard to believe and noticeable only to Falk, but there was a change in Bo at Michigan.

"Bo was a lot more volatile at Miami," Falk said.

The difference was subtle. Something like measuring the difference of getting wetter in Lake Superior than in a backyard swimming pool. But it was apparent to Falk.

Bo was still incurably passionate about football, his job, his team, and how he attacked each aspect of life. He had simply enhanced all of his talents, which resulted in a confidence truly unshakable.

"Bo had become an excellent teacher," Falk said. "He would chew you out if you made a mistake. Then he'd take the time to explain what you did wrong and how he wanted something accomplished. When the incident was over, it was forgotten. You just better remember not to make the same mistake again.

"Bo would 'fire' someone almost every day. Then he would re-hire the person before practice was over. That was just Bo. He knew how he wanted things to be done and was upfront with all the people he led. You never had to wonder about what Bo wanted. That's the sign of a great leader."

The subtle change in Bo was reflected in the command he had established over the storied program of Michigan football.

"Whenever there's a coaching change, it takes a while for the new staff to establish the program they want to run," Falk explained. "Once they do, it becomes their program and then it's a matter of maintaining that standard."

Bo did it in lightning speed with the stunning upset of No. 1 ranked Ohio State in the final game of the 1969 season. From that day forward, it was Bo's program. He was able to shape his players—present and future—along with his staff and the Michigan alumni into the program fully vested in Bo.

The fire inside Bo was as scorching as it had been while he coached at Miami. But it had been five years since Falk had witnessed Bo's passion, and it was obvious to him that Bo had grown.

As the 1974 season approached, Falk was receiving his own cram course in all of the traditions that live nowhere else but Michigan.

When he first came to Ann Arbor, he knew only two things. He knew that Bo Schembechler was the head coach. And he knew that almost everyone in Ohio hates Michigan.

Two of the most celebrated traditions infused into all new players and members of the football staff are the Marching Band and the mystique of The Tunnel. On game days, the two distinctively singular entities combine to create an almost surrealistic experience for any coach, player, or staff member that takes a step onto that field.

"A lot of people don't know how much Bo loved that band," Falk said. "He felt it was an essential part of every Saturday. He actually used it to our advantage."

Organized with nearly 30 members in 1896, the Michigan Marching Band now features 235 members and is one of the most celebrated units in modern college football.

As with all incoming freshman players and new staff members, Falk had to learn the lyrics and melody to "The Victors" long before the first kickoff of the season. Short, rousing, and loaded with the impact of a jackhammer, "The Victors" is the most celebrated college fight song in America.

Written by Louis Elbel in 1898 following a Michigan upset of the powerful University of Chicago coached by the legendary Amos Alonzo Stagg, "The Victors" has withstood every test of time.

"The Victors" is played when the band takes the field after exiting The Tunnel. It is raucously sung by the team in the locker room after each victory. Legendary band director Dr. William Revelli taught each freshman player to sing the song with as much vigor as he performed it.

And each player, coach, and staff member better know every word and note long before the season starts.

"Bo would set up special times after practice for the band to come over and play for us," Falk said. "Sometimes during breaks of two-a-day practices, we were made to stand up and sing 'The Victors.'"

* * * *

Another familiar favorite played constantly each Saturday is the "Let's Go Blue" chant. And that's where The Tunnel provides a stimulating special effect that almost feels spooky.

The Tunnel is a 300-foot gauntlet leading from the locker rooms to the field. For both teams, there's only one way out to the field and one way back.

When the team is returning to the locker room after completing its pregame warm-ups, the band congregates at the back of The Tunnel and begins to play "Let's Go Blue."

"When the players are running up that tunnel and hear that music, you can see their feet almost floating above the ground," Falk said. "There's a lot of bumping and grinding going on, and you can just feel all the excitement building up."

Once inside the locker room, the team can still hear the band playing before taking the field.

"When you hear all that and feel all that, every player in the room knows he's into something bigger than he ever dreamed," Falk said.

No one forgets his first trip down The Tunnel. And that swirling rush of adrenaline stays with each individual for the rest of his life. Michigan All-American and All-Pro tight end Ron Kramer still shivers at the feeling.

"The first time I did it, I thought I was going to pee in my pants," Kramer said. "There's no feeling like it. It's impossible to put into words."

Dan Dierdorf, a Michigan All-American tackle and member of the Pro Football Hall of Fame, treasured every trip through The Tunnel.

"One minute you're in darkness, and the next you're in the middle of 110,000 people," he said. "It seems like the whole world is watching."

When both teams get tangled in The Tunnel at the end of the first half or after the game, needless to say the trash talk, taunting, and "accidental" elbows to the ribs turn into a game itself.

Through the years, Michigan has used the mystique of The Tunnel for even the slightest advantage before the first kick.

One minute you're in darkness, and the next you're in the middle of 110,000 people. It seems like the whole world is watching. *—Dan Dierdorf*

Falk's first trip down The Tunnel came during the season opener against Iowa in 1974. He was only 23 years old and probably more nervous than the players around him.

"Like all the players, I remember jumping up and touching the Go Blue banner that the Varsity Club holds at the center of the field," Falk said. "I'm a little too old to get up that high now, but I still take off my hat and hit it as I run across the field."

Falk also got his first experience of singing "The Victors" in the locker room after that first Iowa game. Michigan jumped to a 14–0 first-quarter lead and finished with a 24–7 victory.

The following week Colorado came to The Big House for a nationally televised game with Keith Jackson calling the play-by-play. Bill Mallory, who succeeded Bo at Miami of Ohio, was the head coach for Colorado. Milan Vooletich, who had lived next door to the Falk home in Oxford, was one of his assistants.

During the Colorado walk-through of the field on Friday, Falk led his former coaches through The Tunnel onto the field.

"This isn't that impressive," Falk remembers Vooletich saying.

Jackson was a veteran who had broadcast countless memorable games at The Big House. He was following the visiting coaches a few steps behind and smiled.

"Just wait 'til tomorrow," he promised in his trademark dramatic droll. "Just wait 'til tomorrow."

Colorado got the message loud and clear as Michigan scored in each quarter in a relatively easy 31–0 rout.

* * * *

Falk was getting a taste for another Michigan tradition. The Wolverines had notched four shutouts during their 10-game winning streak leading to the traditional season-ending classic with Ohio State in Columbus.

Bo always prepared for the next Ohio State game every day of the season. He had a schedule on the wall of the team meeting room. At Sunday meetings, he finished his message to the team by analyzing how it had progressed during the prior week. He would talk about the upcoming game. Then he'd finish his weekly assessment by pointing to the last game on the schedule.

"Men, we're not good enough," he'd say. "Not good enough to play this team down here. We must play better. We must work harder."

The week before the Ohio State showdown, Michigan exploded for a 51–0 whipping of Purdue.

"Men, we are now ready," he began his Sunday session. "We are now ready for Ohio State. We are primed. We are ready."

This was Falk's first trip to the Horseshoe, and it left an indelible imprint on his mind.

"My whole life I had dreamed about going to the Rose Bowl," Falk said. "I thought there was no other thing bigger in sports than the Rose Bowl. Coming from Ohio, of course, I always followed Ohio State and Woody Hayes. But I was true blue Michigan now. And we had a chance at going to the Rose Bowl with one more victory."

Bo was still chaffing over the 1973 game in Ann Arbor that ended in the classic 10–10 tie. Both teams finished with 10-0-1 records, but a vote by Big Ten Conference athletic directors gave the Rose Bowl berth to Ohio State.

At Columbus, the Wolverines indeed looked as if they were good enough by jumping to a 10–0 lead in the first quarter. The defense was impenetrable the entire game. Only once did the Buckeyes get inside Michigan's 26-yard line. But that drive resulted in a 25-yard field goal to lift Ohio State to a 12–10 victory and another Rose Bowl bid. Each team ground out 195 rushing yards. Michigan out-gained Ohio State, 96–58, in the air.

The loss meant that the 1972-73-74 teams had lost only two games and tied one. And none of those players had gone to a bowl game. The situation only infuriated Bo more as he continued his drive to open up the Big Ten to more bowl bids. It was later that year that the conference ruled in favor of any Big Ten team to play in a bowl to which it was invited.

"Every conference team should get down on their knees and thank Bo for what he did for everybody," Falk said. "That opened the door for all the bowl games we have today."

While Falk suffered defeat in his first trip back to his home state, he got his first up-close look at the rivalry that has dominated college football for decades.

And the best was yet to come.

Chapter **6**

1975: Open Bowling

Bo's persistence to open the Big Ten to postseason games beyond the Rose Bowl finally paid off on January 1, 1976, when Michigan played in the Orange Bowl for the first time.

Despite a brilliant 30–2–1 combined record from 1972 through 1974, no Michigan team had played in a post-season bowl.

Now that Bo had helped to rectify that dilemma, he had one more item on his checklist before heading to Miami to take on mighty Oklahoma. He called on Falk to handle the situation.

"Falk," he said with usual authority. "Do you realize that the three previous Michigan teams were cheated out of going to a bowl game despite having one of the finest records in all of college football?"

A rhetorical question…yes. The time to joke with Bo…no.

"I want these young men to get every bowl gift that's allowed by the rules," Bo continued. "And I want our men representing the University of Michigan in a fashion they have earned."

Falk was ordered to purchase blazers, slacks, shirts, and neckties for every player and staff member on the team.

While working in the equipment room a day later, Falk received a phone call from Athletic Director Don Canham's secretary.

"Jon, you better come down here right away," she said. "Mr. Canham is pretty upset about something. He wants to talk to you right now."

Falk was puzzled but made it to Canham's office in double time. As soon as Falk arrived, Canham exploded.

"Who told you to buy these blazers, these slacks, these shirts, and these neckties?" he demanded. "Do you realize how much all of this costs?"

Rarely at a loss for words, Falk chose the next ones carefully.

"I'm sorry Mr. Canham, but Bo told me that due to the fact Michigan hasn't been to a bowl game in four years, he wanted the team to look nice and represent the University of Michigan properly in the Orange Bowl."

Canham picked up the invoice and flashed it at Falk.

"Do you realize what this costs?" Canham repeated. "Get out of my office right away."

As Falk walked out, Bo was walking in.

"Boy, what did you do?" Bo asked Falk.

"I guess the price for all the outfits I purchased for the team totaled up to a little more than he wanted to spend," Falk said. "But I want you to know before you go into his office that the lambs are being led to the slaughter right now."

Bo instructed Falk to wait in his office for a few minutes until he returned. Needless to say, Falk was worried because that was the first time he had been confronted like that by Canham.

When Bo returned to his office smiling, Falk felt a little more at ease.

"Big Jon, the first thing I want you to know is that you're not getting fired," Bo cracked.

That was a relief. Now that he was past that hurdle, he wanted to know what he had done wrong.

"Well, there was a little misunderstanding with Don about what we want to do," Bo said. "I explained to him what we were doing. Go ahead and get everyone sized up, and get the clothes."

At a basketball game that evening, Falk spotted Canham in his usual seat. He was apprehensive about saying anything but finally mustered enough courage to speak to the boss.

"I want to apologize for the misunderstanding we had today," Falk said. "I realize I should have talked to you first."

Now recovered from the sticker shock, Canham put an arm around Falk and told him there was no need to apologize.

"When the University of Michigan goes to a bowl game, we're going to look like the distinguished representative the university is," Canham said.

Bo always had a knack for getting his point across. He obviously had hit the mark with the athletic director.

In addition to the off-field apparel Falk had purchased, he also had to buy 100 special-grip shoes for the slippery turf of the Orange Bowl.

"At Michigan, if there's something legal that helps you to win a game and we can get it, it will be done," Falk said.

While the shoes prevented a lot of slipping, they weren't enough to prevent a 14–6 loss to Oklahoma, which finished the season as the top-ranked team in the two wire service polls.

* * * *

The 1975 season was the start of Rick Leach's fantastic run as a four-year starter at quarterback.

"Good athletes are like stallions," Falk said. "You don't want to tame them. You just want to control them a little. You want a stallion to run and kick his heels. You want him to know he's the best horse in the race, but you don't want him running out of control. Don't break them down. Let them run and kick. That's the kind of athlete Rick Leach was."

Leach will always be remembered for his heroics on the football field. But he also wound up being the Detroit Tigers' No. 1 pick in the 1979 free agent draft.

"One year Bo let Rick out of a spring practice early so that he could play in a baseball game," Falk said. "Michigan had to beat Minnesota to qualify for the NCAA Tournament. I drove him over to the baseball locker room in his football uniform so he could hurry up and change into his baseball uniform. He came up in the last inning and drove in the winning run. Not too many players are talented enough to play in the Rose Bowl and the college baseball tournament."

The 1975 season had its share of memorable moments. After starting the season with two ties and a pair of victories, Northwestern came to Ann Arbor with a 2–0 conference record. Bo was confident in his team, but on the night before the game, he became possessed by the idea that Northwestern might upset the Wolverines in The Big House.

Around 11:00 PM at the hotel where the team was staying, Bo went to all the players' rooms telling them how good this Northwestern team was and how important it was for Michigan to win the game. In his pregame talk before kickoff, he again dug deeply to implore their best efforts.

"Northwestern is coming to beat us," he screamed. "We can't let this happen. I'm not gonna let it happen, and neither are you."

When the team broke from The Tunnel to touch the "M" banner at midfield for the start of the game, their feet barely touched the ground.

Needless to say, Michigan did not let the unthinkable happen. Before anyone blinked, Michigan was up 34–0 and finished with a 69–0 victory.

Running backs Harlan Huckleby, Rob Lytle, and Gordon Bell combined for a rare single-game accomplishment. Each gained at least 100 yards—Huckleby (157), Lytle (105), and Bell (100).

Perhaps the best run of the season, however, didn't result in a touchdown or even a first down. In fact, it actually fell a few yards short of its intended purpose.

The run didn't come from Huckleby. It didn't come from Lytle. And it didn't come from Bell.

The run that may have saved the season was a near 100-yard gallop by Falk who wound up at his destination a split second after the play was ruled complete.

Michigan was hosting Baylor after opening the season with a victory at Wisconsin and a 19–19 tie against Stanford. Baylor had a pesky team and was playing well before the nearly 105,000 fans that packed The Big House. The Wolverines took a 14–7 lead into halftime, but Baylor refused to be intimidated.

In the second half, Baylor was moving the ball when one of the Michigan players on the sidelines yelled something at Falk.

"Hey, Jon, look down at the goal line," the player shouted. "One of the pylons is missing."

No one knew for sure what had happened to the plastic goal-line marker, but evidently one of the members of the marching band had accidentally kicked it out of place during the halftime performance.

Falk wasn't really concerned about why the pylon was missing. He was simply intent about getting another one down on the goal line before anyone in uniform got close to the vacated area.

The missing pylon was supposed to be standing in the northeast corner of the stadium across the field from the Michigan bench. With the way Baylor was moving the ball, Falk realized he had to act quickly.

He sprinted down the sideline toward the south end of the stadium. He then circled behind the Baylor bench and dashed up The Tunnel as if the entire Baylor team was chasing him. Falk knew there was an extra pylon in a storage room near the locker room. He had to retrieve it, and then put it in its proper place before anyone got near the northeast goal line.

As soon as he grabbed the pylon, Falk reversed his field and charged out of The Tunnel full speed ahead. As soon as he hit daylight, he veered right as sharply as a Huckleby cut could ignite the stadium crowd into a full-tilt frenzy.

As Falk was making his mad run toward the goal line, he glanced to his left and noticed a Baylor runner heading straight to the spot that Falk was aiming for.

"I was about 10 feet from the goal line and getting ready to put that pylon down when this Baylor back put his head down and slid into the corner," Falk said.

The referee had his eyes fixed on the corner of the end zone, obviously looking for the pylon that still wasn't there. Suddenly realizing the pylon was missing, he marked the ball out of bounds just inside the 1-yard line.

On fourth down and less than a yard to go for the game-tying touchdown, the Michigan defense refused entry to the end zone. The Wolverines had held and took over the ball on downs.

"I saw the play coming in that direction," Falk said. "I was running as hard as I could. As it turned out, it was a great thing that Baylor didn't score."

Eventually Baylor did score another touchdown and was successful on the extra point. The game ended in a 14–14 tie, but at least Michigan remained undefeated. Michigan ran off a seven-game winning streak before getting stopped by Ohio State in the final game of the regular season. The one-loss season allowed Michigan to play Oklahoma in the Orange Bowl.

The day after the Baylor game, Michigan team physician Dr. Gerald O'Connor had to fly to Dallas. He returned a few days later and showed a Dallas newspaper account of the Baylor game to Falk.

In the story, Baylor coach Grant Teaff placed no blame on the referee or Michigan for the missing pylon that could have caused a controversy.

"Through no fault of Michigan, the pylon was missing," Teaff said. "In the films we watched Sunday morning, we saw this Michigan guy running out of The Tunnel as hard as he could with a pylon in his hand. He just couldn't get there quick enough, and the ref ruled our runner out on the half-yard line."

Years later, Teaff became president of the College Football Coaching Association. Falk had reason to call him on a matter and asked if the former coach recalled his game at Michigan.

"We played hard and could have beaten them," Teaff recalled. "I remember watching film of the game and seeing this Michigan guy running like a freight train down the sideline trying to replace a missing pylon."

Falk couldn't help chuckling.

"You want to know something, sir?" Falk asked. "I was that guy."

It may not have been the most graceful run and it certainly was not the quickest, but Falk's mad dash that turned up a split second late may have been the best play to happen all season.

* * * *

On the day before the season finale against Ohio State, Falk got his first "in your face" encounter with the man he had so admired as a youngster—Woody Hayes.

It was cold and snowy that Friday afternoon when the Buckeye bus pulled up to the stadium for practice. Bo had instructed Falk and associate athletic director Don Lund to inform the legendary coach that the tarp was on the field and there would be no practice.

"Coach Hayes rolled his jaw about three times," Falk said. "Then he took his index finger and stuck it into my left shoulder blade. It still hurts today."

"Every time I come to Michigan, all they wanna do is screw me...screw me," Hayes growled.

"Yes sir, Coach Hayes, but you still can't practice because the tarp is on the field," Falk persisted.

Hayes proceeded down The Tunnel and managed to talk the groundskeepers into removing the tarp from half the field. Falk immediately returned to Bo's office to tell him the Buckeyes were practicing.

***Every time I come to Michigan, all they
wanna do is screw me...screw me.***
—*Woody Hayes*

"Where?" Bo demanded.

"In the stadium," Falk replied.

Bo shook his head and couldn't hide a smile.

"He doesn't miss a trick, does he?" Bo said. "He doesn't miss a trick."

Before Saturday's game, Bo instructed Falk to go to the visitor's locker room and tell Coach Hayes to take the field first. Upon the first knock, the door opened and there stood Woody staring straight into Falk's eyes.

"Sir, Coach Schembechler asked for you to take the field first," Falk said.

Woody said nothing. A few tense moments later, he slammed the door shut in pure Woody fashion that almost cost Falk a finger in the door. Falk told Bo and again was ordered to deliver the message. Again Woody opened the door and once more slammed it shut.

Three minutes later, with Falk still standing in The Tunnel, Woody opened the door and led his team out without saying a word.

"Coach Hayes was an intense guy," Falk said. "When I came to Michigan, Coach Schembechler told me, 'Whenever we play Ohio State, take care of them. Give them whatever they need. We want to beat them, but we respect them. Whatever they want, you better take care of it. And take care of Coach Hayes.'"

As he did before all Ohio State games, Falk toured the locker room reminding all players that they would never experience more fierce hitting than what they were about to face. Leach was getting the first of his four shots as the starting quarterback against the Buckeyes. Before the kickoff, Falk grabbed Leach's facemask and told him to "tighten it up." Leach liked it a little more loose in order to call audibles at the line.

On the first play, Leach rolled left on the option and precisely pitched the ball to a trailing back. The defender assigned to Leach was indifferent to the pitch. His job was simple—complete the play by knocking the quarterback into Monday morning.

Before the next possession, Leach visited Falk to have his chin strap tightened.

Michigan limited two-time Heisman Trophy winner Archie Griffin to 46 yards. The Wolverines held a 14–7 lead with five minutes to play when a critical third-and-15 pass was completed to Brian Baschnagel to keep the game-tying drive alive. Ohio State scored again to win, 21–14.

Years later, Falk was visited by a sports equipment sales rep who introduced himself as Brian Baschnagel. In the middle of their conversation, Falk put the name and face together.

"Hey," Falk shouted. "You're the S.O.B. who caught that third-and-15 pass back in '75."

As the pair reminisced, the late, celebrated Michigan radio broadcaster Bob Ufer entered the locker room. It didn't take him long to recognize Falk's visitor.

"You're the S.O.B. who caught that third-and-15 back in '75," Ufer said.

Now all three were laughing and sharing old Bo and Woody stories. When it was time for Baschnagel to leave, he shook hands with both men.

"You know, Brian," Falk said. "You wouldda made a great Michigan Man."

Chapter **7**

1976: Woody Passed the Ball

L ike all great coaches, Bo never counted a victory until the clock quit ticking.

Once in a while, though, up would jump a stunning exception. And when that opportunity arose against Ohio State, Bo squeezed it like a fresh lemon.

The 1976 Michigan–Ohio State game was predictable. As usual at Columbus, it started with a bizarre incident even before the team boarded the bus for the game.

The water at the hotel where the Michigan team was staying had been "mysteriously" turned off early Saturday morning. No water for players to take showers or brush their teeth. Even the toilets didn't work.

Bo and everyone connected to the team took the matter personally.

"Hey, if that's the way they want to play this game, then that's the way we'll play it," Bo said. "Dirty, mean, and ornery. All day long. There'll be plenty of fresh water in Pasadena when we get there."

"Every time we go to Columbus, something screwy happens," Falk said. "You never know what to expect."

Perhaps even more unexpected than the convenient drought at the hotel was the final play of the first half. Bo seized the opportunity and magnified its significance to his team.

The game was scoreless and crammed with the clean, bone-rattling ferocity featured in every Michigan–Ohio State game. Both defenses were viciously precise as time ticked down in the first half.

With only moments left, Ohio State mounted a drive that took the ball inside the Michigan 30-yard line. With time for one last play, Woody Hayes spurned a long field-goal attempt. Instead, the Buckeyes attempted a desperation pass into the end zone that defensive back Jim Pickens intercepted as time expired. Michigan had stopped Ohio State's best drive and would receive the second-half kickoff.

"The feeling was unbelievable as we ran off the field," Falk said. "Every Michigan player suddenly felt 6 inches taller."

Inside the locker room, the players were hooting and hollering like sailors coming home from six months at sea. They didn't need to rest at the half. They couldn't wait to get back on the field. Amid the euphoria, Bo took the floor.

"Men, gather around me," he shouted. "I want you to know something right now. It's over. It's over. It's gonna be Michigan today. It's gonna be Michigan!"

Time seemed to stand still as the players waited for the answer from Bo.

"Because we just made Woody pass the football!" Bo shouted.

Again the players exploded with cheers heard probably all the way to Cleveland.

"The confidence and emotion that Bo showed at the half just instilled those players with even more confidence in themselves," Falk said. "Bo could read a team. He knew what they were feeling and always had the right words for every situation. He wasn't gonna let this one slip away."

The second half was yet to unfold, but everyone in that room was convinced the game was waiting to be taken.

And no one had to wait long.

Michigan took the second-half kickoff and surgically structured an 80-yard scoring drive. Later in the period, Michigan put together a 52-yard scoring drive. On the try for the extra point, holder Jerry Zuver sprang to his feet and raced around the right end for a two-point conversion to make the score 15–0.

Falk knew that the Buckeyes were starting to feel desperate when Woody would not allow the Michigan ball boys to stand at the line of scrimmage. Each team is allowed to have two ball boys on the opposing side of the field. They are responsible for quickly getting a fresh ball into play for the offense.

"Woody wouldn't allow them inside the 30-yard line," Falk said. "He didn't want any Michigan people walking in front of his bench. Somehow Woody got it into his head that the boys were stealing signs and relaying them to our coaches. Every time we had a ball exchange, we couldn't get it in fast enough because the boys weren't on the line of scrimmage."

Falk tried to diplomatically settle the problem by talking to Ohio State equipment manager John Bozick.

"If somebody has to stand next to our ball boy, that's fine," Falk told Bozick. "But we've got to get fresh balls into the game. I know it's tough to talk to Coach Hayes now but something needs to be done."

Bozick looked at Falk and laughed. "We're in the middle of a game," Bozick said. "We're at home...we're playing Michigan...we're losing...and you want me to go talk to Coach Hayes?"

Falk could certainly identify with his friend's prickly predicament.

"All I'm saying is we've got to be able to get our balls into the game or we're not gonna let your boys on our sideline either," Falk said.

Somehow the sticky situation seemed to settle itself. Wet or dry balls, on that day it didn't seem to matter for Michigan.

The kicking team had practiced the two-point conversion play the previous week. A Michigan victory meant both teams would finish 7–1 in the Big Ten. Michigan would get the Rose Bowl nod for winning the head-to-head competition, and Bo was taking no chances. Michigan scored again in the fourth quarter to make the final score 22–0.

Ironically, earlier in the week *Detroit Free Press* sports writer Joe Falls wrote a column predicting Michigan would beat Ohio State 21–0.

"See what I've always told you, Jon?" Bo said to Falk after the game. "Those sportswriters don't know anything. Ol' Bo had a little surprise for them today."

Bo devoted a portion of practice to game-planning for Ohio State each day of the season. Of course, when game-week practice for Ohio State rolled around, all the football facilities and offices transformed into wartime battle stations.

That year, Bo actually initiated a significant segment of his Ohio State game plan before the first day of practice in late August. Tom Skladany was the Buckeye punter. He had a leg of steel and could boot a ball as high and as deep as a Reggie Jackson home run. Skladany's leg was a lethal weapon, and Woody was the master of using him perfectly.

"You know, Jon," Bo mentioned to Falk before the first practice, "they've got a machine now that can kick a ball 40 to 50 yards in the air. Why don't you go out and buy one for us?"

Bo was as meticulously thorough at providing for his team as he was in his relentless drilling of the offensive line.

"If we could buy the moon to beat Ohio State, would you do it?" Bo asked Athletic Director Don Canham.

"Go tell Falk to write up the purchase order—one moon coming up," Canham replied.

That's precisely what Falk did. A couple of months later when the bill came in, Canham called Falk.

"My God, Jon," Canham laughed. "The moon costs that much? But it was worth it."

For 15 minutes before every practice, regardless of the upcoming opponent, Michigan would simulate the Ohio State punting game against the Wolverine punt return unit. The "moon" machine would cough up 40- to

50-yard spirals and Jimmy Smith would pick his way through tacklers behind the wall of blockers in front.

On game day, Smith and his bruising buddies in front of him made the price of the moon look like chump change. Skladany punted the ball eight times for a 52.2-yard average. Smith negated the brilliant performance by gobbling up 91 yards in punt returns to keep Michigan in good field position.

"That's what it takes to be a great football coach," Falk said. "The great ones always look ahead. Bo knew every player on the Ohio State roster like he knew the telephone number of his mother. That was every year. Even when he got out of coaching.

That's what it takes to be a great football coach. The great ones always look ahead.
—Jon Falk

"The same holds true for equipment managers. The good ones are always thinking of something that will help the team and then telling the boss about it. That's what you're trained to do. Do your job to make it the best team possible."

As much as he had anticipated a victory over Ohio State, Falk never realized how sweet it would taste. Michigan hadn't beaten the Buckeyes since 1971. The Wolverines lost in 1972, tied in 1973, then lost two straight before snapping the string.

"Anyone who coaches Michigan circles that Ohio State game," Falk said. "That's the way it is. You are always judged on that Ohio State game. Every fan wants to know what a coach's record was against Ohio State.

"Bo was fanatic about it. Every year—even after he left coaching—he studied each player on that team. He always built them up to say how great they were. That was his way of letting his players know what a tough game they were in for and how much it means to each school."

A few weeks after that victory, Bo and Falk were at a restaurant when a stranger approached.

"We all love you, Bo," the stranger said. "But if you win just one game a year, please make sure it's Ohio State."

After the stranger left, Bo asked Falk, "I wonder how much they'd love me if I was 0–10 going into the Ohio State game."

Three days before going to Columbus, Bo and Falk had to defuse a situation in Ann Arbor that threatened to leak game plans to the enemy before Saturday's game.

At Tuesday's practice, which marked the first day of hitting, Falk noticed a red light beaming from the second story of a house on State Street across from the practice field. Interestingly, as the offense moved the ball down the field, the beam of light curiously followed.

"Hey Coach," Falk said. "I think there's a camera up in that window."

Bo dispatched Falk to investigate. Falk ran across the street and knocked loudly on the door. When no one answered, he shouted, "Sir, if you have a camera and are taking pictures, we are not allowing that today."

A voice shouted back at Falk, "Go away…this is private property."

Falk reported back to Bo, and the two raced across the street. Bo was slightly less diplomatic. "Open this damn door!" Bo shouted. "You're not taking pictures of our practice during Ohio State week. I want that camera."

A voice again responded, "Go away. I called the police. I'm not opening the door 'til the police get here."

Not a good enough answer for Bo. "I want this damn door open, and I want it opened now!"

At that moment, an Ann Arbor police officer was walking up the steps.

"What's going on here, Bo?" the officer asked.

Bo explained the situation and told the officer he wanted that camera confiscated "immediately."

The door slowly opened. Falk sensed the man inside figured the officer would protect him from Bo.

"Give me those films and camera," the officer demanded.

The man argued that the material was private property.

"Oh, we'll give them back," the officer said. "We're just going to hold on to them…until Sunday."

Bo got word that the incident had been initiated by the United Press International (UPI). At Monday's weekly meeting with the press, Bo was still angry.

"Anybody here that represents UPI better get out," he began even before discussing Saturday's victory. "I am not talking to you. No press person is ever gonna take pictures of us practicing. Especially not before the Ohio State game."

Something bizarre always happens before the Ohio State game. Win or lose, after it's finished, there's always something to laugh about.

The victory over Ohio State capped a spectacular regular season smudged only by a 16–14 loss at Purdue. Of course, everything accomplished was done in typical Bo fashion—with a defense stingier than Ebenezer Scrooge on a bad hair day and a ground game that sent plenty of enemy defenders to Monday morning dental appointments. Michigan notched five shutouts and outscored opponents 426–81.

Before the next season started, Don Nehlen was hired as the quarterbacks coach and recruiting coordinator. Nehlen knew a lot about quarterbacks. Of course, Bo had some pretty strong ideas about quarterbacks, too.

Upon announcement of Nehlen's appointment, one of the local papers ran a story that said, "Michigan brings in a passing coach."

"Hey Bo," Falk said before a staff meeting on the morning the story ran. "I didn't realize we were going to be passing around here."

Bo grabbed the paper and charged into the staff room.

"Okay Nehlen, let's get a couple of things straight here right now," Bo said. "I read in the paper this morning where you're gonna be the new passing coach at Michigan. Let me tell you one thing, Donnie Nehlen—we are not going to pass the football. We're gonna run the ball…run the ball…and then run it again. We run the ball at the University of Michigan."

We're gonna run the ball…run the ball… and then run it again. We run the ball at the University of Michigan.

—*Bo Schembechler*

Naturally, Nehlen was stunned, but he was calmed by Falk that evening. Nehlen was staying at Falk's apartment until his family settled in town.

"That's just Bo's way of welcoming you," Falk said. "You should have seen mine."

Nehlen went on to become head coach at West Virginia University and implemented a lot of Michigan's schemes. He hired Rich Rodriguez as an assistant. In December 2007, of course, Rodriguez succeeded Lloyd Carr as Michigan's head coach and at least had some familiarity with the traditions through Nehlen.

* * * *

Michigan's trip to the 1977 Rose Bowl allowed Falk to realize one of his childhood dreams. He had always watched Woody and his troops play proudly in Pasadena under the New Year's Day sun.

Now it was Michigan's turn, and Falk was part of it. The responsibilities of transporting all of the equipment for 100 players and about 40 staff members for 10 days to the other side of the country were enormous. It's a whole lot easier to flip on the TV and watch the game at home after celebrating New Year's Eve.

But the rewards for participating in a Rose Bowl dwarf any amount of challenges.

"It wasn't everything I dreamed about," Falk said. "It was far, far better. That's why I always tell players to savor every minute of every bowl game they play. It's just so hard to get there, and you never know when you're going to get the opportunity to come back again."

Traveling to any bowl game is a major undertaking that Falk came to appreciate for 33 straight seasons. That first taste of the Rose Bowl only made him hungrier for more.

On TV, he had always watched Bob Hope serve as master of ceremonies at the Dinner of Champions to honor the competing teams. He would listen to Hope interview Woody Hayes, and Falk wondered what that must feel like.

"I loved Bob Hope," Falk said. "Getting there to see him in person would mean that we had arrived."

Not only did Falk get the opportunity to experience the Dinner of Champions, he also had the opportunity to meet the Hollywood icon in his dressing room before the show.

"I gave him a Michigan Rose Bowl sweater," Falk said. "He was really gracious and told me that he liked Ohio State because he was raised in Ohio. But then he said he liked Michigan, too. He said he really enjoyed watching how we played."

In the game, Michigan took a 6–0 lead but lost 14–6 to a strong University of Southern California team. Late in the fourth quarter, Michigan drove to the Trojan 17-yard line but ran out of downs in their potential game-tying drive.

On the flight back to Michigan, Falk remembers Bo's honest appraisal of the game.

"We played hard," Bo said. "But you must remember, Jon, 22 of those USC players are going to the NFL."

Despite the loss, Michigan had made it to the dance. There would be several more. And Falk has never forgotten to savor every moment.

Chapter **8**

Curtis Greer: "What Are You Gonna Do About It?"

From his distinguished Michigan career, Curtis Greer learned that trust is earned, not merely given.

That's why the former All-American defensive lineman, who spent eight years in the NFL, felt confident having his undergraduate son, Brandon, work for Falk as a student assistant equipment manager.

"I say thank you to Jon Falk," Greer said. "Big Jon is just like Bo—honest and oozing with integrity. Both taught me how to do things the right way—

the Michigan way. You can coach your kids, but others raise them. I knew Jon would teach him the right things in life that you can't find in the textbooks."

Of course, Brandon did fairly well with the books, too. After graduating from Michigan's College of Business, he earned a law degree from Michigan.

"I know he's not gonna go to Wall Street and screw things up," Greer smiled proudly. "Jon helped, and I thank him."

You can coach your kids, but others raise them. I knew Jon would teach him the right things in life that you can't find in the textbooks.
—Curtis Greer

A graduate of Detroit Cass Tech High School, Greer and teammates Harlan Huckleby and Tom Seabron were part of the fabulous 1975 recruiting class that also featured Rick Leach, Russell Davis, and Jerry Meter. The following year Cass Tech's Roosevelt Smith joined the Michigan family.

All learned quickly that Falk was a man they could trust.

"Jon Falk isn't just the equipment manager," Greer said. "I view him as the vice president of operations for Michigan football for 37 years. Nothing gets done 'til Jon Falk gets it going. No practice. No uniforms. No balls. No busses. Nothing. He makes everything happen."

What he does behind the scenes, however, is what separates Falk from a mere job description.

As a freshman, Greer observed upperclassmen such as Calvin O'Neal, Greg Morton, and Tim Davis. He watched how they acted—on the field and in the locker room. He noticed the relationship they had with Falk. He felt the admiration they felt for Falk.

Greer came to the conclusion that Falk was "one of the most integral ingredients to our success."

"He's a conduit between the coaches and players," Greer said. "In good times and tough times, a player could go into his office just to get things off his chest. We talked about school. We talked about football. We talked about family. We talked about Bo. If we were bitching, he'd listen."

And when a player was finished, Falk always asked the same question—"Now what are you gonna do about it?"

"That's the way he is," Greer said. "Bitching is alright to clear your mind. But it doesn't solve any problem. How you tackle a situation is what matters. Big Jon helped you find the strength to do something about it."

Greer particularly appreciated Falk's honesty even when his message wasn't exactly what a player wanted to hear.

"That's why everybody admired him," Greer said. "He never worried if a player didn't like to hear what he was saying. It was always the truth. He was never a yeller. But he always got his point across. I remember him saying so many times to a player: 'Son, don't screw this up.'"

Now a successful businessman living in New Jersey, Greer credits Falk with teaching him to do things the right way.

"Jon Falk touched all of us," Greer said. "Besides Bo, he was the only one who touched all of us. He was an integral part of all the success we enjoyed."

When Greer faces a problem today, he stops to ask himself—"Now what are you gonna do about it?"

Chapter **9**

1977: The Equipment Is Where?

Falk didn't have to wait long to savor his second Rose Bowl experience. However, it came with a sticky situation that had to be resolved before the team plane touched down for practice in Los Angeles.

In 1977, for the ninth time in the last 10 years, Michigan played Ohio State for the Big Ten title and a trip to the Rose Bowl. For the second straight

year, Michigan held the Buckeyes without a touchdown in a 14–6 victory at
The Big House.

Everything was rosy. The Wolverines were anxious to take on Washington.

But a funny thing happened on the way to Los Angeles that sent Falk scurrying before Bo and the team arrived.

Falk left for Los Angeles on an 8:00 AM flight one day before the team
departed. Four huge, boxcar-sized containers filled with all of the team's uniforms and equipment were loaded onto a cargo plane scheduled to arrive
ahead of Falk. When Falk touched down in Los Angeles, he and his assistants
immediately drove to Citrus Junior College where the equipment was supposed
to be waiting. The team was scheduled to have its first workout the following
afternoon.

Just one problem—the containers were nowhere to be found. Falk was
teased by one of the Citrus staff members that he had met the previous year.

"Guess you're traveling light this year," he said.

"What do you mean?" Falk asked.

"Well," the local responded, "you didn't send as much equipment as you
did last year."

Falk immediately dashed to his car and drove to the air cargo facility at the
Los Angeles Airport.

"I called Detroit, and they said the containers left this morning," the representative said.

"So where are they?" Falk persisted.

The representative scratched his head and shrugged his shoulders. "Sorry…I
don't know."

For Falk, this was a fourth-and-20 dilemma with only a few seconds left
on the clock.

"Wait a minute," Falk pleaded his case. "This is a life and death situation—
my life or my death. If the Michigan football team gets out here tomorrow and
finds no gear, Bo is gonna kill me."

A myriad of Falk's emotions were melting into a foreboding feeling of
anger, frustration, despair, and fear for his life. A cargo supervisor was standing nearby and overheard the unusual conversation.

"Hey," he said. "You're from the University of Michigan? I graduated from Michigan. I love Michigan football."

Falk eyed him guardedly.

"Well, if you love it that much, how the hell are you gonna get me out of this mess?" Falk said.

The supervisor fired up his computer and started pecking the keyboard for what seemed like an eternity to Falk.

"Everything got sent to Chicago first, and then Chicago blew it," the supervisor finally said. "They put everything on a plane for Las Vegas where it's sitting right now."

Falk forced a smile.

"That's not gonna do me any good," he said. "I don't think Bo will want to fly up to Vegas to practice."

The supervisor got on the phone with one of his colleagues in Las Vegas to check on cargo flights for Los Angeles that day.

"Just one…going out tonight," the voice said. "It's a produce jet filled to the gills with all fresh fruit for the farmer's market."

The supervisor gave Falk a thumbs-up sign and told his colleague that some people would just have to wait for their watermelons and peaches. He was ordering the Michigan equipment to be sent on that plane.

The plane arrived at 1:00 AM PST, 20 hours after Falk and his assistants had left home. They had not slept. They had not even been to the hotel. They immediately loaded the trucks with all the gear and delivered it to Citrus Junior College. They finished by filling each locker with the appropriate travel bag.

Falk finished his work at 8:00 AM. The team was due in at 9:00 AM, so he stretched out on the floor of a hallway to the locker room. He rested his head on a travel bag and caught one hour of much-needed sleep.

He was awakened by a jab to the ribs from one of Bo's shoes.

"Get up, Falk," Bo said. "What the hell did you do last night? Big night in L.A.?"

"Why don't you take a deep breath, coach, and go to your locker?" Falk said. "Everything is in there ready and waiting for you guys. And you're not gonna believe how it got here."

Dedication—that's what we like here.
—Bo Schembechler

Upon hearing the adventure, Bo laughed at the comedy.

"I knew I had the right man for the job," he said. "Dedication—that's what we like here."

* * * *

The 1977 season was a near repeat of the previous year.

After winning the first three games, Michigan took a No. 3 ranking into the game against No. 5 ranked Texas A&M at The Big House. The Aggies had an impressive running game and an outstanding field goal kicker in Tony Franklin.

Equipment manager Billy Pickert was a good friend of Falk's. While conversing with Pickert as the Aggie truck was being unloaded, Falk was astounded at the number of footballs they had brought.

"Billy, you've got 36 new footballs for the game tomorrow?" Falk asked.

"We heard that when you kick a ball into the stands here, you don't get it back," Pickert said.

"Well, here's the solution for that, Pick…don't score," Falk cracked.

When Pickert packed the truck after Saturday's game, he had 35 balls left. After taking a 3–0 lead into the second quarter, Texas A&M was shut out as Michigan exploded for a 41–3 victory.

Two more victories later, including a 56–0 pounding of Wisconsin in Madison, Michigan roared to the top spot in both wire polls. The Wolverines took their No.1 ranking to Minnesota the next week where water literally splashed all over their parade.

It was a beautiful sunny afternoon on Friday when Michigan worked out on the field at Minnesota. The groundskeeper told Bo after practice that the field would be watered and the excess sucked out.

"Bo, they don't have a sucker for field water here," Falk said. "This is natural grass."

"The man said they were gonna suck the water out, Jon," Bo said. "They'll suck it out."

Not only was the water not sucked out, when Falk arrived at the stadium at 6:00 AM, the sprinklers were still running. The muddy quagmire spewed water onto the track that surrounded the field. Falk called Minnesota Athletic Director Paul Giel at 7:00 AM.

"Mr. Giel, I think you better get over here and check this field out right now," Falk said.

Falk was suspicious of the incident but nothing could be proved. Minnesota featured a burly team that pounded the ball up the middle. Michigan featured quarterback Rick Leach and tailback Harlan Huckleby, who ran to the outside.

Not a good formula for a muddy field.

Falk took Bo to the field as soon as he got off the team bus. His dress shoes sank two inches into the ground.

"We're screwed today, Jon," he said.

Michigan wore half-inch steel-tipped cleats that Falk figured would be perfect on a regular field. They weren't. Michigan runners slipped and slid like novice ice skaters, and Minnesota shut out the nation's top-ranked team 16–0. It was the first shutout suffered by Bo's teams in nine years. On the bus after the game, Falk sat next to Bo.

"You know your shoes didn't hold up today," Bo said.

"Yes sir, I'm sorry," Falk said.

Then Bo poked him in the chest and smiled.

"It wasn't the shoes today," Bo said. "We didn't come to play. That's what makes me upset. We didn't come to play. Sometimes when you're successful, you forget about all the things you have to do to maintain that success."

Michigan rebounded with three more decisive victories before the annual clash against Ohio State. And in the shoe department, Falk felt confident. The Wolverines had their "Tiger Paws" for the slick Tartan Turf field at Michigan Stadium.

Before the season started, Falk talked to Ara Parseghian. The Notre Dame coach told him that they had found some shoes made in Canada that stood up well on slick turf.

Bo ordered Falk to get six pairs air-shipped to try in practice. Players using them in practice made pinpoint cuts with footing as solid as a statue.

"Jon," Bo barked. "Go order 250 pairs of these right away."

This time Falk went straight to Athletic Director Don Canham, who was stunned by the $10,000 price tag.

"For shoes?" Canham asked.

"You know how slippery that field is, and you know we can't afford to lose any games because of a slippery field," Falk replied.

Canham laughed and said, "Write the purchase order."

The shoes were air freighted in time for the first game of the season during which Michigan went undefeated at home.

The week before the Ohio State game, an article appeared in the *Columbus Dispatch* that said, "Woody Discovers the Secret to Michigan Shoes." The article explained that while watching films, Woody detected that visiting teams were slipping, but Michigan players moved swiftly and remained steady as a rock. Woody immediately ordered the same shoes that Michigan wore for all of his players for the big game.

"It's the same philosophy over there," Falk said. "Whatever it takes to win."

During Ohio State's workout in the stadium on Friday, Falk was walking up The Tunnel when he noticed some Buckeye players darting out of the Michigan locker room.

"They got the same shoes we do," Falk heard them saying as they raced back into their own locker room.

"Hey, get out of the Michigan locker room!" Falk yelled. "If you wanted to get into that locker room so bad, you should have come to school here when you had the chance."

So both teams—so to speak—were on equal footing. What mattered more than the shoes, of course, were the players who wore them.

Michigan went ahead 7–3 in the second quarter and never trailed in a 14–6 victory. It was Michigan's second straight victory over Ohio State, and in neither game had the Buckeyes scored a touchdown.

Perhaps the player who made the most of his shoes that day was Michigan linebacker Mel Owens who made a game-saving tackle with about 5:30 left to play.

Ohio State tailback Ron Springs broke into the open and was speeding all alone down the eastern sideline. Owens flashed from the west side of the field and finally made a diving stop by knocking Springs out of bounds on the 8-yard line. Ohio State fumbled the ball away and was stopped on its final possession as Michigan held on to victory.

"I don't know where I got that speed because I don't run that fast," Owens said to Falk after the game.

"Well, you must have had angels picking you up because you did it," an ecstatic Falk replied. "Let me tell you right now, anything you want from Michigan you earned today."

More than 30 years later, Owens keeps the picture of that game-saving tackle on his cell phone.

"It may not seem like much at the time, but when an equipment manager can make a suggestion to the head coach—like those shoes—then he feels like he contributed a little something to the victory," Falk said.

Certainly Owens and all of his teammates would agree.

After the game, Woody held his press conference in a little room outside of the locker rooms in which a tractor was stored. He leaned up against the tractor to situate himself directly under the drip of a leaky roof.

"This is what happens when we come here to play," he said. "A man has to get his clothes wet."

Before each Michigan game, Woody used every sliver of psychological warfare to inspire his team. Ohio State equipment manager John Bozick was instructed to put a small rip into the back of the bombastic coach's hat. During a fiery pregame speech, Hayes then would tear his cap to symbolize what he wanted done to the Wolverines.

All great coaches are master dramatists. Woody and Bo in the same building at the same time were worth the price of admission. All of the theatrics mattered little that day. Michigan was off to its second straight Rose Bowl where Falk first had to resolve the mystery of the missing gear.

Michigan rallied from a 17–0 halftime deficit but lost to Washington 27–20. Late in the game, quarterback Rick Leach led a determined drive to the Washington 8-yard line, but a diving interception snuffed the dramatic comeback bid.

Nonetheless, Michigan made the Rose Bowl. And as Falk learned quickly, he enjoyed every moment.

Chapter **10**

Rob Lytle: Always the Team

Falk and the assistant coaches were on bed-check assignment during two-a-day summer camp in 1975. It was their job to ensure all players were in their South Quad rooms before curfew in order to be fresh for the next day's grueling practices.

Hearing no sound coming from the room of Rob Lytle and Gordon Bell, Falk entered to discover neither of the roommates present. Word spread quickly about the pair of MIAs. All players who had checked into their rooms confirmed that the two had returned to the dorm with them.

Big trouble could be brewing if word got back to Bo.

Returning to the missing players' room, Falk and running backs coach Chuck Stobart hoped that perhaps their eyes had failed them. Upon opening the door, Lytle and Bell were tucked in their beds.

For a dash of excitement to break the monotony of the grinding practices, Lytle and Bell had climbed out the window and stood on the ledge just before Falk made his first trip through.

Feeling duped—yet refreshingly relieved—Falk could do nothing but smile at the little "tempest in a teapot."

During his 38 years at Michigan, Falk has worked with more than a thousand players. He takes pride in treating each one equally. But it's impossible not to have a few favorites along the way.

"Rob Lytle was a true leader," Falk said. "Not just because he was a captain. Hook, line, and sinker, Robbie bought in to Bo's program that no one person was bigger than the team. I creid when he died in 2010."

That was never more apparent than during the 1975 season when a decision by Lytle prompted Bo to say, "In all my years of coaching, Rob Lytle was one of the most unselfish players I've ever seen."

Bo was sitting on a pair of aces with Lytle and Bell battling for the starting tailback job. In 1974, they alternated starts and carries during a game. Bo knew the power of the weapons sitting in his arsenal and had to devise a plan for both to be in the game at the same time.

During the summer of 1975, Lytle decided to drive to Fremont, Ohio, for a few days at home. Even before he arrived, Bo had called Lytle's mother and told her he wanted him back in his office by 11:00 AM the next morning.

Lytle's first reaction was a sudden case of nerves. Earlier that week, he had been involved with a harmless off-field incident that he knew would upset Bo.

"It was amazing," Lytle smiled. "Bo knew everything that was going on with his players everywhere in town."

When he reported the next day, the door to Bo's office was closed. He still could hear his coach's voice yelling and his fist pounding the desk.

"I have to follow this?" Lytle wondered.

The door opened, and a tall man emerged—although he may have stood even a few inches taller before encountering Bo's wrath. Bo had heard some rumors about certain Michigan zealots offering gifts to players that extended beyond NCAA rules.

"That was not gonna happen with Bo and his players," Lytle said. "At least I felt a little relieved that he wasn't gonna get on me for what I had done earlier in the week."

Instead, Bo asked his star running back for a favor. He wanted to move Lytle to fullback so that he and Bell could work out of the same backfield.

"We're making changes in our offense, and we think this could be something special," Bo said. "I can't move Bell there, but I can move you. It means that I'm asking you to give up everything you came to Michigan for."

Lytle didn't blink. But he was a little unsure.

"I don't have an issue with that if it helps the team," he said. "But are you sure you want only a 200-pound fullback?"

Bo was unconcerned. He knew the size of Lytle's heart. Bell wound up leading the Big Ten with 1,063 yards rushing and a season total of 1,390. From his fullback spot, Lytle totaled 769 yards in the Big Ten and became the first Michigan fullback to crack 1,000 yards for the season with 1,040.

For the 1976 season, Lytle moved back to tailback and led the Big Ten with 1,136 yards and 1,474 for the season.

"That's the kind of kid Robbie was," Falk said.

In 1976, Lytle was a co-captain with Calvin O'Neal. With a little bit of coaxing from Falk, he rewarded the confidence his teammates had placed in him.

Michigan started the season ranked No. 1 in the nation. They led the parade for eight straight weeks until being upset at Purdue, 16–14. Following the game, Bo was livid.

"You blew it," he shouted in the hushed locker room. "You blew it all today."

"I had never seen Bo explode like that before," Falk said.

After packing the equipment, Falk stopped at Lytle's locker to tell him the season wasn't over.

"If we beat Illinois next week and Ohio State after that, we win the Big Ten and go to the Rose Bowl," he told Lytle.

Lytle pondered a moment and then called the team's attention to the center of the room. He explained the situation to the players and finished his talk by extending his hand. All the players gathered in the center to stack hand upon hand.

"Illinois…then Ohio State," was all anyone said before heading to the showers. Michigan went home to hammer Illinois 38–7 and then traveled to Columbus to humiliate the Buckeyes 22–0.

Jon wasn't afraid to talk to players if he thought it was for the good of the team.

—Rob Lytle

"Jon wasn't afraid to talk to players if he thought it was for the good of the team," Lytle said. "He knew when to needle them and knew when to pat them on the back."

After Lytle fumbled in a game early in his career, Falk taped a handle to a football and placed it in Lytle's locker before the next practice. "We just want to make sure you have a handle on the situation by next week," Falk said.

"That was Big Jon," Lytle said. "And that's why everybody loved him."

Chapter **11**
1978: Another Rivalry Game

he 1978 season revived a celebrated rivalry that had been dormant for 35 years when Michigan signed a long-term contract to play Notre Dame.

Almost every Division I team points to a particular rivalry game on the schedule each year. Some schools have a couple. Michigan is loaded with three.

That's a giant gulp of target games for a coach to get his team particularly stimulated. But that's the way it is when you've won more games than any school in the history of Division I football.

The annual game with Notre Dame marks the meeting of arguably the two most colorful names in college football history. There's the in-state rivalry game against Michigan State with bragging rights and recruiting implications hanging in the balance. And, of course, there is "The Game" with Ohio State that more often than not determines the Big Ten championship and captures the imagination of football fanatics across the country.

"When a youngster comes to Michigan, he knows he's gonna get the opportunity to play one of the toughest schedules in the country," Falk said. "That's part of the package that makes going to Michigan so special. It provides lifetime opportunities that a young man can't get anywhere else. If a young man plays football at Michigan and goes on to get his degree, a lot of doors open that other people can't get into."

Nonetheless, red-letter games can be particularly taxing to coaches in an age when the number of football scholarships has been drastically reduced and parity of conference play has increased.

"Back when Bo and Woody coached, it really was a case of the 'Big Two and Little Eight' in the Big Ten," Falk said. "You couldn't go to sleep against the other teams, but you sort of knew it was eventually gonna get down to the Michigan–Ohio State game."

Now there are so many land mines on the schedule that are impossible to ignore. And for Michigan each year, games with Notre Dame, Michigan State, Penn State, and Ohio State are high-energy affairs.

"A lot of people wonder why we even play Notre Dame," Falk said. "But it makes for a game that the whole country wants to see. I always tell our guys that this is one of the reasons you came to Michigan. You're always on stage."

For Falk, the early-season game against Notre Dame serves as a good barometer for how the season will unfold.

"If you beat Notre Dame, you're generally gonna have a pretty successful season," he said. "They're a lot like Ohio State. Notre Dame, Ohio State, Michigan… we all recruit a lot of the same kids. Ask any of the men who have coached in these games, and they'll tell you how much it means to their programs."

While playing in South Bend is always a challenge, Falk appreciates the way Michigan has been treated when visiting.

"They do a good job," he said. "They let the game be determined on the field the way it's supposed to be."

The revival of the colorful rivalry in 1978 had Michigan traveling to South Bend for the first meeting between the schools since 1943.

Rick Leach led the way for the Wolverines. He ran for Michigan's lone first-half score. Then he fired three touchdown passes in the second half when the defense held the Irish scoreless in a 28–14 victory.

"Like I always said, Rick Leach was a stallion," Falk said. "You wanted him on your side in big games."

Later, Falk had the opportunity to establish a relationship with Lou Holtz when Holtz coached at Notre Dame.

At home after the 1987 game when Michigan lost 26–7, Falk received a call from the Notre Dame equipment manager Gene O'Neil. He asked if Falk would return to the visitors locker room to see if Darrell Gordon had left his watch there. It was a gold-plated watch with diamond-studded numbers.

"The young man obviously didn't buy it at Wal-Mart," Falk said.

Falk told his Notre Dame counterpart he would look for the watch, but chances of finding it were "slim and none."

Upon returning to the pitch-dark locker room, Falk sniffed around and made the discovery. He called South Bend to say he would send the watch overnight on Monday.

On Tuesday, the elated Irish player received his watch. On the same day, Falk received a phone call from Lou Holtz, along with a letter a few days later.

"Darrell was really worried," Holtz told Falk. "That's a very expensive watch. You could just as easily have called back on Saturday and said it wasn't there."

Falk pondered a moment. Whenever speaking to a person of great respect, he chooses his words carefully.

"Coach Holtz," Falk said, "that would have been the hardest thing to do when I held it right there in my hand. What I did was the easiest thing."

Over the phone, Falk could hear Holtz chuckling.

"You've been raised pretty well by Bo and those guys at Michigan, haven't you?" Holtz said.

You've been raised pretty well by Bo and those guys at Michigan, haven't you?

—Lou Holtz

Falk had a similar experience with Michigan State coach George Perles after the 1990 game. Michigan went into the game ranked No. 1 in the country and suffered a 28–27 loss following a controversial call on an attempted two-point conversion with six seconds left in the game.

Midway through the third quarter, Michigan State's telephone lines between the headsets on the field and the pressbox broke down. A frantic Bob Knickerbocker, Michigan State's equipment manager, came dashing across the field seeking Falk's assistance.

"Big Jon, you've gotta help me…you've gotta help me!" he screamed. "Our phone lines are down, and George is gonna fire me if we don't get them fixed."

Despite being tied 14–14 in the spirited game, Falk raced up to the press-box to make some repairs and then went over to Michigan State's side of the field to make the final adjustments for putting the Spartan staff back on line.

With 1:59 left in the game, Michigan State's Tico Duckett scored on a nine-yard run for a 28–21 lead.

Led by quarterback Elvis Grbac, Michigan capped a 71-yard drive with a 6-yard touchdown pass to Derrick Alexander to make the score 28–27.

Going for the victory with a two-point conversion, Desmond Howard dropped the ball in the end zone on a pass in which he appeared to have been tripped by a Michigan State defender, although no interference was called. The following day, Coach Gary Moeller received an apologetic phone call from Dave Parry, the Big Ten's head of officials, for the controversy that resulted from the lack of a pass interference call.

Nevertheless, the score stood, and Michigan's No. 1 ranking disappeared. After the game, Falk went into the visitor's locker room to talk to Knickerbocker.

"Coach Perles wants to personally thank you for all you did for him today," Knickerbocker said.

As the two equipment managers approached the shower area, Perles asked, "You're the man [who] got my phones back up?"

"Yes sir," Falk said. "That was me."

Perles eyed him for a moment.

"We were doing pretty well without my headset," Perles joked. "All my coaches got pretty mad when the phones came back and I could talk to them."

Then Perles shook Falk's hand.

"I always wondered if there were first-class people [who] worked down here at Michigan," Perles said. "Today I met one of them, and I want to thank you for what you did for us."

"That meant a lot to me," Falk said. "Games last for maybe three-and-a-half hours," he said. "Friends last forever, and that's part of this business, too. We remain friends today. In fact, Bob Knickerbocker is one of my best friends."

The 1978 game against Michigan State was also filled with controversy. This one, however, burned off the field.

Throughout the week, quarterback Rick Leach was harassed with threatening letters and phone calls that went unresolved and, fortunately, unfulfilled.

"The FBI got involved," Falk said. "So did the Ann Arbor police. We had so many plainclothes men around the bench I thought maybe we had sold tickets for on the field."

It would have been easy for Bo to say that the added commotion caused Michigan to stumble, 24–15. In the locker room after the game, however, speaking to Falk, Bo summed it up succinctly. "It was the Michigan State defense—that was the real nemesis."

Fortunately for the Wolverines, Ohio State lost to Purdue. The two archrivals went undefeated the rest of the way to set up another season-ending showdown at Columbus.

And for the second straight trip there, the water was "mysteriously" out of order again on Saturday morning.

The Michigan defense was spectacular. Taking a 7–3 first-quarter lead, the Wolverines shut down the Buckeyes the rest of the way for a 14–3 victory to earn their third straight Rose Bowl trip.

While victory, of course, was sweet, little did anyone realize that the Bo vs. Woody rivalry had ended.

Bob Hope again hosted the Dinner of Champions affair in Los Angeles. During the affair, word started circulating that Woody Hayes had punched a Clemson player in the Gator Bowl. By the time Michigan returned to their hotel, speculation was rampant that the legendary coach was going to be fired.

"Bo loved Woody," Falk said. "And, man, we all loved to beat him. But Bo had tremendous respect for the man and taught us to always respect him and his team. That's just the way it was, and we all felt sad about what we were hearing."

The Rose Bowl will be remembered for the "Phantom Touchdown" that USC's Charles White scored. While replays of the short-yardage play show that White had fumbled the ball that was recovered by Michigan's Jerry Meter on the 1-yard line, the referee ruled that the running back had broken the plane of the goal line before fumbling. USC held on for a 17–10 victory.

"No home run, but that was still the Rose Bowl," Falk said. "And that's another memory for life."

Chapter **12**
The New Phone Man

Soon after Falk arrived at Michigan, he was called into Bo's office.

"What do you know about telephones, Falk?" the coach asked.

Falk thought he was joking, so he played along.

"I can make calls…I can answer them…and I'm pretty good with dialing long distance, too," he cracked.

Not the kind of phones Bo was talking about. And he wasn't joking.

Bo was referring to the headsets coaches wear to maintain contact from the pressbox to the field during a game.

"Do you know how they're wired?' Bo asked. "Do you know how they work?"

Falk, of course, had to plead his ignorance.

"Well, you better learn," Bo said, "because you're the new phone man."

Along with his responsibilities for all of the football equipment, Falk was placed in charge of establishing the lines between the phones for both home and road games.

Falk tackled his new assignment with his usual vigor. He even scheduled a few training sessions with a company that sold the products. Those were still the early years of in-game phone communication. The phones basically operated on hot wire, and each school provided equipment to the visiting team.

For a variety of reasons, including weather conditions, crowd noise, and other unforeseen circumstances, the systems were not impeccably reliable and created many frantic moments before and during games for Falk. Bo demanded a plan that would eliminate all such uncertainties. He also wanted to take his own system on the road.

"Jon, I want a headset that keeps the crowd noise out so I can hear better," he said. "You're the phone man. Take care of it."

Falk quickly did some shopping and came up with a $350 pair of headsets that the company offered to Bo to try for a week.

"Now Bo, I've got to ask one favor," Falk said. "You have to promise me that you won't throw these babies to the ground."

Bo looked at him suspiciously.

"What are you talking about?" Bo said. "I don't throw headsets to the ground."

Falk looked back and couldn't resist smiling.

"What do you mean you don't throw headsets to the ground?" he said. "Bo, let me tell you. If you're not the one throwing headsets to the ground when you get mad with a referee's call or a player makes some dumb mistake, then there's a guy out there [who] looks just like you and he's giving you a bad name."

Bo looked at Falk sheepishly and finally broke into laughter.

As expected during the game, Bo happened to disagree with one of the official's calls. Just as he was reaching to the headset with his right hand, Falk jumped in front of him and crouched into a basketball defensive stance with both hands extended.

"It looked like I was waiting to steal the ball," Falk said.

In an instant, Bo spotted him. He removed the set from his head and held it in his hand.

"Damn you, Jon," was all Bo said. "Damn you."

As technology advanced, Michigan switched to a highly sophisticated wireless system. To ensure the system's efficiency, Falk established a relationship with Bob Wierzbicki, an AT&T retiree who lives in Ann Arbor. Wierzbicki volunteers his time as the official Michigan football phone man and is onsite for all home and road games.

When it comes to phones—that was Falk's best executive decision.

Chapter **13**

1979: No. 1 Meets No. 87

alk was speaking to a hulking figure on the Michigan bench before a game early in the 1979 season. He called a freshman over to meet the visitor.

"I want you to meet this man," Falk told Anthony Carter.

Carter shook the gentleman's hand. He was shy and always polite.

"Did you used to be a player?" Carter innocently asked.

As the visitor smiled, Falk told Carter to look up and down the Michigan bench and pick out No. 87. Carter did as instructed.

"I don't see anyone wearing No. 87," Carter finally said.

Again the visitor smiled.

Did you used to be a player?
—Freshman Anthony Carter upon
his introduction to Ron Kramer

"And you won't," Falk said. "Because it belongs to him. This is Ron Kramer. Two-time All-American and one of the greatest players in the history of Michigan football. His number was retired in 1956."

Falk was proud to have made the memorable introduction.

"Who would have thought at the time that Anthony Carter would go on to grab three All-American honors?" Falk said.

Kramer died on September 11, 2010 shortly before Michigan defeated Notre Dame.

Perhaps even more stunning, who would have thought that a receiver would earn such distinction under "always run first" Bo? The magically humorous moment was over in an instant, but it still remains one of Falk's fondest memories.

The summer after Bo recruited Carter to Michigan, Bo was going over numbers to be assigned to players with Falk.

"I want this young man to wear No. 1," Bo told Falk. "This young man is going to be the next Johnny Rodgers of college football."

Actually he wasn't. He was better.

Playing in only his eighth game for the Wolverines, Carter hooked up with quarterback John Wangler to create one of the most magical moments in the 130-year history of Michigan football.

At The Big House with 55-seconds left in the game, Indiana scored a touchdown to tie the score at 21–21. On the sixth play after the kickoff, Wangler hit Lawrence Reid with a pass near midfield. Reid was scrambling toward the Indiana sideline but couldn't run out of bounds fast enough to stop the clock.

Somehow—and no one knows how for sure—the ball popped out of his hands and into those of Indiana head coach Lee Corso. The irate coach heatedly argued that the ball had been thrown intentionally out of bounds to stop the clock.

"Of course, we didn't see it that way," Falk said. "More importantly, neither did the referees."

Now Michigan had the ball on the Indiana 45-yard line with 6 seconds to play. With one play left, Wangler dropped back to pass and hit Carter, who had cut into the middle. The freshman broke one tackle and eluded two others when he stumbled and looked as if he would fall. He miraculously regained his footing and raced into the end zone as the fans swarmed the field. No extra point was needed, and the game belonged to Michigan, 27–21.

"Lee Corso is a good man," Falk said. "He knows college football and knows how to pump up the game. Whenever I see him now, I always tease him that he made the second-best catch of that game."

That one game—that single play—immortalized Carter for Michigan fans forever. And there were three more years yet to come.

Of course, Carter earned the legendary status that his acrobatic magic brought to the memorable touchdown. But Falk also remembers the coolness of Wangler, who triggered the drama.

"John Wangler was one of the toughest competitors ever to wear the Michigan uniform," he said. "I still picture him standing back there, waiting for just the right instant to get the ball to Carter."

Playing North Carolina in the Gator Bowl after the regular season, Wangler was tackled on a sprint out and suffered a severe knee injury. By that time, he had already passed for 204 yards.

Not only was Wangler unable to play the rest of the game, his football future at Michigan was in serious jeopardy after undergoing radical surgery. He demonstrated his passion for Michigan by promising he would return for his senior season.

"I never saw anyone rehab himself as hard as John did the entire seven months before fall practice," Falk said. "He was in the trainer's room every day. He promised himself he would be back in 1980, and he wouldn't let anything stand in his way."

Because of Carter's slight build, defenders were trained to hit him hard then grab his jersey to pull him down before he could break away for extra yardage. Bo was concerned that Carter might end up with a helmet implanted into his chest. He instructed Falk to purchase some tear-away jerseys.

"I was able to come up with some material that would almost disintegrate when you touched it," Falk said. "Anthony would go through seven or eight jerseys a game. We had 15 for him each game—home and away. A tackler would come up and grab that jersey, and he'd be left with a handful of material while watching Anthony sprint down the field for extra yards. Defenders looked like they were grabbing at a ghost."

The next year the NCAA outlawed the material. By then, Carter had put on a little more bulk, and his technique became more refined.

Lifted by the thriller against Indiana, Michigan hammered Wisconsin the next week, 54–0. After taking a 17–0 lead into the half, Michigan exploded for 23 third-quarter points as Bo emptied the bench. Wangler completed 10-of-13 passes, and running back Butch Woolfolk scored three touchdowns, including a 92-yard run.

Even a defeat at Purdue the following week didn't eliminate Michigan from title contention. But its bid for a fourth straight conference championship was snapped by Ohio State. Led by first-year coach Earle Bruce, the Buckeyes scored the winning touchdown on a return of a blocked punt in the fourth quarter for an 18–15 victory in Ann Arbor.

Michigan had to settle for a berth in the Gator Bowl and suffered a 17–15 loss.

But the Carter legacy had been firmly established. And it certainly was not a one-catch story.

Chapter **12**
Trophy Games

One of the first assignments given to Falk after being hired by Bo was to "keep" the Little Brown Jug and the Paul Bunyan Trophy.

Over the years, he's done a pretty good job. Of course, the coaches and players might have had a little something to do with keeping both treasures in Ann Arbor almost every year.

"I just tell the boys to go out and win it, and I'll keep it safe," Falk cracked.

More than a century old, the Little Brown Jug goes to the winner of the Michigan-Minnesota game and has spent enough time in Ann Arbor to qualify for permanent residency. The Jug is held for a year by the winning team, who is then responsible for bringing it to the game the following season.

"I never knew how important the Little Brown Jug was until we lost it," Bo said.

Bo's teams manhandled the Golden Gophers in their first eight meetings before surrendering the Jug in 1977 in Minnesota. Michigan entered the game with the nation's No. 1 ranking. The Gophers, obviously, seemed unimpressed and handed Bo his first shutout, 16–0.

Of course, Bo never did anything in an understated fashion. During his 21-year career at Michigan, Bo's only other loss to Minnesota was a 20–17 decision at home in 1986.

The battle for the Little Brown Jug is the granddaddy of all college football trophy games. Now there are approximately 60 such trophy games across the country.

None, however, enjoys the history of the Little Brown Jug.

The battle began in 1903 when coach Fielding Yost took his Michigan team to Minnesota. Yost was concerned that the Gophers would not provide pure water to the players on his team. He ordered a member of his staff to purchase a jug to prevent any problems.

After Minnesota scored late for a 6–6 tie, pandemonium erupted in the stands. The game was called by the referees with time left on the clock. In their haste to leave, Michigan left the jug on the field. It was discovered later by Minnesota equipment manager Oscar Munson. He gave it to his athletic director. On the jug, the Gophers painted, "Michigan Jug—Captured by Oscar, October 31, 1903." They also painted the score: "Minnesota 6, Michigan 6."

Yost sent a letter requesting the Jug's return. Minnesota's athletic director wrote back, "If you want it, you'll have to come up and win it." Through the years, Michigan has made the Jug its own.

The Jug disappeared from Michigan's trophy case from 1930 to 1934 when a replica jug was used. The real Jug was accidentally discovered behind a clump of bushes at an Ann Arbor service station. The authenticity of the original was confirmed by a flaw on one of the sides that could not have been duplicated.

The Jug is not particularly attractive, and most of the time it sits in the equipment room in a locked box in Schembechler Hall under Falk's watchful eye.

But its significance springs to life each autumn when the two teams tangle.

In 2003, Michigan traveled to Minnesota riding a 14-game winning streak over the Gophers. Playing at the Minneapolis Metrodome, Michigan fell 14 points behind before all the players had their cleats tied. In the second half when things still looked darker than a Minnesota winter midnight, Falk ran over to the Minnesota equipment manager to explain the postgame procedure for the transfer of the Jug.

"When you beat us, I'll have the Jug out of its box," he told him. "We'll have the case in a hamper and roll it over to you from our locker room."

Late in the third quarter and throughout the fourth, the Michigan offense suddenly rose from the dead. Behind the determination of quarterback John Navarre, the Wolverines rallied for a 38–35 victory in one of the school's biggest comebacks. Michigan followed that comeback with a 27–24 victory in 2004.

Then the inevitable happened. In 2005, the 16-game victory streak was snapped with a 23–20 defeat at The Big House.

Glen Mason was the Minnesota coach and a good friend of Falk. During the Minnesota workout on the Friday before the game, Mason visited with his friend.

"The Little Brown Jug?" he asked. "As far as I'm concerned, it's a myth. I've never seen it. None of my staff has ever seen it. Certainly, none of my players have seen it. Nobody at Minnesota has seen it for I don't know how long. How do we know it even exists? As far as I'm concerned, it's just a myth."

Mason, of course, was teasing. But steroids hadn't even found their way into Major League Baseball the last time the Jug had spent any real time in Minnesota.

Nobody at Minnesota has seen it for I don't know how long. How do we know it even exists? As far as I'm concerned, it's just a myth.
—Glen Mason

With time running out, a Gopher tailback broke for 63 yards to set up a field goal to snap a 20–20 tie. The Minnesota players charged across the field to claim their trophy. They swarmed the Michigan bench and hoisted the Jug high.

After the game, Falk visited Mason in the visitor's locker room.

"Hey Jon," Mason shouted as he spotted Falk. "You know, that Jug isn't a myth. We have it right here. I can see it. I can touch it."

Falk was dejected about the loss but felt good for his friend.

"Let me tell you something right now, Glen," Falk said. "You take good care of that Jug. Don't break it. Don't let anybody who might drop it handle it. You enjoy every minute of it. Because I'm telling you right now, we're coming to take it back."

Mason not only was careful with the Jug, he placed it on a seat next to him on the plane ride back to Minnesota. Players and staff kept walking to the front of the plane to touch the treasured trophy.

"Don't you drop it," Mason told everyone. "My friend Jon back in Michigan said he'd kill me if anything happened to it while it was with us."

Mason took the Jug with him to a restaurant that evening. Fans in the restaurant lined up for the opportunity to see the Jug in person.

"Every time someone touched it, I saw your face, Jon," Mason said over the phone the next day. "Now that wasn't a very pleasant experience. Especially when eating my dinner."

The Jug's stay in Minnesota was brief. Michigan rebounded with three straight victories.

* * * *

Even though it's closing in on 60 years, the Paul Bunyan Trophy is still in its infancy compared to the Little Brown Jug. Nevertheless, it carries significant importance.

The trophy was initiated by Governor G. Mennen Williams in 1953 to signify yearly supremacy in the state between Michigan and Michigan State. And once again, the trophy has established deeper roots in Ann Arbor than in East Lansing.

The trophy features an approximate 2-foot sculpted figure of Paul Bunyan with his axe. He stands on a map of Michigan with one foot planted in the Upper Peninsula and the other in the Lower to signify the state's rich lumbering history. The trophy's base is a little over 4 feet tall.

"Coach Carr always called it 'the ugliest, nicest trophy in the country,'" Falk said. "It doesn't matter how big or awkward it may look…you better keep that trophy in your town rather than give it up to the other school."

When Michigan is holding the trophy and the game is in East Lansing, the custom is for Falk to pack it on the truck on Thursday evening to unload into the locker room on Friday. The trophy is kept in the locker room. The exchange is made after the game—either for celebration or surrender—in the locker room.

As holder of the trophy, one year the Michigan State equipment staff forgot to pack the trophy in its truck for the game in Ann Arbor. Following the Michigan victory, Falk went into the Spartan locker room to claim the trophy.

"Hey," Falk said. "You got Paul?"

The hesitation in response was all Falk had to hear.

"We forgot to put him on the truck," the equipment manager said. "He's back in East Lansing."

Falk did not raise a commotion because the equipment manager was a friend. The commotion came when Falk returned to the Michigan locker room and the players were shouting for Paul Bunyan. On Monday, Falk was struck by an idea that illustrated the importance of the awkward-looking symbol of victory.

Falk accompanied an empty semi-truck with the Michigan logo painted on its sides to East Lansing to pick up Paul. Paul had a pleasant trip home where he remained for the next several years.

It's always good to have Paul and the Jug tucked away securely in Ann Arbor.

Section 3

1980s

Chapter **15**

George Lilja: I'll Take That One

Doug James couldn't have picked a better time to have a shirt plucked right off his back.

The theft occurred on November 15, 1980, in front of 105,831 people at The Big House and who knows how many millions watching Purdue play Michigan in a national telecast on ABC-TV.

George Lilja was an All-American center for the Michigan team who made it to the Rose Bowl and beat Washington for Bo's first bowl victory. He anchored a powerful offensive line and wound up playing in the NFL for the Browns, Rams, Jets, and Cowboys.

Apparently the Purdue defensive line had trouble containing Lilja because one of the defenders grabbed his jersey and ripped it from top to bottom. With his shoulder pads flopping, Lilja raced to the sidelines in search of a new jersey.

With all the extra jerseys packed in the equipment room, Falk had to improvise quickly to get Lilja back into the game.

Those were the days of considerably more football scholarships, so Bo was stocked four and five deep at each position.

Falk quickly perused the sidelines for the first player that resembled Lilja's physique.

"Hey, No. 73," he shouted. "Get over here on the double."

When James reached Falk, the spontaneous equipment manager took the shirt off the freshman's back.

"Lilja needs this shirt," he said. "His got ripped, and we gotta get him back in the game right now."

James was standing shirtless on the sidelines when the crowd started to cheer as No. 73 trotted back to the huddle. That evening he received calls from family back in Louisville, Kentucky. They said they saw him make some big blocks on TV. They just didn't know he was a center.

"That's how quick Jon was doing his job," Lilja said. "Whatever the situation, he always seemed to come up with a solution."

Lilja doesn't believe the title of equipment manager suffices when applied to Falk's talents and responsibilities.

"Jon is the kind of person who reached out to every player on the team," Lilja said. "He's got that kind of personality that makes him easy to talk to. He never cared if a player was a walk-on or an All-American. He treated both the same."

More important to Lilja is Falk's character, which was molded by a man Lilja trusted so much.

Jon was always big on all of the traditions at Michigan. He's been around so long he's become a tradition himself.   *—George Lilja*

"Jon embodies everything that Bo wanted to get done," Lilja said. "He embraces Bo's principles and shares his work ethic. Jon was always big on all of the traditions at Michigan. He's been around so long he's become a tradition himself."

While many coaches have tried to mimic Bo, Lilja is convinced there'll be no one else quite like him.

"When a player came to Michigan, Bo was just their coach," Lilja said. "By the time the player graduated, he was their best friend. That's pretty much the same for Jon."

Chapter **16**
1980: "You Got a Problem?"

By 1980, Falk had learned to carefully walk the tightrope between his relationships with the coaching staff and those with the players.

His primary responsibility was to the head coach. Bo had established a program that had already withstood the test of time. The program was basically founded upon football fundamentals—execution, toughness, dedication, and loyalty. Nothing fancy; it simply worked. And Bo was in command of every aspect.

Falk also felt a loyalty to the players. It was his job to make them feel comfortable enough in their roles to extract the most from their talents. He has never betrayed the confidence he has built with them and run the risk of losing their trust.

Most importantly, Falk learned well from Bo that no one person is bigger than—in Bo's words—"the team…the team…the team."

So without giving names, Falk confided to the coach that an undercurrent of unrest was beginning to surface with some of the players.

The season began with a lackluster 17–10 victory over Northwestern. Victory was nice, but Bo was dissatisfied. With the weapons Michigan possessed, the game shouldn't have been that close.

The following Saturday in South Bend, a 51-yard field goal by Notre Dame's Harry Oliver on the game's final play lifted the Irish to a 29–27 victory.

The wind was furious all day. It was blowing straight into the kicker's face just before the ball was snapped.

"I kept yelling, 'Blow wind! Blow!'" Falk said.

Then another miracle of Notre Dame suddenly stilled the sky.

"It was unreal," Falk said. "I never saw anything like it. Just before he booted the ball, the wind stopped blowing. Give the kid credit, but I still have never seen anything like it."

At The Big House the following week, South Carolina, led by Heisman Trophy winner George Rogers, handed Michigan another loss, 17–14. In practice the next week, rumblings in the locker room started to surface.

So you want me to tell every Michigan football player [who] played here before you that our practices are too hard?
—Bo Schembechler

Big or small, Bo had one way to treat every problem—meet it head-on without giving it a chance to fester. Bo called captain Andy Cannavino into his office. The meeting was anything but subtle. The eruption in Bo's office was felt all the way to the Student Union.

"You're the captain of this football team, Cannavino," Bo barked. "What's going on?"

Cannavino, of course, was somewhat stunned and quickly had to gather his thoughts.

"The players are thinking they are practicing too hard," he blurted out. "We're hitting too hard, and we need to lighten up."

The fuse had been lit, and the coach was ready to explode.

"So you want me to tell every Michigan football player [who] played here before you that our practices are too hard?" Bo shouted. "The players don't want to practice like they used to? The sacrifices they made to build this program don't mean anything?

"Well, I'm telling you right now, Cannavino, you're the captain of this team. If I ever hear any more talk like that, you will not be the captain one day longer. You will start by telling all of those players that we'll do it the way we want it done. And it's gonna be up to you to help turn this thing around."

The meeting, obviously, served its purpose. Michigan reeled off victories against California, Michigan State, Minnesota, and Illinois. Still, the team sputtered at times and wasn't quite meeting the expectations Bo felt had to be realized.

In the eighth game of the season in Bloomington, Indiana, all the pieces to the puzzle finally fell into place.

The offense was proficient and the defense was spectacular in a 35–0 blanking of the Hoosiers. The following week Michigan traveled to Madison, Wisconsin, and posted an even more spectacular 24–0 shutout. One final game stood between Michigan and Ohio State to decide the Big Ten championship for the 11th time in the last 12 seasons.

That was against Purdue, a traditional spoiler, even when playing on the road.

Purdue quarterback Mark Herrmann had already established himself as the NCAA's all-time passing leader. It was up to defensive coordinator Bill McCartney to devise a scheme to stop him.

The Michigan defense was riding a string of 10 straight scoreless quarters. On Monday, it installed a defense designed to stop Herrmann, and the team practiced it for two days. On Wednesday morning, McCartney visited Bo's office to tell him he wanted to adjust the game plan by adding a sixth defensive back.

Bo looked as if he was hearing that the game had been cancelled. He was shocked perhaps even more than Cannavino had been in the early-season meeting that helped to turn the team around.

"McCartney," Bo said. "Do you realize this is Wednesday? We only have today and tomorrow to practice this. And on Friday, all we can do is talk about it."

McCartney had anticipated the boss' response.

"We can do it, Bo," he pleaded. "I studied film of every move Herrmann makes. I know this sixth defensive back is gonna be effective. Bo, I had this vision."

Bo always had confidence in the assistant coaches who served him. But this was a risky departure that demanded faith, trust, and maybe even a good shot of luck.

"Well let me tell you, McCartney," he said. "If this doesn't work, you better have a vision for another job on Monday."

Not only did the defense work, it was spectacular. Purdue was limited to 129 yards passing and added just 65 on the ground. Michigan clobbered the Boilermakers 26–0 and was headed to Columbus riding a streak of 14 straight quarters without allowing a point.

The string was snapped at 15 when Ohio State kicked a second-quarter field goal. That was all the scoring for Ohio State, however. Ali Haji-Sheikh also kicked a second quarter field goal. Anthony Carter scored on a 13-yard pass from John Wangler in the third quarter for a 9–3 Michigan victory.

The victory sent the Wolverines to their fourth Rose Bowl in five seasons. It was the sixth try for Bo, and he finally left Pasadena with a Rose Bowl Trophy under his arm after a 23–6 victory over Washington. Butch Woolfolk led a bruising running attack with 182 yards. Anthony Carter caught five passes for 68 yards and a touchdown.

Once again, however, it was the defense that provided the foundation.

The defense allowed two second-quarter field goals and ran its consecutive no-touchdown quarters to 22.

"By the end of that season, we could have played the whole Russian army and held them scoreless," Falk said. "The turnaround was amazing. And it was done by the whole team, not a couple of individuals."

That early-season meeting that no one but the team knew about certainly left its imprint on history.

"That's the way it was with Bo," Falk said. "Look a problem straight in the eye and then do something about it."

It's a lesson Falk has carried for life.

Chapter **17**

John Wangler: A Fair Deal

J ohn Wangler made Falk the ultimate offer he couldn't refuse. And after Wangler delivered, Falk delivered, too.

Michigan was practicing for its sixth Rose Bowl under Bo, whose teams had dropped their first five appearances. After the team arrived in California to prepare for the 1981 classic, Wangler set the stakes.

"I told Jon if we beat Washington, I want my helmet and jersey," the fifth-year senior quarterback said.

Despite starving for that first Rose Bowl victory, Falk told him that according to the rules, he couldn't technically give them to him. Perhaps, however, something could be arranged. Under the direction of Wangler, Michigan defeated Washington 23–6.

"I wanted that helmet and jersey real bad," Wangler said. "I have them displayed in my home today, along with various other pieces of memorabilia."

Wangler, of course, carved his name into Michigan folklore by tossing a pass to Anthony Carter, who zig-zagged down the field to score the winning touchdown that nipped Indiana, 27–21, with no time remaining in 1979.

But his gutsy play throughout his career was even more impressive.

After suffering a serious knee injury midway through the second quarter of the Gator Bowl the previous season, Wangler underwent surgery and had to endure painful rehabilitation in order to be ready for the 1980 season.

"Nobody rehabbed as hard as John Wangler," Falk said. "Other guys may have worked just as hard, but no one surpassed him. He was full of guts…full of determination. He promised himself he would be back."

As always, Wangler credited the coaches, his teammates, and all the devoted people at Michigan.

"Jon Falk is definitely one of them," Wangler said. "Big Jon is a legend. He's one of a kind."

Wangler should know. He spent five years as a player, three as a graduate assistant under Bo, and also one summer as a worker under Falk. Along with a handful of other players, Wangler spent the summer before his final season sorting equipment, painting the football building, and anything else Falk could cook up.

"Mel Owens and I were the supervisors," Wangler said. "Anthony Carter and a couple of other players worked under us."

There was an incident when Wangler and Owens pulled rank and left for lunch. When they returned, they discovered the entire varsity bathrooms totally covered with fresh paint.

"They painted everything," Wangler said. "I mean everything. They painted the walls, the sinks, the toilets, the urinals. They even painted the mirrors."

When Falk showed up to check their progress, he shook his head and nonchalantly said, "Looks like we're gonna be busy. There's plenty of work for everyone the rest of the summer."

Wangler came to appreciate Falk's offbeat humor and peculiarities.

"I really came to appreciate him during my fifth year," Wangler said. "He was always charged up. Always unflappable. He has this passion for Michigan football. He told us more stories about players and games and traditions that only he can remember."

During his final season as leader of the team, Wangler found himself spending more time with Falk in his office.

Jon is like a security blanket. You always know you can go back to Ann Arbor and share old stories.
—John Wangler

"The beautiful thing about Jon was how you could talk to him," Wangler said. "Sometimes it's hard for a player to talk to a coach. Jon made it easy to get things off our chests. Sometimes coaches would be yelling and screaming. Jon would lend a calming effect."

Wangler also appreciates the link that Falk provides from Bo to all subsequent coaches.

"Jon is like a security blanket," Wangler said. "You always know you can go back to Ann Arbor and share old stories. It'll always feel like home. You still feel like you're part of the program."

Wangler recalls those Fridays before games when Falk played the classic Bob Ufer tapes with the highlights of Michigan football.

"He had those tapes blaring," Wangler said. "You could hear them throughout the whole building. It was one of his ways to pass along all the legacies that are so important to the program."

Like all former players returning to Ann Arbor, Wangler never fails to visit Falk on one of his stops.

"Just knowing he's there to connect all the dots is important," Wangler said. "There will never be another Jon Falk."

Chapter **18**

Brad Bates: Earning the Trust

From one tip of the ball to the other, Brad Bates understands all the nuances of major college football. And he got his education the old-fashioned way—he earned it.

From a walk-on player for Michigan to graduate assistant under Bo to his current position of athletic director at Miami of Ohio University, Bates grabbed bushels full of knowledge along the way.

One of the most important lessons he learned is that while wins are the obvious measure of success, no university remains in the upper echelon of major college football for decades without complete commitment from players, coaches, and the entire football staff.

"Players have to play and coaches have to prepare them to give their best, but so much goes on behind the scenes to make it possible," Bates said.

That's why Falk remains so vital to the success Bates enjoys today.

As a walk-on player to a team loaded with four- and five-star "can't miss" recruits from around the country, Bates didn't arrive at Michigan with a resume filled with press clippings. Walk-ons are grunts. For the opportunity to run through The Tunnel and stand on the sidelines in full uniform during home games at The Big House, they withstand the bumps, bruises, and blood of daily practice with only a popcorn kernel of a chance to step onto the field during a game. And when each new semester arrives, they reach into their pockets to pay for tuition and books like most of the other students who sit in the stands on Saturdays.

It takes guts to be a walk-on and a heart full of determination. Most walk-ons disappear somewhere during their freshman year. Those who stick it out have a chance to earn a scholarship. When they do, they proudly carry the distinction for life. Bates got that feeling by earning a varsity letter in 1980. He had the guts.

Now a distinguished athletic director for Miami of Ohio University, he has a well-rounded perspective of major college football that few of those five-star players do.

"The beautiful thing about Jon was that as long as a player followed the rules and put in his best effort, he never cared if the player was a five-star recruit or a walk-on," Bates said. "He treated everyone the same. Jon never treated any player based solely on talent. He read your heart."

Bates appreciates the sensitive position of any equipment manager. The equipment manager spends more time with the players than any person in the program and must walk the fine line of being a liaison between coaches and players.

"When it comes to Jon, the title is misleading," Bates said. "He truly has the pulse of the team. Sometimes a player runs into a problem that no one knows about. Maybe his parents are getting a divorce, or maybe there's a health problem in the family. They know they can confide in Jon. In a diplomatic fashion, Jon can make the coaches aware of the situation."

Bates is grateful for the experience that the University of Michigan provided for his personal success.

"It takes so much more than players for long-term success in any program," Bates said. "Jon Falk is one of those persons who taught me so much. I realize the influence he's had on me in my job every day."

Jon never treated any player based solely on talent. He read your heart.
—Brad Bates

Chapter **19**

1981: Locker Room Lessons

There may be no more luxurious way to enjoy watching college football's most storied team than in the elegant new sky boxes at Michigan Stadium.

But throughout his Michigan career, Falk has enjoyed a postgame ringside seat that no amount of money can buy.

After each home game—win or lose—Falk is the last man sitting with the head coach in his office long after the locker room has emptied for another week or off-season.

From Bo to Mo to Lloyd to Rich Rod, the postgame session is a priceless treasure that Falk is proud to have earned.

The sessions offer an unusual window into some of the nuances of coaching major college football. Even more important is the opportunity to understand the leadership qualities that are demanded of each man entrusted to lead a program as tradition rich as the University of Michigan.

It's not all about Xs and Os. It's more about the life lessons that each young man can take from the game and use wisely once he leaves the field.

"I've always regarded that opportunity as one of the most precious privileges ever given to me," Falk said. "It's something that will live for me the rest of my life.

"There's so much going on in a head coach's mind. We all have issues and situations in our lives. We all have responsibilities. Some on the job. Some at home. A head coach has the same situations. But he's also responsible for his staff, for more than a hundred young players, to the athletic director, the university, the alumni, and the fans."

So Falk sits and listens. And he learns. He weighs each word carefully in his mind before offering his own opinion.

"Win or lose, I learned to wait until the coach speaks first," Falk said. "It's his time to clear his mind."

Postgame conversations are always easier after victories. Everyone is smiling, and the team is undefeated for at least another week. Meetings after losses are painful and subdued.

Character, sometimes, is more deeply developed in defeat than in victory. One particularly memorable meeting came after the 14–9 loss to Ohio State at The Big House in 1981.

It was a game of squandered opportunities. Michigan amassed 431 total yards to Ohio State's 264. Four times the Wolverines drove inside the Buckeye 10-yard line and had to settle for three field goals.

After the game, Falk was busy finishing his assignments in The Tunnel. He looked up to see Woody Hayes walking toward the visitor's locker room alone. Woody had been replaced by Earle Bruce after the 1978 season.

"Coach Hayes," Falk acknowledged him. "I'm Jon Falk—equipment manager for Michigan."

Woody had become much more subdued in retirement.

"Well, another great Ohio State–Michigan game today," Woody remarked.

Falk, of course, courteously smiled.

"Well coach," Falk said, "a friend of mine is sitting about a hundred feet from here, and he didn't think the game was worth a damn today."

Woody smiled with compassion.

"Well, I'll call Bo on Monday," he said. "I'm not gonna talk to him now."

Upon completing his duties, Falk returned to Bo in the locker room. Bo was sitting quietly, obviously replaying in his mind so much of what had transpired on the field. Without question, Falk maintains, it was one of Bo's most bitter losses.

"You know," Bo said, "I really don't want to go home tonight. Millie's got a house full of people, and I don't really want to talk to anybody."

Bo had to drive to Detroit to tape his TV show at 11:00 PM. "I've got a few hours to kill," Bo said. "What do you have going tonight?"

Falk said his time was open and asked what the coach had in mind.

"Let's go over to your place," Bo said. "We can talk and just relax."

Falk was living in his apartment on the Michigan golf course at the time. The two sat for a couple of hours talking about almost everything but the football game that Michigan just lost.

"I've got a video of the game if you want to watch it," Falk said.

Bo was interested, but only in watching Ohio State's final drive.

Late in the game with Michigan leading 9–7, Ohio State intercepted a pass in its own end zone. Under the direction of quarterback Art Schlichter, the Buckeyes methodically drove 80 yards for the game-winning touchdown.

Bo kept flipping the tape back and forth on certain plays during the drive. After watching the winning touchdown for about the sixth time, he shut off the recorder, finally convinced Ohio State had won. He put on his coat and left for his TV show without saying a word.

The 1981 season started with some serious twists and turns. Ranked No. 1 for the season-opener, Michigan dropped a 21–14 decision at Wisconsin. The following week Notre Dame came to Ann Arbor as the nation's top-ranked team and was easily handled by Michigan 25–7. Navy visited The Big House and tested the Wolverines before finally succumbing 21–16.

In the locker room on Sunday morning, Falk overheard a few players discussing which senior bowl games they were going to attend after the regular season.

"What the heck are you guys talking about?" Falk demanded. "What do we care about any senior bowl game? All we care about at Michigan is the Rose Bowl. Why are you guys talking about senior bowl games now?"

Falk's outburst was nothing more than a whisper in the wind compared to Bo's message at the Sunday night team meeting.

"There has to be an attitude on how the team is shaped," Falk said. "That Sunday night, Bo pretty much performed an attitude adjustment."

Following that performance, the Wolverines won five of their next six games leading up to Ohio State. The victory over Illinois came after Michigan yielded 21 first quarter points and then proceeded to dissect the Illini from all angles in a 70–21 rout.

Instead of playing in the Rose Bowl on New Year's Day, the Wolverines settled for the Bluebonnet Bowl on New Year's Eve against UCLA.

A controversy brewed before the game and—not so surprisingly—Bo successfully managed to make his point.

It was the year when there was a move to use a 25-second down clock displayed on the field. No team had employed it during a game that season. Field officials, at the time, clocked the 25 seconds on watches held in their hands. As instructed by Bo, Falk told the bowl representative that the 25-second clock would not be used.

Upon taking the field for pregame practice, the 25-second clocks were working on both sides of the field.

"Did you tell them we were not going to use those clocks?" Bo asked Falk.

Falk explained he told the representative, but the committee now decided to use them.

"Not in this game!" Bo was emphatic. "We didn't practice with them, and we're not going to use them."

Bo told UCLA coach Terry Donahue that Michigan was not taking the field as long as those clocks were working.

Needless to say, Bo was successful with another attitude adjustment. Michigan also had its way with UCLA, hammering the Bruins 33–14.

"Attitude adjustments were always one of Bo's specialties," Falk said.

Chapter **20**

1982: Where's "Go Blue Go?"

Some call it tradition. Others call it superstition. Maybe it's a slice of discipline or plain old-fashioned habit.

Whatever it's called, the world of sports is filled with behavioral peculiarities that some coaches and players believe are absolute necessities when preparing for a game—especially a game such as college football that relies as much on emotion as it does on physical superiority.

One such routine for the Michigan football team demands that each player tap the "Go Blue Go" sign attached above the locker room door on the way to the field before each half of every game—home and away.

Nobody knows for sure when the practice started, but it's mandatory procedure for every member of the team.

So what happens if the team is playing on the road and somehow the sign is missing? That was a dilemma Falk had to resolve before a game at Illinois in 1982.

"Maybe we would have scored 70 points without that sign," Falk said. "But what if we had been shut out? All the possibilities didn't amount to a half-cup of two-day-old coffee. We simply had to have that sign, no matter what it took."

All it took was a pinch of Harry Houdini and a splash of James Bond mixed with some middle-of-the-night maneuvering for Falk to ensure that sign was ready for Saturday before one player took a step onto that field.

The locker room that Michigan was using was next to another room used by the Illinois track team. Falk was suffering from a bout with the flu on Friday and was in his bed sleeping before suddenly awaking to make an emergency call to Dennis Hammond, one of his student assistants, who was on the trip.

"I don't know what you're doing, but we've got to go over to the stadium right now," Falk said. "I left the sign in that track locker room, and we have to make sure we get it."

When the two arrived, the sign was nowhere to be found.

"Somehow we have to get a sign up there tomorrow no matter what it takes, or there'll be a target pinned to my back," Falk said.

They jumped in the car and drove to a 24-hour K-Mart. Of course, neither believed that a K-Mart in Champaign, Illinois, would somehow miraculously have a "Go Blue Go" sign for sale.

But creativity isn't prohibited even in an all-night K-Mart in Champaign. And if ever there was a need for one flash of genius, this was certainly the time.

Falk purchased a piece of wood the size of the sign. Then he bought two cans of paint—one yellow and one blue. They walked up and down the aisles to find a pair of brushes, a package of white paper plates, and letter stencils from which to form the words. They took the material back to the hotel and began their work as spur-of-the-moment artisans.

By 2:00 AM, they had the letters cut and traced onto the wood that they had painted blue. Hammond was instructed to wake up at 4:00 AM to paint the letters a yellow that was the closest to maize they could find. Before anyone reached the locker room, the sign was finished and as dry as desert sand. Falk attached it above the door to the field, and the game proceeded as if nothing had happened.

Despite yielding a whopping 515 total yards to the Illini, the Michigan defense held them scoreless in the third and fourth quarters. In fact, the only scoring in the second half came on a pair of third-quarter field goals by Ali Haji-Sheikh that provided the 16–10 victory.

With one minute left to play, Illinois drove to the Michigan 5-yard line with four plays left to punch in the winning touchdown. On the first two plays, quarterback Tony Eason's passes were dropped. He connected on a third down 3-yard strike to take the ball to the 2.

Keith Jackson was handling play-by-play for the national telecast. When Illinois lined up for fourth down, Jackson looked to the Michigan sideline and spotted Bo shouting with his arms straight up in the air.

"He knows it's gonna be a running play, and he just called the defense," Jackson forecasted excitedly.

The Illini tried to punch the ball up the middle and were stopped as time expired.

"People ought to know, you just don't run on Michigan at the goal line," Jackson observed.

Not even Falk believes the return of the "Go Blue Go" sign stiffened the Michigan defense on the game-deciding play. But he wasn't taking chances. He had done his job, and the players did the rest.

The outcome ensured that one more victory out of the final two games would earn the Wolverines their fifth Rose Bowl berth in the last seven years.

With Steve Smith passing, Anthony Carter catching, Lawrence Ricks running, and Haji-Sheikh kicking, Michigan settled the championship the following Saturday by burying Purdue 52–21 at The Big House.

People ought to know, you just don't run on Michigan at the goal line.

—Keith Jackson

Michigan lost to Ohio State 24–14 at Columbus in the first game between the two giants that didn't decide the conference championship and a berth in the Rose Bowl.

In the Rose Bowl, Michigan was held scoreless in the first half and fell to UCLA, 24–14. The Wolverines finished the year with an 8–4 mark and at least made it to the bowl game that has always set the standard.

And the "Go Blue Go" sign made it to every game.

Chapter **21**
The Dufeks: A Time Warp

The Dufek boys add a whole new meaning to that old saying, "Those who play together, stay together."

Papa Don played fullback for Michigan under coach Bennie Oosterbaan and was named Most Valuable Player in the 1951 Rose Bowl when the Wolverines beat California 14–6. Don Jr. and brother, Bill, played for Bo.

Don Jr. was an All-American strong safety who played in the 1976 Orange Bowl and wound up playing for the Seattle Seahawks. Bill was an All-Big Ten offensive tackle who played in the 1977 and 1979 Rose Bowls. All three still live in Ann Arbor and remain passionately loyal to their school.

The three have known Falk since the day he arrived at Michigan in 1974 out of Miami of Ohio. And overwhelmingly, the Dufeks are proud to call Falk a friend.

"When I was a freshman, I didn't even know Jon was in his first year," Bill said. "I didn't realize we were pretty close to the same age. Now he just seems like part of the family."

Don Jr. arrived at Michigan one year before Bill and had the "distinction" of living in one of the rooms in the building at the University golf course where Falk had an apartment.

"Jon has always been a little different," Don Jr. said, smiling. "It's hard to imagine how one man can have so much energy and do so many different things at the same time. I'm not sure anyone has more passion for Michigan football than Big Jon."

I'm not sure anyone has more passion
for Michigan football than Big Jon.
—Don Dufek Jr.

Don Jr. was part of Falk's first team that had to endure the major "laundry bag experiment."

When Falk arrived, players had become accustomed to leaving laundry on the floor in front of their lockers. Falk wanted to make the switch to laundry bags to add order and efficiency to the locker room.

"I went to Bo and asked if we could distribute laundry bags to each player with their names on them," Falk said. "A player can stick all of his dirty laundry into the bag, hand it in, and it'll be returned clean in the bag the next day."

Bo listened to his rookie equipment manager. "What's the matter with you?" was his first response. "Don't you like to work?"

Falk carefully chose his words when explaining that perhaps Bo was missing the point.

"That's not the case," Falk said. "It's a system whereby all the equipment can be accounted for in an orderly fashion. It worked for us at Miami of Ohio."

Again Bo pondered.

"We'll try it for two weeks," Bo said. "If I hear one complaint from one player, your experiment is over."

Obviously, the system worked because it's still in operation today.

"Players get to know," Falk explained, "that if they don't turn their things in properly, they have to wear wet underclothes and socks the next day for practice.

"Once in a while, I'll walk through the locker room reminding players that it isn't much fun putting on wet stuff the next day. They get the message."

Bill appreciated the way Falk would always take time to talk to players during a particularly tough day.

"You could be out on that practice field getting ripped by Bo or one of the coaches and then come into the locker room and get a little word of encouragement from Jon. Maybe that was part of Bo's plan because it always seemed to work."

Both Dufek boys remain amazed at all the Michigan history Falk seems to carry in his back pocket.

"As soon as he got here, he studied all of the Michigan traditions," Don Jr. said. "He makes it seem like he was around for Tom Harmon. He knows the players, the teams, the big plays, and everything else about Michigan football. That's why the coaches have him talk to all the new players when they get here. He's darn near a coach himself."

All the Dufeks appreciate the simple fact that Falk is still there.

"It's almost like a time warp," Don Jr. said. "He was there pretty much for Bo's beginning and then stayed on through all the coaching changes. That says a lot about his character."

In fact, character, the Dufeks believe, may be Falk's greatest gift.

"He was hired by Bo," Don Jr. said. "He loves people, just like Bo did. That says everything."

Chapter **22**

1983: Going to the Dance

Though Michigan missed going to the 1984 Rose Bowl, there were significant consolations.

Michigan finished second in the Big Ten with its lone conference loss to 1983 conference champion Illinois, 16–6, at Champaign. Michigan's 8–1 conference record included a 42–0 shutout over Michigan State at East Lansing and a 24–21 victory over Ohio State.

The Wolverines' efforts were rewarded with an invitation to the Sugar Bowl where, despite a 9–7 loss to Auburn, Falk picked up a lifelong memory.

And this one has nothing to do with football.

During Bowl Week, the host committee staged a dance for all bowl participants and various dignitaries. Falk had two ladies he wanted to escort to the fancy affair. The problem was he had no tickets. His lone option was to speak to Athletic Director Don Canham.

"Mr. Canham, I'm sorry to bother you, but I brought my mom and grandmother on the trip," he said. "I sure would like to take them to the dance."

Despite Canham's reputation for being financially stringent, his heart was softer than warm yogurt.

"You want two tickets, you got 'em," Canham said.

He pulled them out of his pocket, and Falk felt as if he had hit the lottery big prize.

"One more thing, Big Jon," Canham said. "You tell your mom and grandma to save a dance for me."

Canham made good on his promise to dance with the ladies. He even gave each one a kiss for good luck.

"They were thrilled for weeks," Falk said. "They couldn't stop talking about how nice Mr. Canham was."

In the game, Auburn displayed its punishing running attack highlighted by Heisman Trophy winner Bo Jackson. The Tigers totaled 301 rushing yards and controlled the ball for more than 23 minutes of the second half, but the Michigan defense yielded only three field goals.

"Bo Jackson was one of the most gifted natural athletes I have ever seen," Falk said. "I believe he could have picked any sport and been a star."

After Bo retired from Michigan and became president of the Detroit Tigers, he was approached by Jackson. The versatile athlete found his way into Major League Baseball playing for the Kansas City Royals.

"Coach Schembechler," Jackson said to Bo. "I never had the opportunity to meet you. I just want to let you know I still have bruises from that Sugar Bowl we played. Without a doubt, that Michigan defense of yours was the hardest hitting bunch of guys I ever faced."

Bo smiled at the compliment. He always took particular pride in the defenses he created and the marks—literally—they left on opponents.

The Sugar Bowl trip also featured an incident that would influence future policy on the way Michigan transported equipment to and from long road trips.

Without a doubt, that Michigan defense of yours was the hardest hitting bunch of guys I ever faced.
—Bo Jackson to Bo Schembechler

It was brutally cold that December day when the team departed for New Orleans from Detroit Metropolitan Airport. The wind-chill factor was a frigid 40 degrees below zero.

Falk and his young assistants needed more than an hour to pack all of the personal luggage and necessary football equipment into the belly of the plane for the 10-day trip. In addition to the staff and various officials, the team consisted of 105 players. Breath expelling from the mouths of Falk and his boys looked like smoke from the stacks of Ford's Rouge Plant in the heydays of the American automobile industry.

Finally finished, Falk boarded the plane. The one seat unoccupied was next to Bo.

"What the hell took you so long to load this plane?" Bo demanded.

Falk looked squarely at the impatient coach.

"Bo, don't yell at me right now," Falk said. "My ears are so cold that if your voice starts to vibrate, my ears are gonna crack off."

Bo laughed, but the seed had been planted. A few years later, Bo would have Falk truck all equipment to games in which the team traveled by plane. Bo never liked his team to wait, particularly after a game.

Steve Smith completed his record-setting career for the 1983 team. An outstanding passer and equally dangerous runner, Smith was a prototype for the modern dual-threat quarterback. Like all senior quarterbacks wishing to enhance their performance, Smith looked for any advantage to make his throws more accurate and swift.

Before practice one day, Smith asked Falk for a pair of light quarterback shoulder pads. Quarterback pads were lighter than the tailback pads that Bo insisted his quarterbacks wear. Smith believed the lighter pads would provide more flexibility.

"Coach is not gonna put up with that," Falk warned him. "He'll find me and tell me to get that boy in tailback pads."

Smith was insistent. He could feel a hot hand.

"He'll never notice," Smith said. "And wait 'til you see my passes."

Against his better judgment, Falk complied.

Not five minutes after taking the field, Bo had seen all he needed to see.

"Falk!" Bo screamed. "Get those quarterback pads off Smith and put him back in tailback pads. I will not allow my quarterbacks to get hurt."

Falk looked at Smith and laughed. "I told you, Steve," he said. "You just wouldn't listen."

The light pads allow a quarterback to get his arm up and throw a little easier, especially if he throws a lot.

"At Michigan at that time, we used to run a lot and throw a little," Falk said. "Today, all the pads and uniforms are streamlined. Players want the freedom to move around quickly. They don't like to feel restricted. The shirts are so tight now it's hard for a defender to grab them."

Despite the shoulder pads and a run-first offense, Smith finished his career with a handful of passing records that stood until the game shifted to its more wide-open attack. And despite defeat in the Sugar Bowl, the 9–3 season was solid.

Good enough, in fact, for Falk's mother and grandmother to dance in New Orleans.

Chapter **23**

Anthony Carter: The Snake Is Real

Anthony Carter's Michigan career provided enough highlights for a Cecil B. DeMille movie.

One of his most memorable experiences with Falk, however, occurred far from The Big House where Carter's acrobatic heroics came to be expected.

The incident occurred at a dump site during a summer when Carter was working for Falk. The two were disposing of trash from the locker room when Falk spotted a snake crawling near a dumpster.

"Snake! Snake!" Falk yelled in an effort to alert Carter.

"Snake" was the nickname Falk had pinned on the magical wide receiver, so Carter kept staring at his boss wondering what he wanted as a real reptile kept slithering closer.

"I mean a real damn snake," Falk shouted. "Jump out away from there."

Falk neither wanted his friend to be bitten by a snake nor run the risk of having to tell Bo what happened to his prized receiver. Having been raised in Florida, Carter wasn't quite as alarmed about a snake as his Midwest-bred cohort.

He's the kind of guy you could talk to if something was on your mind.
—Anthony Carter

"He kept yelling and yelling," Carter recalled with a smile. "It was just a little ol' garter snake."

Carter carries many memories from his three-time All-American Michigan career. The most precious ones involving Falk occurred off the field.

"Jon is a jack of all trades," Carter said. "I had skinny legs and weighed between 140 and 150 pounds when I got to Michigan. I always had to talk him into giving me three or four extra pairs of socks to cover my legs.

"He takes care of all the equipment, but he also kept all the guys laughing. He's the kind of guy you could talk to if something was on your mind."

Carter enjoyed the teasing that Falk peppers on all the players. And once in a while, Carter liked to give a little back.

"You can leave that Jug at home," Carter cracked as the team was preparing for a trip to Minnesota.

At stake was the Little Brown Jug that belongs to the winning team for a year. Falk is passionate about maintaining the Jug and the Paul Bunyan Trophy that goes to the winner of the Michigan–Michigan State game.

"We're gonna win it," Carter assured. "Just save yourself the bother."

The Wolverines, indeed, held onto the Jug and Paul Bunyan throughout Carter's four-year tenure.

Watching the 2005 Michigan game at Iowa on television from his home in Florida, Carter was stunned by the accidental sideline hit to Falk that resulted in a serious broken leg.

"I called him in the hospital just to check," Carter said. "When he told me he'd be alright, I felt relieved."

When watching a Michigan game on TV, Carter has a routine.

"The first person I look for is Big Jon," Carter said. "When I see him, I know we're ready to play."

Chapter **24**

1984: How Cold Was It?

As one particularly curious barroom philosopher once posed the question, "How cold does it have to get 'til it can't get any colder?"

It was exactly that kind of frigid January night in 1985 when six layers of clothes were no match for the snow and sleet and icy temperatures that chilled the bones of any brave wanderer to venture outside.

It was the perfect night for relaxing in front of a fire. Since Falk had no fireplace in his apartment, however, he decided to drive to Detroit for an evening of entertainment.

Visibility was minimal, and traffic, of course, was slowed to a crawl on the eastbound I-94 Freeway. He debated about getting off the freeway at the next exit and returning home for an evening of television.

As Falk neared the outskirts of Ann Arbor, he spotted a man trying to thumb a ride. He said to himself, *"That guy's wearing a hat just like Bo's."* And the car parked behind him also looked like Bo's.

Falk pulled off to the side of the freeway and walked toward the shivering figure that, in fact, happened to be Bo.

"He was shaking from head to toe," Falk said. "His nose looked like a red balloon, and his cheeks looked like they were painted with rouge."

As Falk approached, the frozen face flashed a look of relief.

"I've never been so happy to see your ugly face in all my life," Bo cracked.

"Bo, you better treat me nice now," Falk responded. "My car is still running, and it's warmer than the Fourth of July inside."

Bo was on a mission. There was no time to waste.

"I'm going on a recruiting trip," Bo said. "Get me to the airport."

The pair got into the car, and Falk turned the heat switch to high. Bo's hands were still shaking, but at least he was beginning to thaw. It was the perfect time to commence complaining.

"I want you to know right now," Bo barked. "I've been on this highway for the last 45 minutes and not one S.O.B. stopped to pick me up. Three state trooper cars passed me. Not one, Jon...three! You'd have thought one of them would stop to see what I was doing, but no...they all just zipped by."

With the warmth, Falk could sense Bo was coming back to life.

"Well Bo, you gotta remember now," Falk cracked. "You were only 6–6 last year."

Bo forced a smile and said, "Why you S.O.B!"

The time for small talk was over. Bo had business, and there was no more time to waste.

"Now here's what you're gonna do," Bo ordered. "You get me to the airport as fast as you can. And I want my car running in my driveway before I get back."

"Well Bo, I've got some plans," Falk said.

"Well, your plans just got changed," Bo concluded.

Falk proceeded to get Bo to the airport in time for his flight. He then contacted a friend at a service station to have Bo's car towed. The car was repaired in the morning, and Falk had it parked in Bo's driveway before noon.

For many schools, a 6–6 record with an appearance in the Holiday Bowl against eventual national champion Brigham Young University would be an acceptable season. But never before did Bo have to endure a .500 season in his life. And he promised himself it would never happen again.

The 1984 season started as if it could manage a .500 record playing only with helmets and cleats. Led by quarterback Bernie Kosar, Miami of Florida visited The Big House as the nation's top-ranked team. The Hurricanes took a momentary 7–6 lead early in the third quarter before saying good-bye to the game and their No. 1 ranking as Michigan beat them 22–14. Michigan snagged six interceptions and recovered two fumbles in a balanced attack that offered promise to the season.

"I did not think we could beat Miami," Falk admitted. "After a win like that, you start to think that we might be pretty good."

Only once during the year, though, did Michigan manage to post back-to-back victories.

The play that probably defined the entire season occurred against Michigan State. Not only did the Spartans walk out of The Big House with only their second win over Michigan in the last 14 tries, but the Wolverines left with their championship hopes dashed.

Diving to recover a fumble, quarterback Jim Harbaugh suffered a broken arm that sidelined him for the rest of the season.

"Jimmy was a tough, wiry kid," Falk said. "He was a leader. Very charismatic. When he was just a little boy and his father, Jack, was an assistant here, I used to get footballs for Jimmy to fool around with during practice. When you lose your No. 1 quarterback—especially a leader like Jimmy—you've got serious problems."

Two weeks later Michigan was shut out at Iowa, 26–0. It was the first shut-out Michigan had suffered since the 1977 loss at Minnesota.

"The whole week after that loss we could hear the rumblings," Falk said. "Some of the press and a lot of fans called the Michigan offense a Model T Ford. Some were saying that time had passed Bo by. They didn't know Bo. When there's a challenge…that's when he digs in. It was just hard to do without the No. 1 quarterback."

In the Holiday Bowl against a tough Brigham Young team, Michigan held a 17–10 lead early in the fourth quarter before yielding a pair of touchdowns that sealed the Cougars' No. 1 ranking.

It was a long off-season. But Bo promised himself never to suffer another season such as that. And it began that frigid January night on a cold ride to the airport with Falk at the wheel.

Chapter **25**
1985: "Did You Rob That Bank?"

Waiting for that single opportunity to play in a game for the University of Michigan demands dedication, perseverance, and patience. Once in a while it even requires a trip to the local police department to prove your innocence in a bank robbery charge.

That's the way it happened for Pat Moons, who made the most of his opportunity to kick against Ohio State in the victory that sent the Wolverines to the 1986 Fiesta Bowl.

Moons was a place-kicker who had never seen the field before his senior year in 1985. A good student and reliable member of the team, he showed up slightly late for practice before the fourth game.

Falk had to return to the locker room to retrieve a piece of equipment. When he walked through the door, he thought he had entered *The Twilight Zone.*

The room was filled with characters completely out of place. The ensuing chaos was dizzying. He blinked his eyes and shook his head to wake himself out of this dream.

There were two members of the local SWAT team, three Ann Arbor police officers, and three University police officers. All had weapons drawn and aimed at one young man in the middle.

Falk knew all the officers and couldn't understand why they had weapons drawn inside of his locker room. And why were they pointed at one of the members of the team?

"What's going on here guys?" Falk asked.

"We've got a bank robber here, Jon," one of them barked. "Stand back. We don't want anyone hurt."

Straining to see the surrounded suspect, Falk broke into a laugh when he recognized the face.

"That's no bank robber," he said confidently. "That's Pat Moons. He's a kicker on the team."

The officers were not swayed.

"We're sorry, Jon," one said. "He's been positively identified for robbing a bank here in Ann Arbor, and we're gonna have to arrest him and take him in."

Falk was as equally determined as the officers.

"This isn't right," he said. "This is just not right. This is not a bank robber. This is Pat Moons. He's a kicker on the Michigan football team."

Falk ran out to the practice field faster than anyone playing in the backfield. It was time to bring Bo into the situation.

"Bo, the police are arresting Pat Moons for robbing a bank," Falk said.

Bo looked at Falk as if he had told him that he had just swallowed a football.

"What the hell are you talking about?" Bo asked. "Are you going crazy on me now here during practice?"

Falk managed to convince Bo to return to the locker room. On the way, he told Bo to be careful because all the weapons are drawn.

"What the hell's going on here?" Bo demanded upon entering the room.

"Bo, we have a positive ID that this man here robbed a bank in Ann Arbor," one of the officers said.

Bo walked up to Moons and stared straight into his eyes.

"Moons," he said. "Did you just rob a damn bank?"

Moons, of course, was shaken but answered the coach directly.

"No sir," he said. "I was at the bank. That's why I was late. But I sure didn't rob it."

Bo turned to all the police officers and raised his arms as if he had just cracked a case easier than a peanut shell.

"There you have it men," he said confidently. "Pat Moons said he did not rob the bank. You have the wrong man. Now all of us have to get back to practice."

__Moons, did you just rob a damn bank?__

—*Bo Schembechler*

Slightly smiling, one of the officers told Bo they still had to take Moons to the station in order to clear the matter. Bo didn't like it, but he told Moons to go with the officers peacefully, and everything would be worked out.

"The law will take care of itself," Bo said. "You'll be alright. I'll talk to you later, Moons."

Moons, in fact, had been at the bank that was robbed. A witness had seen Moons running to his car because he was late for practice. However, the identification of him as being the robber was incorrect.

As the season progressed—with no bank robbery charge hanging over his head—Moons continued to practice patiently and got the surprise of his career on the Saturday Michigan hosted Ohio State at The Big House.

Mike Gillette was a gifted place-kicker who handled all kicking duties. On the Friday before the game with Ohio State, however, he broke a team rule.

"That was one thing with Bo that never changed," Falk said. "If a player broke a team rule, he had to suffer the consequences. It didn't matter who the player was—first stringer or walk-on who had splinters from sitting on the bench. Bo never bent the rules for anyone."

Gillette was benched for the biggest game of the season. After four years of waiting, Moons was in the game.

"I can't even imagine what was going through his mind the first time he took the field," Falk said. "He had never stepped on the grass during a game, and now he was out there against Ohio State. Whatever was going through his mind sure turned out to be pretty good."

Moons kicked two field goals and converted on all three extra-point attempts as Michigan dumped the Buckeyes 27–17.

The only major glitch in that season came at Iowa in the sixth game on the schedule. Stories by then had circulated from Iowa that coach Hayden Fry had the visitor's locker room painted totally in pink. Apparently it was a psychological ploy to subconsciously make the visitors more docile and less enthusiastic about playing a hard-nosed game.

When confronted by an attack—physical or psychological—Bo always had a counter.

"Now you know this locker room we're going to be using is pink," Bo said to Falk early in the week. "When you get down there, I want you to go out and buy all the butcher's paper you need to cover every inch of that room. I mean every inch. I don't want to see one speck of pink."

Falk took a deep breath.

"My God, Bo," Falk said. "That's an awful lot of footage to cover in just one day."

Bo eyed him and then repeated his command.

"I want every inch covered with white paper," he said. "Remember…no pink! I know I have the right man for the job."

Falk purchased eight rolls of white butcher's paper as soon as he arrived in Iowa Friday morning. He and three student assistants finished the job before the team arrived.

Bo walked the entire room inspecting each inch like a grizzled drill sergeant.

"Good job, Jon," he said.

And that was it.

Iowa entered the game rated No. 1 in the country. Michigan was No. 2. At the time, it was only the 19th time in NCAA history for such a meeting to occur.

The Wolverines rolled into Iowa City with a defense that had allowed only one touchdown in five games. They extended that mark to one in six games before they left. However, the Hawkeyes kicked four field goals and hung on for a 12–10 victory. The only other smudge on the Michigan record was a 3–3 tie at Illinois.

On the trip back to Ann Arbor, Bo dismissed the mystique of the pink.

"That loss had nothing to do with anything in the locker room," Bo said. "They simply outplayed us."

With the victory over Ohio State, Michigan finished the regular season with a 9–1–1 mark and a berth in the Fiesta Bowl against highly regarded Nebraska.

Again, a stellar defense and a 24-point third quarter explosion powered the Wolverines to a 27–23 victory. Moons kicked two more field goals and added three extra points.

Not picked by any writer or football publication to finish in the top 20 before the season began, Michigan wound up ranked second in both wire polls.

"Not bad for an old Model T," Falk cracked. "Don't ever stir a hornet's nest when the hornets are still around."

Chapter **26**

Paul Jokisch: Stern and Loose

The easiest way for Paul Jokisch to measure Falk's value to the Michigan football program is simply turning to Bo.

"Bo was very astute," said the acrobatic, giant wide receiver and former Parade All-American in both football and basketball. "Not just in football but in all aspects of life. Bo knew Jon was a little quirky. But he also understood his value to the football program. He knew he could trust him. He never had to worry about Jon getting his job done."

That's high praise from Jokisch, who sometimes felt that Bo possessed some mystical power to know what every person under his charge was doing each moment of the day.

Jokisch experienced Bo's uncanny power in 1984 after driving back to Ann Arbor from Christmas break when the team was preparing to play in the Holiday Bowl against No. 1 Brigham Young University. His car broke down near the intersection of M-59 and M-23. He frantically sought the help of a stranger living on a nearby farm.

"I'm gonna be late reporting, and Bo's gonna kill me," Jokisch told the man. "Is there any way you can help?"

The two managed to get the car started, and Jokisch reported to the football building one hour after the scheduled time for all team members to arrive.

Jokisch raced into the building hoping to report without Bo seeing him. He was dashing up a hallway and almost made it when he happened to glance up and saw Bo glaring coldly from his position at the end of the hall.

"It had to be the worst timing in the world," Jokisch laughed. "I told him my car had broken down."

Those were the last words Jokisch was able to manage before Bo exploded, and Jokisch began to think that maybe it would have been better if the car hadn't started at all.

Assistant coach Bob Thornbladh was passing and stopped to put an arm around his shaken player. "Don't worry," he said. "He didn't mean what he said."

When Jokisch reached the locker room, Falk was scurrying around handling equipment and firing out his usual quips like Groucho Marx in one of his classic movies.

Finally, Jokisch could smile.

"Jon just has a way to make people laugh," Jokisch said. "Bo was such an intense person. Jon had his own way of keeping a locker room loose. Don't think for a second Bo didn't realize that. That was part of Bo's master plan—stern and looseness."

Jokisch believes Falk, in his own way, is just as astute as the legendary coach.

"Jon is not always politically correct with what he says," Jokisch said. "But you always knew where he was coming from. Bo appreciated that. That's why he had so much confidence in Jon."

 **_Nobody knows more about Michigan tradition than Jon._**

—Paul Jokisch

Like every player who has served with Falk, Jokisch marvels at the stories about Michigan tradition that Falk loves to tell.

"Nobody knows more about Michigan tradition than Jon," Jokisch said. "And nobody cares more for Michigan football than Jon."

The friendship Jokisch feels for Falk will last a lifetime.

"He's the kind of friend that you might not see for 20 years," Jokisch said. "And when you meet, it's like you never left. That's real friendship."

Despite the wave of new people who now occupy Schembechler Hall, Jokisch still feels part of the tradition.

"With Jon there, a little piece of me is still there, too," he said.

Some traditions never change—stern or loose.

Chapter **27**

1986: You Can't Rush History

Falk learned an unforgettable lesson in 1986. There shall be no plaque before its time.

Shortly after mid-season, Falk was struck by an idea he considered not only brilliant but also foolproof. Bo was on a speed path to become the winningest coach in the history of Michigan football, and Falk devised a plan for every person on the team to share in the historic feat. To allow everyone to feel part of the celebration, he collected a couple of bucks from each player who chose to contribute. The collection totaled about $350, allowing Falk the freedom to buy the nicest plaque on the shelf.

On November 8 in West Lafayette, Indiana, Michigan yielded only a meaningless fourth quarter touchdown in a 31–7 rout over Purdue. It was Bo's 165th Michigan victory, tying him with the legendary Fielding H. Yost.

The table was set for the following Saturday with Minnesota coming to The Big House. The Wolverines were ranked No. 2 in the nation with nine straight victories, including impressive wins over Notre Dame and Florida State. They had defeated the Golden Gophers eight straight times and 17 times in their last 18 meetings. And Bo really had no idea about the impending personal historical meaning of the game or the gift from his team.

It was like Falk holding four of a kind in stud poker only to lose to a royal flush.

"It was such a beautiful plaque," he said. "It was engraved with all the right numbers. I had Minnesota and Michigan on it with just a little space left to fill in the score. That was the mistake—the score."

A funny thing happened on the way between making the plaque and presenting it to Bo.

Minnesota just happened to get in the way.

Minnesota turned four Michigan turnovers into 17 points and kicked a 30-yard field goal with no time left on the clock for a stunning 20–17 upset. The Minnesota victory snapped Michigan's 13-game winning streak dating back to the previous season.

"I can still see Rickey Foggie running around right end for 30 yards to set up that field goal," Falk said. "We not only lost the Little Brown Jug but also the plate on a $350 plaque."

Falk sensed even greater danger. Especially with the Wolverines traveling to Columbus the next Saturday with the Big Ten title to be determined between the two for the 18th time in history.

After the devastating loss to Minnesota, quarterback Jim Harbaugh committed a cardinal sin against Bo's methodical planning for the annual attack against Ohio State. In the hushed locker room after the game, Harbaugh "guaranteed" a victory over Ohio State to the media.

"I heard the young man may be biting off a little more than he can chew," Bo said to Falk in his office. "I guess it's better than him saying we're gonna lose. If he said it, then by God, we have to push him so he can stand up to it."

The whole team got an unexpected lift at practice that Thursday. Any visit from Bo Derek is always easy to take. The beautiful movie star stopped by to say she was rooting for them on Saturday. She and husband, John, had flown to Detroit and were driving back to Los Angeles after picking up a car they had ordered.

"She was pretty easy to look at," Falk said. "Especially after the practices we put in for Ohio State."

Going to Columbus, however, is always an adventure.

"You can always count on something screwy happening there," Falk said. "If it's not the water getting turned off in the hotel, it's the headsets going out or something else totally bizarre."

This time it happened to the equipment truck long before the team got to town.

With Falk riding in the cab, the semi carrying all the equipment on Friday morning was involved in an accident. Going down a hill near the stadium, the truck lost its brakes.

"I looked up and another semi was getting ready to enter the intersection," Falk said. "We were pulling for that semi to make it through before we got there, or we would have been broadsided. The truck almost cleared the intersection, but we hit part of its side."

Police were sent to the scene and asked what the truck was carrying. Falk told them it was filled with Michigan football gear.

"You mean all the Michigan equipment is right here on this truck?" the officer asked. "I'm awfully sorry sir, but we're gonna have to impound this truck for 48 hours."

Of course, he was joking. Wasn't he, Falk hoped?

"But that didn't keep passers-by from giving us the one-finger salute when they found out what we were carrying," Falk laughed. "Needless to say, it was not the index finger."

Checking the stadium early Saturday morning, Falk found the field to be hard and dry, so he distributed the appropriate shoes to the players. Once the game started, the sideline phones to the pressbox failed. Falk was racing between the field and pressbox desperately trying to restore service. He saw little of the first half during which Michigan players were slipping all over the field. After the sun broke through the morning clouds, frost on the field melted, making the surface slippery.

"I want every man on this team wearing his wet shoes in the second half," Bo ordered the players. "Jon's going around to check everyone, and no one will be allowed on that field without his wet shoes."

Whether it was the wet shoes or sheer determination to uphold Harbaugh's guarantee, Michigan owned the second half.

Trailing 14–6, Michigan took the second-half kick and put together an 83-yard touchdown drive. Michigan was the first Big Ten opponent to score a touchdown in Ohio Stadium all season. Jamie Morris added a second third-quarter touchdown. Thomas Wilcher added a third in the fourth quarter.

With 3:17 left in the game, the Michigan defense stopped Ohio State on the

Wolverine 28-yard line. A 45-yard field goal attempt by Matt Frantz sailed wide left, and Michigan held on for a 26–24 victory.

Michigan was going to the Rose Bowl. Harbaugh made his guarantee good. And the plaque celebrating Bo's 166th Michigan victory was that much sweeter coming against Ohio State.

"You never want to lose a game," Falk said. "But years later, the plaque probably meant more to Bo with the record coming against Ohio State."

Michigan dropped a 22–15 decision to Arizona State in the Rose Bowl. With an 11–2 record, however, the Wolverines finished in the top 10 of both wire polls.

* * * *

The season marked a logistical change for Michigan, and this one also involved a truck. Bo grew tired of having his players wait for hours after boarding a plane as the equipment was loaded. For trips that required air travel, he wanted a truck to leave a day ahead of time for the equipment to be ready in the locker room before the team arrived.

"I saw Iowa drive in here with a semi all decorated with Iowa symbols and records and all kinds of other stuff," Bo told Falk. "Why don't you go out and get something done like that for Michigan?"

Falk contracted a moving company that painted and stenciled the sides of the semis in brilliant maize and blue.

"You'd be surprised how many calls we get asking if they can rent the truck for personal moving purposes," Falk said. "We generally send the truck out to move the belongings of a new coach coming in. It's available to the public through the trucking company."

Just don't try to get it during the football season. That's when Falk is the captain of the truck.

Chapter **28**

Jamie Morris: Quite a Welcome

It's one of those unsolved questions that may have no right answer:

What do you say to a naked man upon meeting him for the first time?

That was the dilemma Jamie Morris faced when reporting to the University of Michigan as a fresh recruit out of Ayer, Massachusetts, in 1984.

Upon arrival in Ann Arbor, Morris reported to running backs coach Terrell Burton in the football office. After a few words of encouragement, Burton sent the eventual record-setting tailback to Bo for his official welcome to Michigan.

Despite his somewhat diminutive size, Bo liked his new recruit. He liked his determination and the way he conducted himself. Bo shared his plans for Morris with him and then sent him to the locker room to be fitted by Falk for his first Michigan uniform.

Any first meeting with Bo became an event permanently chiseled into a young player's mind. At least for an instant, however, even that memory-making moment was upstaged by Morris' first meeting with Falk.

"I walked into the locker room and saw him riding one of those workout bikes that was equipped with a big fan," Morris said.

Nothing unusual about that until Morris noticed that Falk was riding the bike naked.

"Come on over here, Little Fella," Falk instructed. "Let's get you fitted up."

Feeling a little strange, Morris did as he was told. Recalling the incident, he still chuckles.

"I came from a small town in Massachusetts," he said with a smile. "I was new to the city, new to the university, new to the program, and I wasn't sure how to react. The third person I met at Michigan welcomed me naked and was about to size me up for a uniform."

Obviously, the oddity of that first meeting did nothing to dissuade a friendship that has flourished for decades. Having worked for the University's athletic department, Morris saw firsthand what Falk means to the football program after so many years.

"Jon's main job is taking care of all the equipment," Morris said. "But it's impossible to measure how much he means to the program. He's the kind of guy who goes around the locker room always trying to encourage the players. He's good at reading personalities. He knows when a player needs a pat on the back or a kick to the butt. Jon has a knack for keeping players fired up. Nothing means more to Jon than the success of Michigan football."

He knows when a player needs a pat on the back or a kick to the butt.
—Jamie Morris

It's easy for Morris now to reflect on Falk's gift for reaching out to help young players adjusting to their new lifestyle and properly representing the University of Michigan.

"It can be tough on players who are far away from home during their freshman year," Morris said. "No matter who you are, you sometimes get a feeling for wanting to be back home.

"Jon just has a way of putting them a little at ease. He'd always say something like, 'Home is great and you can always go back home. But you have an opportunity to represent one of the greatest institutions in America. There's only a handful of young men as privileged as you.' After a while, a player comes to understand and begins to feel like he fits. Jon was always great at bringing a smile to someone's face."

Falk also serves as a daily reminder of the traditions of Michigan football and the responsibilities of upholding them. He knows the stories behind all the big rivalry games and makes sure that all the players—and coaches—are suitably informed.

"He always preached about the importance of certain games—the Little Brown Jug game with Minnesota...the Paul Bunyan Trophy game with Michigan State...the battle with Notre Dame...and more stuff about the Ohio State game than everything written in all the history books combined," Morris said. "When any of those games were coming up, you could see the intensity in Jon's face."

All that tradition was passed down to Falk. And he's always eager to share.

"He not only knows it, he lives it every day," Morris said.

The degree of exuberance about Michigan tradition is matched by Falk's meticulous detail for issuing proper equipment.

"If he gave you a pair of socks, he expected you to be responsible for them," Morris said. "If he gave you a jock a little too big, he'd say, 'You're just gonna have to grow into it.'"

Even to this day, Morris is amazed at the detail of Falk's control.

"We always traveled with two pairs of shoes for the games," Morris said. "One for a dry field, and the other for a wet one. If Jon saw a player slip just once, within a minute he'd have another pair of shoes on him."

Another of Falk's characteristics has left a lasting impression on Morris.

"I used to work for him during the summers painting the football offices and stenciling in different slogans for the upcoming season," Morris said. "He loves tradition but doesn't waste time looking back. He has an optimistic outlook and always is looking forward to that next game."

Morris now regards Falk more as a member of his family than merely another person working for Michigan football.

"That's because he's never changed," Morris said. "He still has the same intensity today as he had when I came here. That says a lot for the man."

Chapter **29**

1987: Heartfelt and Heartache

Falk remembers the 1987 season for a lot more reasons than any particular football game.

On December 5, he was married to Cheri Boychuck-Winkle. One week later, Bo was hospitalized for his second heart operation.

Getting married during the football season when working for Michigan demands pinpoint planning. The date has to fall between regular season wrap-up and bowl game preparations that take the team out of town. Michigan was scheduled to play Alabama in the Hall of Fame Bowl in Tampa, Florida, on January 2, 1988.

"Now that was good timing," Falk teased Cheri. "How many couples get married, then go on an all-expenses-paid honeymoon? And play in a bowl game, besides."

At the wedding reception, Bo toasted the newlyweds.

"Here's to all the wives who have fed Big Jon Falk over all these years," Bo said. "Cheri, now it's your turn."

Obviously, the Falks got used to the timing of their wedding because they kept celebrating the anniversary of their honeymoon year after year after year at bowl games.

Unfortunately for Falk, the team, and all Michigan fans, Bo did not coach the team against Alabama. He was back in Ann Arbor recovering from quadru-ple bypass heart surgery. It marked the second such time Bo had been knocked out of a bowl game. The first was at the Rose Bowl in 1970.

"I always used to tease Bo that I was the cause of his heart attack," Falk said. "He just couldn't get over the fact that I was finally getting married."

Even before his setback in December, Bo suffered a health issue in May that almost caused Falk himself to have heart failure. About 7:00 AM, there was a knock on the back door of Falk's equipment room When he opened the door, there stood Bo bent over gasping for breath. He was holding his body some-where between his heart and stomach. He kept repeating, "Help! Help!"

"Oh no," the words fell from Falk's mouth.

"It's not here," Bo pointed to his chest. "It's my stomach."

Falk got him into his car and made the short trip to St. Joseph Hospital in record time. Bo was yelling and cursing from pain. When Falk looked over, Bo's head had flopped down onto his chest.

"Bo, wake up!" Falk yelled. "You're not gonna faint on me, damn you. You're not fainting on me today."

I always used to tease Bo that I was the cause of his heart attack.
—Jon Falk

Bo looked up and rolled his eyes. "Damn near fainted, didn't I?" he said.

Fortunately, the problem wasn't with his heart. He had developed a kidney stone and had to remain in the hospital until 5:00 PM when the pain finally subsided.

Getting into the car, Bo took his fist and jabbed Falk in the ribs.

"You thought that was it, didn't you?" Bo teased Falk. "You thought that was the big one."

Finally, Falk could afford to smile.

"I don't know if I thought that or not," Falk said. "But a few hours ago, I never would have dreamed that the two of us would be laughing like this right now."

Bo recovered fully for the start of the 1987 season in which Michigan finished with a respectable 8–4 record. Three of the losses, however, were to Notre Dame, Michigan State, and Ohio State. Those losses alone make the season unacceptable.

The fourth loss came to a spunky Indiana team at Bloomington. Bill Mallory was the head coach and a friend of Falk since their time together at Miami of Ohio. Two weeks before hosting Michigan, Indiana had upset Ohio State. Falk visited Mallory in his office the day before the game.

"I see you have a scalp there," Falk remarked, referring to the Ohio State hat sitting on Mallory's desk.

"Nice of you to notice," Mallory said. "And tomorrow I'm gonna get yours." Falk pulled his cap tightly down to his ears.

"I don't think so, coach," Falk said. "You're not getting this one."

In a driving windstorm with heavy rain, Indiana scored the go-ahead touchdown in the third quarter and held on for a 14–10 victory.

"Mr. Falk, Coach Mallory said you're gonna give your hat to him?" one of the Indiana assistant equipment men said in the Michigan locker room after the game.

Falk removed his hat and handed it to the young assistant.

"Give it to Bill, and tell him great game," Falk said.

The loss to Ohio State was bittersweet. Earlier in the week, Ohio State had announced that this would be Coach Earle Bruce's final game. The Buckeye players did not agree with the decision and wore headbands with his name sewn on. Bruce showed up in top hat and tuxedo for his finale with the team he loved. Bo had become good friends with Bruce and was also upset with the decision.

Michigan squandered a 13–0 lead, and the teams were tied 20-all late in the fourth quarter. Matt Frantz, who had missed a game-winning field-goal attempt the previous season in Columbus, kicked a 26-yarder to cap the 23–20 victory.

In the locker room after the game, Falk patiently listened to Bo replay almost every down.

"You know how much I hate to lose to Ohio State," he said. "But if we had to lose today, I'm glad it was to Earle Bruce in his last game."

For the Hall of Fame Bowl on January 2, Gary Moeller pinch hit for Bo as acting head coach. Moeller showed he was up for the challenge by cashing in on a daring call with only 57 seconds left to play.

Trailing 24–21 on fourth-and-3 with the ball on the Alabama 20-yard line, Moeller called time out. Instead of trying for a game-tying field goal, Moeller decided to go for the first down.

He wound up getting far more as Demetrius Brown lofted a 20-yard pass that John Kolesar grabbed in the corner of the end zone for a touchdown.

Just as Bo learned a lot about coaching at Miami of Ohio, Falk made his equipment manager debut at Miami under the tutelage of Bob Purcell. Check out the style of young Falk's trousers.

The full-time equipment crew is ready and smiling before another game. Left to right that's Brett McGiness, Robert Bland, Falk, and Rick Brandt.

Longtime friends Falk and author Dan Ewald before a game.

The rush of taking the field is really only felt by those privileged to represent the University of Michigan.

Former Michigan center President Gerald Ford had the "honor" of staying in Falk's apartment during an outing at the Michigan Golf Course.

Lloyd Carr and Falk had plenty to smile about in the locker room after a victory at Notre Dame.

Falk arranged for Coach Rich Rodriguez to see his first Tigers game.

Falk persuaded Bo to attend a couple of Tigers games after the ol' coach left the baseball team's front office. As president, Bo was instrumental in improving training facilities throughout the organization.

The light at the end of The Tunnel is all you see after stepping out of the locker room at The Big House.

Now that's a wedding party! From left to right: Bo's son Schemy, Bo, Bo's wife Millie, Falk, and Cheri.

"Jamie Morris kept pacing up and down the sideline when the defense was on the field," Falk said. "He kept saying, 'We gotta win this for Bo. We gotta win this for Bo. He's watching every play on TV and we gotta win this for Bo.'"

Morris certainly did his part by rushing for 234 yards.

Bo indeed watched every play without any damage to his heart. He would be ready for the next season, which turned out to be one of his finest.

Chapter **30**
Erik Campbell: One Shirt Owed

Erik Campbell still smiles about the 1985 game at Minnesota when he suffered a concussion from a vicious hit to the head. Carted from the field, he wound up in the locker room lying on a table looking up to see Falk's grinning face.

"Soup" was falk's nickname for Campbell. "Soup," Falk said. "You S.O.B. You owe me a jersey. They had to cut the one you were wearing to take your helmet and pads off."

It hurt too much to laugh, but at least Campbell managed a smile. The zinger from Falk let him know that everything was going to be alright.

From four distinct perspectives, Campbell has been "blessed" by a shotgun volley of Falk's endearingly quirky personality—first, as a highly touted player out of Gary, Indiana; second, as a summer student worker; third as an assistant coach at Michigan; and fourth, as a lifelong friend.

"From each of those perspectives, I can emphatically say that there is never a change in Jon Falk," Campbell said. "He treated me the same as a player as he did when I was a coach. He's the same today as the day I met him. Jon Falk is Jon Falk. That's all you can say. There's no one else like him."

Falk is an outrageously singular individual with an innate gift for helping mold the myriad personalities that comprise a college football team into

Jon Falk is Jon Falk. That's all you can say. There's no one else like him.

—Erik Campbell

a unified whole. The University of Michigan has long been a national football power able to recruit elite athletes from all parts of the country. Some such players from states like California or Florida or New York or Louisiana aren't completely schooled in the storied traditions of Michigan.

And then along comes Falk.

"Every player knows a little bit about Michigan," Campbell said. "They know about The Big House. They love the winged helmet. They know about the game with Ohio State. They've heard 'The Victors.' They know that Michigan wins championships.

"I happen to come from Indiana, so I was a little more familiar with Big Ten football. But there's so much Michigan tradition that even I had to learn. Jon lives that tradition. In fact, that's what he lives for. He takes it upon himself to instill all of it into every single player."

Falk spends a lot of his time walking through the locker room explaining all the tradition that each player is expected to uphold.

"Coaches are too busy teaching techniques that players have to absorb," Campbell said. "They're familiar with all the tradition but don't have enough time to explain all of it."

The entire week before the Ohio State game, Falk plays tapes of prior games broadcast by the voice of Michigan football—the late Bob Ufer. Falk plays the tapes on maximum volume so that even when leaving the locker room it's heard throughout the halls of the football building.

"Jon has an amazing memory," Campbell said. "He remembers all the names, all the numbers, all the key plays. Even all of the critical blocks that set up a big run or pass play. He's probably the best history teacher they have at the university."

Actually, Falk has become a piece of living history himself. He's the single link between Bo and Mo and Lloyd and Rich Rod. That's an amazing string in the volatile world of contemporary college football.

"Jon connects all the dots," Campbell said. "And he does it for only one reason—his passion for Michigan football. There isn't a player who comes to Michigan who isn't touched by Jon Falk. And it comes in a way that's far more important than playing a game of football."

Campbell is now the wide receivers coach for the University of Iowa. His primary area for recruiting is Texas.

"I'm always amazed at all of the people at other universities who know Jon," Campbell said. "Every place I go, someone tells me to remember them to Jon. That's quite an honor."

That's an incredible accomplishment for someone who played only one football game in his entire life.

"And you still owe me a jersey," Falk teases Campbell whenever they meet.

Chapter **31**
1988: How 'Bout Them Boots?

E arly in the 1988 season, Falk popped into Bo's office one morning merely to say hello. Without any prompting, his eyes were drawn to Bo's feet—or more specifically, what was on them.

"Wow, Bo," Falk was surprised. "You've got yourself a new pair of boots."

Not just any pair of boots. They were black and made of genuine leather. Pointed toes and hand-carved on both sides of each boot was the name "Bo."

"Somebody must have given those to you because you wouldn't spend what those things cost," Falk teased. "I could buy a dozen pair of sneakers for what those babies must cost."

Bo lifted his pants to give Falk the full effect.

"Wish you had these, don't you?" Bo said.

The boots were sent by Dallas Cowboys executive Gil Brandt. Bo knew all the important people in the NFL. He knew everyone in college football. Everybody loved him.

Later that afternoon, the assistant coaches arrived early in the locker room to prepare for the daily meeting with players from respective units. Bo would show up a little later to take the team onto the field.

Falk was busy tending to all his duties in the locker room when he got called to Bo's office.

"Falk, get in here," Bo yelled. "I need you to help me with something."

When Bo spotted Falk nearing his office, again he yelled to "get in here right now."

"And close that door," he added.

Falk looked back over his shoulder and then squarely at Bo. "Now wait a minute, Bo," he said tentatively. "You and I are in this locker room alone, and I have to shut that door? What's going on here?"

Falk recognized the squint Bo got in his eyes whenever he was serious.

"What I'm asking you to do is something I want you never to tell anyone," Bo said. "You never tell anyone what you're about to do for me."

Falk didn't squint. In fact, his eyes almost popped from their sockets.

"Bo, you're getting me a little nervous," he said. "Now just what do you have in mind?"

Though no one else was in the room, Bo lowered his voice and said, "Get these goddamn boots off my feet. I can't get them to budge."

Finally, Falk could smile. In fact, he broke into a boisterous belly laugh.

Even with Falk's strength he had to struggle with the boots. Falk turned his back to Bo, put both legs over Bo's knees, and bent forward as if he were riding a horse. It was—to say the least—an outrageously compromising position.

"Now Bo, if anyone walks in here while we're in this position, we're gonna have a little explaining to do," Falk said.

Bo broke into a roar at the same time one of the boots popped from his foot. With the proper technique now discovered, Falk hurriedly removed the second one.

"Bo was beautiful," Falk said. "He was tough and could be ornery, but he had the innocence of a boy in his heart. He could see the humor in life, and I think that's what helped him to be able to laugh at himself."

Bo did a lot of things that people might not have expected. One of his special treats was going to Neil Diamond concerts.

"He'd call me up and say that he and Shemy and I were going to a Neil Diamond concert that night," Falk said. "Of course, I was the driver. He loved Neil Diamond."

The 1988 season didn't start as smoothly as a Neil Diamond concert. By the time it ended, however, the Wolverines were rocking louder than the Rolling Stones.

In the opener at Notre Dame, Michigan held a 17–16 lead early in the fourth quarter. With 1:13 left, Reggie Ho kicked a 26-yard field goal to reclaim the lead for the Irish. Michigan engineered a drive to Notre Dame's 32-yard line with three seconds remaining. Mike Gillette's 49-yard field-goal attempt sailed wide right as time expired to give Notre Dame a 19–17 victory.

Miami of Florida visited The Big House the following week. The defending national champions scored 17 points in the last five minutes of the game for a 31–30 victory.

With Michigan leading 30–14, one of Falk's ball boys who was stationed on the Miami sideline came running across the field.

Asked what he was doing, the boy said, "Coach [Jimmy] Johnson threw me off the sideline."

"Why did he do that?" Falk asked.

"He thinks I'm somehow giving the plays they are running to the Michigan coaches," he said.

This was the old Woody Hayes trick that Falk had experienced before.

"Do you know that much about football?" Falk asked the boy.

"I don't know anything about football," he said. "I'm just trying to keep the balls dry."

Falk told him to follow him across the field so that he could rectify the situation.

Following the Miami heartbreaker, the Wolverines went on a tear. They won three straight games before settling for a 17-all tie at Iowa. They then reeled off six straight victories, including a 22–14 decision over fifth-ranked USC in the Rose Bowl.

One of the more satisfying victories was the 17–3 thumping of Michigan State. Gillette proved how valuable a kicker can be. He scored 11 points, including six on a 40-yard touchdown run on a fake punt.

When Falk visited the Spartan locker room to claim the Paul Bunyan Trophy, he was told that the equipment manager had forgotten to pack it. Falk settled the case of the missing trophy on Monday morning when he drove the Michigan semi up to East Lansing to claim it.

Upon his visit, Falk had the opportunity to tour the Michigan State facilities. Compared to Michigan's, they were the Taj Mahal. When he returned to Ann Arbor, he told Bo about the weight room and workout facilities.

"I gotta tell you, Bo," he said. "They're a whole lot nicer than what we have here."

Bo dismissed Falk's observations."Michigan State doesn't have anything better than Michigan," he snapped.

But it must have stirred the coach to thinking.

He called Falk to his office the next day for a full report. Bo was aware of some rumblings about the visitor's locker room in Michigan Stadium from having read Sam Wyche's description of it in a *Sports Illustrated* article.

"Bo, I gotta tell you," Falk said. "When a visiting equipment manager comes to tell me he needs a couple of extra lockers, I pick up a hammer and a couple of nails and ask him where do you want them."

The seed had been planted. Bo was then determined to do whatever was necessary to construct the finest facilities in the nation for the team he loved so much.

Two years later, Schembechler Hall became a reality. With the addition of the new indoor practice field and renovations to The Big House for the 2010 season, Bo's vision will be forever enhanced.

In the regular season's final game, Michigan needed a fourth-quarter rally to nip the Buckeyes 34–31. The 1-2 running punch of Michigan was devastating.

Leroy Hoard gained 158 yards, and Tony Boles ground out 103. But it was another Demetrius Brown to John Kolesar end zone strike with about a minute to play that sealed the victory.

In the Rose Bowl, the Wolverines had to contend with one of the stingiest defenses in the country. USC led the Pac-10 in rushing defense and passing defense.

Nevertheless, the Michigan offense picked up where it had left off in Columbus. Hoard bullied his way to two touchdowns and 142 yards. Boles added 49, and Michigan scored 13 points in the fourth quarter for a 22–14 victory.

Michigan finished with a 9–2–1 record and a No. 4 ranking in both wire polls.

"Kinda funny," Falk remarked. "We didn't hear any talk about a Model T for the last few years."

Chapter **32**
Vada Murray: My "M" Stuff

A few years ago when the Cincinnati Reds visited Detroit to play the Tigers, Hall of Fame–bound Ken Griffey Jr. called former Michigan safety standout Vada Murray. The two had played football together for the fabled Cincinnati Moeller High School team.

They joked with each other and swapped old stories as only former teammates can. As Griffey was about to hang up the phone, he gave Murray a reminder.

"Don't forget to tell Big Jon to have my Michigan stuff ready when I go out there tomorrow," Griffey said.

After having spent four years with Falk (1987–90), the reminder didn't surprise Murray. In fact, hardly anything pertaining to Falk surprises Murray.

"I don't know how he does it, but Big Jon knows a lot of people," Murray said. "Big-time people."

Reflecting upon his Michigan career, Murray often thinks about Falk. Some of the memories make him smile. All of the memories make him feel proud.

"One of the best things Big Jon does for a young man is make him earn his respect," Murray said. "That young man might not realize what Jon is doing at the time, but it's done for a purpose. Big Jon is always hardest on the freshmen. Getting socks and T-shirts and almost anything out of him when you're a freshman isn't easy. A junior or a senior can get anything he wants. But a freshman first has to be around for a while to earn respect. Big Jon can tell if a player is a Michigan Man. He knows who can be counted on."

Big Jon can tell if a player is a Michigan Man. He knows who can be counted on.
—Vada Murray

Players recognize the fact that Falk was handpicked by Bo for the position.

"That right there tells the whole story," Murray said.

Like so many other players, Murray also appreciates the boundless enthusiasm Falk has for Michigan.

"He's a charismatic person," Murray said. "Always on the go. I'll always remember those Ohio State game weeks when Big Jon would pump up the volume for those old Bob Ufer tapes. You could hear them in Ypsilanti. The players did get pumped."

Another yardstick for the amount of respect Falk has earned can be measured by his familiarity throughout the conference.

"Some schools have gone through two or even three equipment managers since Big Jon has been at Michigan," Murray said. "That's a lot of personnel change. There isn't a coach in the Big Ten [who] doesn't know Big Jon."

That may be the highest form of respect. And he got it the same way he gives it—he earned it.

Murray died on April 6, 2011.

"He was a good player and a tremendous person," Falk said.

Chapter **33**

1989: Good-bye to The Tunnel

Win or lose, Falk treasured all those memorable moments he was proud to share with Bo in the coach's room after each game. Even when the room was filled with nothing but silence, Falk could pick up a valuable life lesson that only he was privileged to learn.

Before the Ohio State game in 1989, the situation shifted slightly. Bo brought his loyal longtime friend into his strictest confidence before the opening kickoff.

"Well Big Jon, this will be the last time I walk down The Tunnel against Ohio State," Bo said.

Naturally, Falk was stunned by the cryptic remark. Despite a quiet undercurrent relating to Bo's future, somehow everyone always believed that Bo would be at Michigan forever.

"What are you saying, coach?" Falk asked.

For the moment, that was all Bo was willing to divulge. He had an immediate issue to tackle. In a few moments, he had that little matter of tangling with Ohio State.

"You'll find out later," Bo said. "But this is my last trip down that tunnel."

The pregame talk to the team was particularly emotional. Bo never revealed the secret he was carrying, but tears welled up in his eyes. Who knows for sure what the players suspected, but their emotions mirrored their leader.

"Walking down The Tunnel with him is a moment I'll never forget 'til the day I die," Falk said.

After the game that Michigan won 28–18, Falk joined his friend for the final trip up The Tunnel.

"Well Big Jon, that was it," Bo said in his office. "I'll never walk down that tunnel for a game again."

Falk knew what his coach was saying. He tried desperately to gather his thoughts for the right words.

"You're getting out?" Falk finally managed to ask.

Bo blurted his answer almost as if to hear the words himself.

"I'm retiring, Jon," he said. "I'm retiring. But don't you tell anyone."

A few days later, Bo made the announcement. First he called the entire staff together in the meeting room in Crisler Arena. There wasn't a dry eye in the room—including Bo's. Later Bo told the world at a press conference. Even some reporters left the room with wet eyes.

There had been whispered speculation about the inevitable. But the thought of Michigan football under the direction of anyone but Bo Schembechler was tough to imagine.

Bo had taken a storied though slightly dormant program and revived it into a national powerhouse with his indelible mark of loyalty, determination, and smash-mouth football.

Though stung by the change, Falk understood the necessity of Bo's decision. The coach had undergone two heart surgeries. The pressure of coaching a high-profile team such as Michigan had become significantly more taxing on his overall physical health.

"I've seen all the responsibilities that the head coach at Michigan has to endure," Falk said. "But until you experience them for yourself, I don't think any of us can fully appreciate the toll it takes."

More important to Bo than any of his personal concerns was his final act of loyalty to the people who had helped preserve the program he had created. He named assistant coach Gary Moeller as his successor. It was critical to Bo for the people he had brought into his program to be able to retain their positions.

Bo learned that lesson from Bear Bryant, the legendary Alabama coach, who shared Bo's passion for the game and also for the men he had hired.

"Bo used to tell me how tough it was for Coach Bryant to step down," Falk said. "He said that Coach Bryant wanted to retire a few years before he finally did but felt responsible for those people who had been loyal to him. When Bo finally devised his plan, he felt comfortable enough to step down knowing all the pieces were in place. That's the way it was with Bo. He worried about everyone."

Bo was able to name Moeller as the head coach, and the rest of the staff was retained. Bo was stepping aside, but his beloved program would remain stable and thriving.

The victory over Ohio State capped a fittingly magnificent final season for Bo. After dropping the opener to Notre Dame 24–19, the Wolverines won their next 10 games to earn the right to play USC in the Rose Bowl.

And until the day he died, Bo blamed himself for the loss to the Irish.

Notre Dame's Raghib "Rocket" Ismail returned two kicks for touchdowns that had all Michigan fans shaking their heads. The Rocket took the second-half kickoff and squirted down the field for an 88-yard TD return. In the fourth quarter, the Rocket struck again on a 92-yard return to put the game out of reach.

Bo's inclination was to squib the second kick to Ismail. He had been burned once and didn't want to risk the chance of being scalded again. Talking to Bo on the headsets before kicking off, the assistant coaches were convinced that Ismail couldn't do it twice.

"I'm the guy who approves those plays," Bo told Falk after the game. "It was my fault. I accept it. If I had to do it over again I probably wouldn't have done it that way. But I approved it, so I take the hit."

Bo was fearless when it came to accepting responsibility for something that went wrong.

"He was always a stand-up guy," Falk said. "He never passed the buck. There were plenty of times when an assistant suggested something that didn't work out right. Bo had the power to take or leave the suggestion. If a play failed, he accepted the responsibility."

For years afterward, however, Falk liked to tease his boss.

"Criminy Bo," he'd say. "Whatever possessed you to kick the ball twice to the Rocket?"

Then both would laugh.

"That was dumb," Bo would say. "What the hell was I thinking about then?"

Michigan traveled to UCLA the following week. The Wolverines scored 10 points in the game's final 10 minutes, capped by a 24-yard field goal by J.D. Carlson with :01 remaining to secure the victory. After mauling Maryland 41–21 the following week, Michigan galloped through the Big Ten season undefeated.

Then came the Rose Bowl, and Falk had one more critical personal assignment before heading west.

On December 7, Falk and his wife, Cheri, became the proud parents of daughter Katie. Two weeks after coming into the world, Katie was on her first airplane trip to Pasadena. Now 19 years old, Katie has attended 19 bowl games.

"There's gonna be a lot more," Falk said. "And Katie already knows to savor every moment."

Chapter **34**

They Come and They Go, Hobbs

Bo had a gift for weeding fact from fiction.

While he appreciated the media hype for the Rose Bowl, all that really mattered was what happened on the field.

The Rose Bowl is always one of those end-of-the-world media happenings. The actual game often gets dwarfed by all the hoopla. The story line for the 1990 edition was written in Ann Arbor shortly after Michigan had dismantled Ohio State.

It was to be Bo's last game as coach of the University of Michigan. The TV execs were drooling, and the spew of hyperbole from the rest of the media could have filled the Grand Canyon.

P.T. Barnum couldn't have devised a better hook. It seemed almost not to matter that two of the nation's most talented college football teams were preparing for a dogfight.

Bo cared little for what the media had to say. He cared only for the team that would always have the privilege of saying it played in Bo's last game.

"Men," he began his pregame talk. "You are not playing this game just for me. You are playing this game for the University of Michigan.

"How am I treating this game? I'm a senior just like all the other seniors on this team. I don't want it played emotionally because it's my last game. It's our seniors' last chance for the privilege of playing for Michigan. This game represents everything that they came to Michigan for. Now let's go out and win this game for the University of Michigan."

That was it. Nothing fancy. Nothing to cry about.

Of course, the pregame hoopla was beyond Bo's control. And how could the players not enjoy seeing another Bo—movie star Bo Derek and her husband John—cheering for the Wolverines on the Michigan sideline?

The captivating beauty had befriended Bo during previous Rose Bowl visits. It was a good time to be the Michigan equipment manager because Falk had the honor of presenting her with a Michigan jersey—No. 10, of course—plus a sweater and various other items of Rose Bowl memorabilia. The Dereks wore the Michigan attire at the game and also at the pep rally they attended earlier in the week.

It was a time of excitement and also a time for nostalgia. Most precious to Bo, of course, was the opportunity to play another big game.

Michigan played determinedly and rallied to enter the fourth quarter tied with USC at 10-all. But the Trojans scored the only touchdown of the fourth quarter and held on for a 17–10 victory.

The pivotal play of the game came with 12:00 left in the fourth quarter. On fourth-and-2 from the Michigan 46-yard line, Michigan punter Chris Stapleton's fake punt gained 24 yards. But the play was called back for a holding penalty. Tacked on was an unsportsmanlike penalty that pushed the ball back to the Michigan 21-yard line.

The play did, however, provide a memory that remains etched in the minds of all who love Bo.

"He got so livid with the call that he tripped on the phone line and fell," Falk said. "Wasn't that classic Bo? Getting so enraged that he fell to the ground in his final game?"

Nevertheless, the Wolverines had their first 10-win (10–2) season since 1986 and earned their second straight Big Ten championship. Bo ended his career as the winningest coach in Michigan football history with a 194–48–5 record.

Shortly after the team returned to Ann Arbor, Bo made the public announcement that he had accepted the position of president of the Detroit

Tigers. Whenever a coach leaves, tradition calls for Falk to immediately remove the man's nameplate from his locker and empty all of his gear.

The assistant coaches couldn't resist the opportunity to play a final practical joke on the man they so much admired. They had Falk remove Bo's nameplate from the locker. All of his workout gear was removed. The locker looked as spacious as the gap between a seven-year-old's missing two front teeth.

Following his press conference, Bo decided to work out his anxiety with a run on the treadmill.

"Falk!" Bo yelled into the telephone. "I came down for a workout, and all my stuff is gone! No shoes. No socks. No shorts. No T-shirt. What the hell is going on here?"

Fighting back his laughter while being urged on by the assistant coaches, Falk regained his composure.

"Hey Bo," Falk said. "They say you're done here. They say you're moving on. You're a Tiger now."

Then in reference to a line from Bernard Malamud's classic novel *The Natural*, Falk said, "They come and they go, Hobbs…they come and they go."

Bo laughed loud enough to be heard all the way to Tiger Stadium.

"He loved telling that story to anyone who'd listen," Falk said.

* * * *

Falk had already established some longtime friendships with a variety of Tiger players and personnel. After just one year under Bo, they unanimously agreed that the improvements he initiated throughout the entire system accomplished more in those 12 months than what had been done in the previous 12 years.

Weight-training rooms were added to the major league club as well as all the minor league affiliates throughout the system. An additional coach was added to each minor league team. Travel conditions were improved for the major leaguers.

"It didn't matter what sport it happened to be," Falk said. "Bo understood athletes. More importantly, he understood men. He knew how to get the most out of every athlete he was around."

Soon after leaving Michigan, a tribute to Bo was held at Detroit's Cobo Hall. The large convention center was packed with former players and coaches. A litany of celebrities from every walk of life attended the affair. The list also included Bo Derek who, of course, illuminated the head table.

Seated at the head table was legendary basketball coach Bobby Knight, one of Bo's closest friends. Knight wore a Michigan baseball cap and a pair of sunglasses as Bo had done for all the games he coached.

A few weeks later when Indiana played at Michigan, Knight borrowed a cap from Falk and walked into Crisler Arena looking just as he had appeared at the tribute dinner.

While at the dinner, Falk reflected on the many things that had transpired and the many talented people he had been privileged to meet since that cold January afternoon in 1974 when Bo told him, "You've got to come to the University of Michigan."

"I've learned a little something from each one of them," Falk said. "I know Bo and Bobby the best. They were so much alike. Both were no-nonsense guys. They were strict disciplinarians with themselves and with their teams. Neither of them would do anything against the rules. They were both squeaky clean. They had no tolerance for those who broke the rules."

Above all else, they took pride in teaching young men how to become productive young adults.

"There's no question Bo and Bobby were teachers first and coaches second," Falk said. "Woody Hayes was the same way. They taught athletes what they had to learn to become successful after they graduated. That was always their big thing.

"Athletics are fine, but you need to know how to apply what you learned in athletics to help you succeed in life. You need to know how to become good citizens of this country. Bobby always said there was no professor at the University of Michigan [who] taught young men about life better than Coach Schembechler. And the same thing can be said about Bobby."

Another quality that coaches like Bo and Knight share is the ability to laugh at themselves. Their sense of humor was sincere.

"Bo could laugh at himself more than anyone else," Falk said. "When he made a mistake, he wasn't afraid to admit it."

Athletics are fine, but you need to know how to apply what you learned in athletics to help you succeed in life.
—*Jon Falk*

In 1976, the team was preparing to play at Northwestern. Part of Falk's responsibilities was to pack the travel bag of each player on the travel list prepared by Bo.

"Coach, you're not taking Harlan Huckleby on the trip?" Falk asked during the final practice.

Bo squinted at Falk as if he was a referee who had just thrown a flag for a 15-yard penalty. "What the hell are you talking about?" Bo demanded. "He's the starting tailback! Don't you know anything at all about football? Why would I leave Huckleby at home?"

Falk sheepishly handed the travel list to the coach.

"I don't know sir," he said. "I was kinda wondering that, too."

Bo perused the paper and strolled over to assistant Terrell Burton.

"I think we better take Huck on this trip," he said before breaking into a belly laugh.

"It was a good feeling to see Bo laugh at himself," Falk said. "It showed the real person inside."

Falk had a similar experience with Knight while driving to a dinner in Bloomington, Indiana. Knight stopped at four service stations without finding a pump that would accept a credit card. Finally, Falk suggested that Knight go into the station and pay cash while Falk pumped the gas.

Falk was still having trouble removing the gas cap when Knight returned to the car.

"What is wrong with you, Jon?' Knight asked. "You gotta be smarter than this gas cap."

Knight removed the cap, grabbed the hose, and inserted it into the tank. No gas was flowing.

"What the hell is wrong here?" Knight asked. "Why won't this hose work?"

Falk turned to the pump, pressed the switch, and the gas began to flow.

"Here coach," Falk said. "You gotta be smarter than this gas pump." Knight looked at Falk and laughed.

Bo's sense of humor was matched by his sense of loyalty to friends and those he trusted. For Bo, there was no greater loyalty than to assistant coaches and members of his staff. He often rewarded their loyalty through generous gifts known only to them.

"He had a contract with Nike that paid him pretty handsomely each season," Falk said. "Bo would divvy up the money among assistants and staff members for the college education of their kids. Since I didn't have any kids of my own at the time, he let me put it toward my sister's kids."

That ability to laugh at yourself and practice loyalty to friends are qualities that separate great coaches from the good ones.

Does anyone doubt that Bo tops the list?

Section 4

1990s

Chapter **35**
Gary Moeller: A Clean House

After 44 years in football as a player and coach at every level, Gary Moeller has spent enough time in locker rooms across the nation to be considered a certified gym rat.

Never during his five years as Michigan head coach and 18 seasons as an assistant under Bo did he ever worry about a locker room run by Falk.

"Jon was always more than prepared," Mo said. "He anticipated problems before they could happen. He had everything in order—uniforms, pads, equipment, and anything else we needed for a game or practice."

It sounds fairly simple, but preparing a team for a run at a championship in a disconcerted locker room is like going to have a tooth extracted by a dentist who forgot to place his weekly order for anesthetics.

There's a rhythm to the locker room that begins as soon as the first player steps through the door. A player has to know that everything he needs for the game is in his locker, ready to go. If anyone has a special need, he must feel confident that the manager can resolve the situation quickly. No coach can afford the disrupted mindset of a team preparing to play a game.

"A lot of equipment managers run a good locker room," Mo said. "What separates Jon from so many others, though, is his enthusiasm for the game and his passion for Michigan. It's important for him to feel a part of the team, and it shows through his enthusiasm. His energy is a real asset because it spreads throughout the whole team."

With Falk, no job is too big and no job is too small. Whatever it takes to make the team a little better, Falk gets it done without anyone noticing.

"We all have seen guys who operate on a 9-to-5 schedule," Mo said. "Once they've put in their time, they aren't going to lift a finger unless they are told. You never have to tell Jon what to do. If something is going to help the team, he just goes ahead and does it. He never had any set hours. The only time he peeks at his watch is when it's getting close to kickoff."

Mo knew he could rely on Falk's unyielding enthusiasm to encourage players and make them feel more at ease.

"He loves to go around the room talking to players before a game," Mo said. "Football—especially at the college level—isn't all Xs and Os. So much of the game is based on emotion.

"I never minded Jon talking to the players just like a coach does. He wasn't going over plays or a particular game plan. He was sharing his enthusiasm with the players. The kids could feel just how important each game was simply by watching how much it meant to Jon."

The kids could feel just how important each game was simply by watching how much it meant to Jon.

—*Gary Moeller*

The locker room is a particularly fascinating study of psychological and physical dynamics. It's a sanctuary where players learn and bond. It's a classroom where coaches teach and discipline. The order of the room reflects the quality of accomplishment.

For Falk, the job of equipment manager transcends his role as mere keeper of helmets, cleats, socks, and jocks.

"I've seen a lot of equipment managers over the years," Mo said. "Without a doubt, Big Jon is one of a kind. He's proud to be part of the team. And every team he serves is fortunate to have him."

Chapter **36**
The Laugh's on Bo

Gary Moeller is not a natural practical joker. But the prank he pulled on his former boss and longtime friend still makes all members of the former Michigan staff smile.

It happened during a practice leading to the start of the 1990 season at a time when Bo was finishing his first year as president of the Detroit Tigers. By then, Bo had come to appreciate the fact that the maybe two losses in a season he had to endure coaching football at Michigan could be matched in a single day by the team of his new sport.

And quite often it was.

It was a beautiful late summer afternoon, and Bo decided to visit a practice of his former team. The only excitement surrounding his new team came from first baseman Cecil Fielder who was in the late stages of his successful run to become the first player in 13 years to hit at least 50 home runs in one season.

Maybe it was a nostalgic musing that brought Bo to the practice. Maybe he missed seeing athletes in helmets and pads hitting each other. Or maybe he just wanted to see his old staff that had served him so faithfully.

He called Mo and asked if he would object to a visit from the old boss. Bo didn't want to impose. He respected the fact that the team now belonged to Mo.

Of course, Mo and all the assistants were anxious to visit with the rookie baseball executive. Mo told him the team was practicing in the stadium that day, and everyone looked forward to the visit.

Before Bo arrived, Mo was struck by an idea that turned out to be pure classic comedy—a perfect segment for the old TV show *Candid Camera*.

Mo called Falk and told him to station one of his student assistants that Bo didn't know at The Tunnel gate. It was the only entry to the stadium that day.

"Whatever you do, you don't let him in until we say so," Falk instructed the young man.

Bo walked sprightly toward the gate after parking his car. Bo loved watching a practice. He could tell from its crispness—or lack of it—how a team would perform on Saturday. This was the team that he had put together before turning over the reins to his good friend Mo.

Falk, Mo, and the rest of the assistant coaches stood unseen in the shadows along one wall of The Tunnel.

"I'm here to watch practice," Bo told the young man at the gate.

Whatever that student lacked in football knowledge he more than compensated for with theatrical flair.

"I'm sorry, sir," the young man informed Bo. "This practice is closed. You can't come in."

Needless to say, Bo was certifiably dumbfounded. Finally, he responded.

"What?" was all he managed.

"I have strict orders that practice is closed, sir," the young man said.

Now Bo's temperature was starting to slightly rise.

"I called Coach Moeller, and he said to meet him at the stadium," Bo said.

Again the young man was mannerly persistent.

"I'm sorry, sir," he said. "I can't afford to lose my job."

By that time, the snickers and giggles kept getting louder in The Tunnel. Falk decided it was time for Bo to join the fun.

"Wait a minute, son," Falk said to his student assistant. "Do you know who this man is?"

The student looked at Bo and then back at Falk.

"No sir," he said.

"Well, this is Coach Bo Schembechler," Falk said with pride and authority.

The student looked back at Bo.

"Oh yeah?" he said. "Where do you coach?"

Mo and the rest of the assistants then burst from the darkness of The Tunnel with grins on their faces as if they had just raided the cookie jar. Finally Bo got the welcome he had expected.

"Everyone got the biggest kick out of that little stunt," Falk said. "Even Bo broke into a belly laugh."

That's the way Mo was. He may have had a droll sense of humor, but he loved to laugh and also was able to laugh at himself. That's an invaluable quality for a head coach at such a high-profile institution as the University of Michigan.

It was a season of transition for the tradition-rich university that viewed head football coaching changes as aberrations to the cosmic system. Those changes are about as normal as a complete solar eclipse of the sun occurring on Christmas Day…and right at midnight.

Bo had been only the 14th head coach since Michigan started playing football in 1891. Excluding the six coaches who served until 1901 when Fielding H. Yost came along to lay the foundation for modern Michigan football, Bo was only the eighth.

Would there be change under a new leader? Of course there would. A football team is like any other structured organization.

"No change at the top goes without the new top exec putting his fingerprints on the organization," Falk said. "That's the way it's supposed to be. The pressure is on him. He's the top guy. When the heat is on, he has to take it."

Bo had developed a championship program based upon fundamentals, consistency, and playing by the rules. The consistency of his excellence captured not only the players who performed on the field but also the vast network of Michigan alums around the nation.

The formula for success was already in place. It was up to Mo to maintain that consistency and fine-tune the machine with some of his personal touches.

But drastic change? Not really. There was no reason for radical re-tooling. Mo had served 18 seasons as Bo's assistant. He had recruited much of the talent that he inherited. And most importantly, he shared many of Bo's qualities and beliefs.

Mo introduced a little more passing into the offense. But like his predecessor, Mo had three basic running plays he could call at any time when necessary to pick up a couple of precious yards.

Mo shared Bo's belief that games were won and lost on both sides of the line. He accepted the Michigan tradition and never strayed from following the rules.

One of the bigger differences between Mo and Bo went largely unseen by the public and was felt only by the staff.

Bo, of course, was anything but subtle. A shout to most people was only a whisper to Bo.

"Bo was special," Falk said. "He created a plan and was religiously focused on getting it done. Most people can't do that. He knew what he expected from everyone, and everyone was supposed to get that job done. He never wavered. You could ask him a question, and he would give you an answer right away. You never went away wondering how he wanted some assignment done."

Mo also had a plan but was more deliberate when making a decision.

"Mo wanted to hear all sides of every situation," Falk said. "He would weigh all the factors and then make a decision. That was just an extension of his personality. He has a different personality than Bo did. Everyone does things their own way."

At the end, though, the results were the same. The program continued to flourish, and the traditions survived.

Mo's football pedigree taught him never to stray far from a road that has led to success. He was the obvious choice to succeed the retiring legend. He had served as an assistant under Bo at Miami of Ohio and 18 seasons at Michigan. He served three years as head coach of Illinois. He was a three-time letter winner as a linebacker at Ohio State and captained the 1962 team. After leaving Michigan, he had short stints in the NFL as head coach of the Detroit Lions and as an assistant coach with the Jacksonville Jaguars.

Mo was familiar with all the nuances of Big Ten and Midwest college football. And he had been schooled in all the traditions of Michigan that made the transition from Ohio State so much easier.

He put his individual imprint on the program. But he recognized the fact that no blueprint for overhaul was necessary.

"How could anyone really expect for anyone to exactly replace someone bigger than life like Bo?" Falk said. "That just can't be done. Coaches like Bo and Woody come along only once in a lifetime. But Mo learned from Bo. He shared his principles. There were some subtle changes, but he was a good extension of Bo."

Chapter **37**
1990: Mo's the Right Man

Falk had demonstrated unimpeachable loyalty to Bo and Michigan football for 16 seasons. The confidence that Bo had demonstrated in him made for a seamless transition during the head coaching change of 1990.

"Bo was able to show all the coaches on the staff that he trusted me," Falk said. "He trusted how I did things. So as those assistants grew, I believe they felt they could place the same trust in me."

With Gary Moeller handpicked by Bo to be his successor, the assistant coaches and the rest of the staff were retained.

"The transition was a little less tumultuous than at other schools," Falk said. "Sometimes you are able to keep a coaching change within house, and sometimes you can't. It was a little easier because everyone knew everybody else and what to expect."

While the portrait of Michigan football wasn't radically altered, there were a few subtle adjustments.

"Mo shared the same principles as Bo but obviously had his own way of doing things," Falk said. "In any job, every time you have a new boss there are bound to be some changes. Each boss has a different personality. Each one possesses different strengths and ideas that they want to pass along to those working for them. Underneath it, though, Mo understood it was his job to maintain the program that Bo had built."

One of the changes Falk noticed from the start was Mo's concern for details.

"Bo was a special kind of person," Falk said. "He knew exactly what he needed to make his program work. He told you what he wanted and expected everyone [who] worked for him to get the job done.

"Bo was more spontaneous. If an issue arose, he confronted it right at the moment. Mo wanted every piece of information before making a decision. Mo rarely made snap decisions. He liked to study things to learn all the details.

"Mo was a very detailed guy. He asked a lot of questions. He wanted to know the ramifications of every situation and expected you to tell him."

Mo understood it was his job to maintain the program that Bo had built.

—Jon Falk

For instance, Mo sought details for making practice schedules. He wanted to know how long it took to pack and unpack the equipment truck for road games. He immersed himself into the usually unseen details of a program that had become one of the most dominant forces in the world of college football.

"Bo was cognizant of all those things but didn't get into all of the details," Falk said. "He had a plan and expected you to know how to make it work. Mo sought a little more input before making a decision."

Nevertheless, their principles were mirror images. Mo had proven himself to be a master recruiter. And once he assembled all that talent, he stressed fundamentals with the same ferocity as his legendary predecessor.

"Bo may have been a little more outwardly vocal, but he and Mo shared the same passion for Michigan," Falk said. "All the players loved Mo. They still do and give him a standing ovation every time he comes back for a reunion. Just like Bo, Mo has a gift for laughing at himself. That's a pretty good sign of a man who has confidence in himself."

No one on the team was laughing after the first game of the 1990 season. Despite totaling more yards than Notre Dame and taking a 10-point lead into the fourth quarter, Michigan lost 28–24 at South Bend.

Nevertheless, Michigan rebounded with three straight victories before suffering a 28–27 loss to Michigan State on a controversial decision by the officials.

Trailing 28–27 after a 6-yard touchdown pass from Elvis Grbac to Derrick Alexander with :06 to play, Mo decided to go for the two-point conversion and the victory. Grbac tossed a pass to Desmond Howard, who was tripped in the end zone and dropped the ball as he hit the turf. No pass interference was called, and the Big Ten office called Michigan on Monday to apologize for the situation.

After a 24–23 loss to Iowa the following week, Michigan rolled over Indiana, Purdue, Illinois, and Minnesota to set up the meeting with the Buckeyes in Columbus.

With time running out and the score tied at 13–13, Ohio State went for a first down on fourth-and-1 on its own 29-yard line. The Wolverines smothered quarterback Greg Frey on an option to take possession. Four plays later, J.D. Carlson ended the game with a 37-yard field goal as time expired for a 16–13 Michigan victory.

The victory gave Michigan a 6–2 conference record, a share of the Big Ten title, and a berth in the Gator Bowl.

Playing Mississippi in Jacksonville, Florida, Mo unleashed the offense for a Michigan single-game record 715 yards. It was Michigan's fourth bowl game victory in its last six appearances.

Michigan's No. 7 and No. 8 finishes in the final two wire polls confirmed the choice of Mo to succeed his former mentor.

Chapter **38**

1991: A Sticky Situation

Desmond Howard's diving fingertip catch in the end zone to beat Notre Dame launched his successful drive to the Heisman Trophy. The reception is one of the most celebrated in the history of Michigan football and is still seen by millions of television viewers every time Michigan plays the Irish.

Even before the game started, Falk was involved in a discussion with the referees during which he made his point without dropping the ball. The officiating crew was comprised of representatives from the Big Ten and Big East Conferences.

Each team is required to provide six footballs to the referees for inspection for use in the game. During Friday night preparations, Falk unwrapped six new balls and secured them safely next to a hot water heater. Evidently, the heater had made the surface of the balls tacky, which prompted the Big East official to say, "I'm not approving these balls for the game."

This was Falk's first such encounter, and he was determined to rectify the situation expediently. "Do you have any other new footballs?" the Big Ten official asked.

Falk returned to the locker room and retrieved six new balls that were still in plastic bags near the same water heater. He removed the plastic and put them in boxes before returning to the officials.

"Something still doesn't feel right," the Big East rep said.

After making his inspection, the Big Ten official said, "Did you do anything to these balls, Jon?"

Falk explained exactly what he had done before bringing the balls to them.

"That's good enough for me," the Big Ten official said. "Let's play."

Neither Howard nor any receiver needed tacky footballs to ensure a better grip. At the time, receivers at many schools were using new gloves that were as sticky as a jar of molasses. "You could take those gloves and throw them up against a wall and they would just stick there," Falk said. "Desmond loved them. He would go through two or three pairs a game."

Howard didn't need any help that year. He was catching anything thrown to him that remained within radar distance. "I teased him after the game that the ball actually stuck to the ends of his fingertips on that catch," Falk said.

The celebrated touchdown came on a gutsy call by Coach Gary Moeller. After calling a timeout, Michigan elected not to attempt a field goal on a fourth-and-1 on the Notre Dame 25-yard line. Quarterback Elvis Grbac pump-faked a pass and then found his favorite target in the end zone.

It was Michigan's second straight victory to start the season. And as Falk always maintains, "When you beat Notre Dame, you are usually set for a pretty good season."

Michigan dropped a 51–31 shootout to No. 1 ranked Florida State following a bye week before mauling their way through the Big Ten schedule without being really contested. Michigan posted shutouts over Purdue and Illinois and also pasted Minnesota 52–6 to keep possession of the Little Brown Jug.

Michigan scored at least 42 points in five victories as Moeller opened the offense to a little more passing. "No question the offense was doing a few more things," Falk said. "Mo still relied on the running game just like Bo, but each coach is gonna run an offense that best fits the kids he recruited."

In the final game of the regular season, Howard put his personal claim on the Heisman Trophy he was destined to win with his "Heisman pose seen round the world." The play came in the second quarter when Ohio State punted to the Michigan 7-yard line. Howard took the ball and split a pair of defenders down the left sideline on his trip to the end zone. Upon his arrival, he broke into his Heisman pose and took the ribbing of his life from happy teammates when he returned to the delirious Michigan bench.

"He said he was debating about doing it while running down the sideline," Falk said. "It must have been a pretty quick debate because he got into that end zone faster than a flea on a sweaty dog. When he got into the end zone, he said he told himself—what the hell."

Michigan hammered Ohio State 31–3 for its fourth straight Big Ten championship.

In the Rose Bowl after a scoreless first quarter, Washington took a 13–7 lead into the half. The Huskies controlled the final two quarters and finished with a 34–14 victory.

In the locker room after the game, Moeller planted a seed for the following season. "I want every person in this room to dedicate themselves to one thing," Mo addressed the team. "There's just one goal. Next year in the Rose Bowl, I want to sing 'The Victors' in Pasadena. Remember SVP—Sing 'The Victors' in Pasadena."

Chapter **39**

Desmond Howard: Earning Respect

Desmond Howard knows about the unwritten rules of sports. More than the ones found in the books, they separate sports from other walks of life. And the 1991 Heisman Trophy winner has learned them well.

One of the most basic of those rules is that respect is earned, not merely given. Unlike jerseys, towels, or pairs of socks distributed freely to every man on the team, respect is earned over a period of time. It demands talent and character on and off the field.

That's one reason for the admiration the former Michigan All-American wide receiver holds for Falk.

"When you go to Michigan as a freshman, he treats you like a freshman," Howard said. "All your press clippings from high school don't mean anything. It's a new game, and Jon wants to see a player earn respect. When you get to be an upperclassman and have followed all the rules, he treats you a little differently."

As a freshman, Howard quickly discovered he wasn't going to get anything before it was earned. "At the time, I wasn't really used to that," Howard said. "Part of his charm is he can be rude and ornery, but that's just the no-nonsense side of the man. That's part of the show. He's got a big job to do and wants all the players to do their jobs, too."

Howard recalls fondly how Falk could sternly address a player directly about a matter and then console him in the locker room after a tough practice.

He was always telling us stories of old games and old players. I think he knows more about Michigan traditions than anyone around there.

—Desmond Howard

"He has a voice that reflects his personality," Howard said. "There's no beating around the bush with Jon. He always speaks directly. Sometimes he sounds funny even when he's not trying to be. He was always telling us stories of old games and old players. I think he knows more about Michigan traditions than anyone around there. I'll never forget that voice."

Howard certainly earned Falk's respect and, in return, pays it to his former equipment manager. "Jon is one of the last Mohicans," Howard said. "He goes all the way back to Bo. Whenever I get back to Ann Arbor, I always go to visit Jon."

That's a slice of respect that Falk treasures greatly.

Chapter **40**

Steve Everitt: No Time Off

leeping on the job is only permissible for firemen and emergency physicians during breaks on the all night shift. At times, however, Falk does some of his best work while snoring and dreaming about how a problem can be solved.

"I can't explain it, but I have a lot of dreams like that," he said. However bizarre—and that's quite the norm with Falk—it worked for center Steve Everitt, who refused to let a little situation like a broken jaw keep him off the field.

Everitt isn't the most celebrated Michigan Man to have played the game's least glamorous position. That distinction belongs to Gerald Ford, who used the experience he gained at Michigan to go all the way to the White House. Arguably, however, Everitt may have been the best. An All-Big Ten performer, Everitt was the Cleveland Browns' first-round pick and the 14th overall selection in the 1993 National Football League Draft.

Everitt suffered the broken jaw against Notre Dame in the second game of the 1991 season. More than the pain he felt while lying on the ground, he almost panicked when his mother bolted from the stands onto the field to check on her son. "Now that I'm a parent myself, I can appreciate how she felt," Everitt laughed.

After a bye week, Everitt was forced to sit out the Florida State game with three steel plates protecting his jaw. He vowed to return for the start of the Big Ten season the following Saturday.

"I asked Jon if there was some way he could come up with a chin strap that could give me more protection," Everitt said.

That—and Falk's dream—was all it took. "I dreamt about a couple of extra straps running up and down each side of the helmet to hold the chin strap in place," Falk said. "I took a helmet and a handful of straps to the shoe repair place. I cut the jaw pad down and added a little extra padding on the bottom so it wouldn't irritate him."

The doctors agreed that the unconventional strapping would prevent further damage and cleared Everitt to play.

"That's a special thrill when you come up with an idea that actually makes a difference on the field," Falk beamed.

While appreciative for the creative moment, nothing about Falk surprises Everitt. "He's one of the top five characters I've met in life," Everitt said. "Jon doesn't get enough credit for all the things he does. The hours he works would kill most people. And it's the way he does it. He takes his job to another level. Just the fact that he's worked for four different head coaches is amazing. That just doesn't happen."

As creative as Falk is in his job, so too is Everitt with his passion for art. Everitt is an accomplished artist and used his talent to inject a sense of calm into players before another tense practice.

"A lot of us used to get to practice a half-hour early and draw caricatures of teammates and coaches and staff that we would show on a projector," Everitt said. "Fun things. Everybody laughed. Jon was one of our favorite subjects."

It's easy to share that kind of humor with a person trusted as a true friend.

"He's a friend for life," Everitt said. "Whenever I get the chance to get back to Ann Arbor or go to a bowl game where Michigan is playing, I always go straight to Jon. He's got almost 40 years with Michigan. That's saying something. Especially when you realize that Bo hired him."

Chapter **41**
1992: A Time of Change

Mo and his 1992 team did make good on their SVP promise the following New Year's Day. They raucously sang "The Victors" in the locker room following a 38–31 win over Washington.

Mo was particularly proud of his team's accomplishment. For everyone to remember the commitment necessary to return from Pasadena victorious, Mo ordered one side of the Rose Bowl ring—given to each player, coach, and member of the staff—to feature the letters "SVP."

"Anyone connected to that team will never forget what those letters mean,"

Falk said. "A lot of sweat. A lot of blood. A lot of sacrifice. And a whole lot of attitude to honor a commitment."

The 1992 Wolverines went undefeated though not unblemished. They captured their fifth straight Big Ten championship but had to endure ties with Notre Dame, Illinois, and—worst of all—Ohio State.

"Duffy Daugherty once said that a tie is like kissing your sister," Falk quipped. "We just happened to throw in Aunt Matilda and Cousin Becky for good measure."

The 9–0–3 record was still good enough for a fifth-place ranking in both national polls. Nevertheless, the 1992 season was spooky for more reasons than the oddity of three ties. It started just as the Wolverines were preparing for the season with two-a-day workouts. On August 4, Bo and longtime top club executive Jim Campbell were fired from the Detroit Tigers when the club was sold. Through Bo, Falk had befriended Campbell over the years. Bo, of course, was more than a friend to Falk. He had brought Falk to Michigan, and that bond of loyalty would last forever.

"Everyone at the University and around the state was stunned," Falk said. "Especially since Bo had done so much in such a short period of time to improve a lot of the working conditions and the whole minor league system."

Bo returned to Ann Arbor, but his unsavory dismissal from the Tigers was forgotten when his wife, Millie, died of adrenal cancer on August 19. "Bo was already going through enough grief when he got leveled by that," Falk said. "Millie was one of the finest and friendliest women anyone had the good fortune to meet. Before I got married, she and Bo would invite me to dinner at their house all the time. Sometimes when Bo went on a recruiting trip, I would go for dinner with Millie and the boys.

"I remember one night when all of us were sitting at the table, and she asked if Bo scared me. I looked over at Bo, who was waiting for the answer. I said, 'I know one thing for sure, Millie—I always run whatever I say to him through my head before I let my mouth start yapping.'"

Soon after Millie's death, Bo made a commitment to raise enough money to make the University of Michigan Hospital the top research center in the country to combat adrenal cancer. He held an annual charity golf tournament for eight years and raised millions.

As with everything he tackled, Bo promised to make the tournament the state's best charity event of the summer. He brought in celebrities like Sparky Anderson, Yogi Berra, Bobby Knight, Ara Parseghian, and enough former Hall of Fame and All-American football players that some groups wound up playing with more than one celebrity.

"Bo did the big job," Falk said. "He made all the calls to invite the stars to play. Now you know that none of them can say 'no' when Bo has them on the line."

Falk made sure that every player in the tournament was properly equipped with the gifts that were presented. For any little glitch that occurred during the day's events, Falk was there to fix it.

The football season that started three weeks after Millie's death certainly didn't erase Bo's grieving, but at least it provided momentary diversion. As a signal for things to come in that strange season, Michigan opened with a 17–17 tie at Notre Dame. Eight victories later, Illinois tied Michigan 22–22 at The Big House. Michigan finished the regular season with a 13–13 tie against Ohio State at Columbus the following week.

"Ohio State had lost the previous four games against us," Falk said, "but I couldn't believe the way the fans reacted. They charged the field and were yelling and screaming and jumping around like they had just shut us out. I saw a story where the president of the school said it was one of Ohio State's biggest victories. They didn't even beat us. That just goes to show how intense this rivalry is."

Before the next season started, Bo met his future wife, Cathy. At the time, Cathy had no idea what her future husband with the short first name and the tongue-twisting last name had accomplished in the world of sports. She also didn't have a clue about the fishbowl she was about to enter with her move to Ann Arbor.

Although the pair met through friends in Florida, Cathy had a home in Pittsburgh. She was arranging her personal business affairs with her lawyer before the move.

"What does your future husband do for a living?" the attorney asked Cathy.

She said he doesn't have a job.

"What did he do in his last job?" the attorney continued.

She said he was fired.

The attorney gave her a concerned look.

"May I ask the name of this gentleman?" he said.

"It's Bo Schembechler," she replied.

The lawyer remained composed, but his eyebrows raised like a 50-yard field goal.

"THE Bo Schembechler?" he asked.

He was certainly the only one Cathy knew and obviously a man the lawyer highly regarded.

And so it was for Bo and Cathy, who lived happily together until Bo's passing 13 years later.

Chapter **42**
1993: Bo Is Back

The most positive change in Michigan football to occur in 1993 had nothing to do with anything that happened on the field. Bo returned to Schembechler Hall, one of the nation's finest football facilities, which was in its third year of operation since Bo had spearheaded the drive to construct it.

He didn't take the head coach's plush office that now overlooks the country's largest indoor practice facility. He settled for a modest office toward the end of the second floor near recruiting secretary Mary Passink, who Bo hired many years ago.

Instead of playbooks for the season in session, the office was filled with new and old football media guides, a scattering of pictures and awards that Bo had accumulated throughout his career, and boxes of footballs and miscellaneous Michigan memorabilia that fans left for the ol' coach to sign.

From that office, he and Howard Wikel ran the charity golf tournament Bo had created to raise funds to fight the war against adrenal cancer, the disease that had taken Millie's life. And with the generous assistance of Passink, Bo scheduled the countless speeches and appearances he made around the country.

The office happens to be one of the first a fresh recruit and his parents must pass on their way to the head coach's office. It was an unexpected bonus for the visitors—and for Michigan's recruiting efforts—who often sought Bo's autograph and a few words from the master.

"His mere presence in the building meant so much to everyone on the staff," Falk said. "When times were tough, just knowing he was there and that you could talk to him meant a whole lot to everyone."

Falk felt like it was a daily family reunion.

"I was so fortunate to have our friendship grow when he was the head coach," Falk said. "When he came back, we had more time to visit. There was a lot less pressure on him, and he was more relaxed."

Bo followed politics closely. And needless to say, he was never shy about voicing his opinions. Discussions ranged from presidential elections to the state of major college football. "He always talked about how there won't be many more head coaches [who] last for 20 years at this level," Falk said. "The pressure from the media and the administration and the alumni is too much. Coaches can probably count on their fingers the number of times they really had fun during the year because of the pressure and responsibility of winning year after year."

He always talked about how there won't be many more head coaches [who] last for 20 years at this level.

—Jon Falk

Bo's presence in the football building was a blessing for Mo and later Lloyd Carr. No other coach in the country enjoyed such a treasure to lean upon. "A lot of people never understood how valuable it was for Mo and Lloyd to have Bo there," Falk said. "Only head coaches can appreciate what other head coaches are going through. They understand all the pressures they face each day of the year.

"Bo was an opinionated man, but never did he walk into the head coach's office to say anything. Mo and Lloyd both would go to Bo's office to seek advice on certain situations, and Bo never refused. But he never cast a shadow over them. He was just Bo."

After having won five straight Big Ten championships, the 1993 season didn't really reach its peak until the final four games. Losses to Michigan State, Illinois, and Wisconsin within a four-week mid-season tailspin killed all hope for a sixth straight title. Only an emotional victory at Penn State soothed the pain.

The game in Happy Valley was the biggest in Penn State history. The Nittany Lions had just joined the Big Ten. They were 5–0, ranked No. 7 in the nation, and feeling as if they could run through the conference without breaking a sweat. It also happened to be the school's 1,000th game.

Michigan went into halftime trailing 10–7 when Mo delivered a simple yet stimulating halftime speech. "Football is a mental game," Mo said. "You played a tough first half. Now you go out and dedicate yourselves to the second half. They are playing Michigan. They do not know about Michigan. We are about to give them a little education on what Michigan football is all about."

In the third quarter, Michigan took a 14–10 lead before Penn State engineered a 79-yard drive to the Wolverines' 1-yard line. And then the lesson was delivered.

Defensive coordinator Lloyd Carr created the theme of "Just Give Us a Place to Stand" before the season started. And that's all that was needed as the defense stopped four straight running plays without yielding an inch. Michigan scored another touchdown and held on for a 21–13 victory.

Falk had a football painted with "Michigan's first win over Penn State, 21–13." He presented it to Mo, who placed it in the defense meeting room next to a sign that read "Just Give Us a Place to Stand."

Losses to Illinois and Wisconsin preceded victories over Purdue and Minnesota before the showdown with Ohio State. And that's the game where Falk delivered a message of his own.

The Buckeyes arrived in Ann Arbor ranked No. 5 in the nation and undefeated in Big Ten play. A victory over Michigan would give them the outright title. As a matter of policy, the conference sends the championship trophy to the site of the game where the winner is playing.

Falk received the trophy on Friday. Before the Ohio State players arrived for their Friday workout, he had strategically placed the trophy outside the visitor's locker room door.

"There's your trophy men," he said as they walked into The Tunnel. "It's all yours. You can take it."

Falk watched them picking it up and holding it over their heads. He knew that if the roles had been reversed, Mo or Bo would have yelled to "get that thing out of here…we haven't won anything until we beat Ohio State." Falk dashed into Mo's office.

"Coach, I was just over there when they were coming out of the locker room," he said. "I want you to know right now, this game is ours. It's gonna be like feeding grain to crappies."

Mo thought Falk was hallucinating.

"Mo, they're no more ready to play Michigan than the man in the moon," Falk said. "They already won their championship and have the trophy. This game is ours."

On Saturday, Falk studied both teams as they went down The Tunnel.

"We were fired up," he said. "I could see it in their eyes. Ohio State was just lugging down The Tunnel. And when they hit daylight, their eyes got big as saucers."

Michigan raced to a 21–0 first-half lead. The Wolverines kept possession of the ball for all but 1:06 of the fourth quarter in a dominating 28–0 shutout.

Riding the wave of that victory, Michigan pounded North Carolina State 42–7 in the Hall of Fame Bowl to finish the year with four straight victories.

Chapter **43**
1994: The Helmets Are Gone

By 1994, Falk had learned to prepare himself for any absurdity waiting in Columbus. "You just can't trust things going right at Ohio State," he said. "Something always goes wrong that has to be fixed immediately."

As always, Falk went to the Ohio Stadium early before the 1994 game. This time he ran into trouble setting up the phone lines between the pressbox and the headsets to be used on the field.

That was a minor glitch compared to the situation waiting for him in the locker room. One of Falk's student assistants came looking for him to deliver the news.

"Did you lock up five helmets last night?" the assistant asked.

Falk had no idea what the young man was talking about, but he was wise enough to head for the locker room immediately. Soon he discovered trouble had already been there and gone. Five Michigan helmets were missing, including those of tailback Tyrone Wheatley, quarterback Todd Collins, and tight end Jay Riemersma. Those were not exactly the players you want to disrupt on game day with Ohio State.

Each of the missing helmets had been placed properly in the appropriate locker along with the rest of the player's uniform on Friday. Falk and his assistants scoured each inch of the locker room only to conclude that the helmets had been stolen.

Falk called the Ohio State University Police who responded quickly to take a report. "The police were good about it," Falk said. "They even apologized on behalf of the university."

Falk accepted the apology, but it didn't help him out of the pickle he found himself in. "If Bo had still been coaching, he would have exploded," Falk said. "He would have been steaming on that field all day. I really wasn't sure how Mo was going to react."

As soon as the team arrived, Falk went directly into Mo's office to break the news. Mo was trying to devise a plan as he quietly listened to the details of the theft.

"Do you have five extra helmets to put on these guys?" he asked.

Falk said he had enough but wasn't confident about how they would fit.

"Fit them the best you can and tell them to go out and play hard-nosed football," Mo said.

The reaction from Mo helped to settle Falk's nerves. He immediately understood why the coach reacted as he did. The game was only a few hours from starting. It wasn't the time for any off-the-field distractions.

When you take a player's helmet, you're messing with the man personally.

—Jon Falk

"When a player gets to the locker room for a game, there has to be a rhythm to the flow of things," Falk said. "The player has to know everything is waiting for him in the locker. The only thing that should be on his mind is what he has to do in the game.

"When you take a player's helmet, you're messing with the man personally. That helmet belongs to that player alone. It has to fit just right, and it becomes part of his identity. Just like a new pair of shoes, it takes two or three days to break in a helmet."

Falk learned his lesson well. When playing in Columbus now, he hires an armed guard to spend the night before the game in the visitor's locker room. Neither helmets nor any other pieces of equipment have shown up missing since.

In the morning of the 1995 game in Ann Arbor, two Ohio State Troopers returned the stolen helmets to Falk. The perpetrators had already been tried and convicted. Falk signed papers allowing them to perform community service in lieu of jail time.

In the second game of the 1994 season, another piece of missing equipment may have inadvertently helped lift Michigan to a comeback victory at South Bend.

As almost always happens, the two teams were in a back-and-forth dogfight. With less than a minute to play, Notre Dame scored a touchdown and an extra point to pull ahead 24–23. With only 46 seconds left in the game, quarterback Todd Collins quickly moved Michigan down the field.

Sensing he may be called upon to attempt a game-winning field goal, kicker Remy Hamilton frantically looked for the kicking net to warm up his leg. He raced to Falk to tell him the net was gone.

"What do you mean the net is gone?" Falk asked.

Suddenly he spotted one of his assistants carrying the net and various other pieces of equipment up the tunnel to be loaded onto the truck. Falk sprinted toward the tunnel but arrived a shade late. Hamilton practiced by kicking air before he was sent onto the field to attempt a 42-yard game-winning field goal.

Falk's pulse stopped for that agonizing moment when he saw the football heading toward the goal posts. Fortunately, the ball sailed through the uprights to give Michigan a 26–24 victory. Touchdown Jesus could feel the sigh of relief coming from deep inside Falk's lungs.

After the game, Falk teased the deliriously happy Hamilton. "If you had warmed up the usual way, you might not have made it," he said. Since that game, Falk has assigned one assistant to guard the net with instructions not to leave until there are all zeroes on the clock.

The following week when all the zeroes appeared, the entire Michigan contingent and the 106,000 people crammed into the stadium stood frozen in time. What was impossible did, in fact, occur. It was the game when Colorado gave a whole new meaning to the Hail Mary pass.

Michigan had the ball and a 26–21 lead with 2:16 left in the game. Failing to run out the clock, the Wolverines punted to make Colorado start from its own 15-yard line with 15 seconds to play. Kordell Stewart hit Michael Westbrook for 21 yards before stopping the clock.

As time expired, Stewart launched the miracle pass into the end zone that was tipped by Michigan's Ty Law before falling into the hands of Westbrook as the game ended 27–26 in favor of Colorado.

"When he let the ball go, I swear it was gonna be short of the end zone," Falk recalled. "But time seemed to stop, and the ball kept floating. When Westbrook raised the ball over his head, all sound in the stadium was suddenly sucked into space."

After the game, Falk went into the Colorado locker room to see head coach Bill McCartney and assistant Elliot Uzelac. Both had served as assistants under Bo.

"That was a big win for us today," McCartney said.

Falk didn't view it quite the same way.

"Let me tell you something, McCartney," he began. "That was a long pass that won the game today. Nothing more, nothing less. Our guys played their tails off, and they beat you. You just happened to win."

Sitting with Mo in his office later, Falk wisely chose not to speak a word.

"You always let the head coach lead the conversation," Falk said. "It was pretty clear to me Mo didn't have much to say. What could anyone say? That loss sticks in my mind more than any other."

Michigan rebounded with two straight victories, including a 40–20 pasting of Michigan State. But the Wolverines suffered three more losses, including the 22–6 defeat at Columbus, to finish the regular season at 7–4.

Michigan handled Colorado State 24–14 in the Holiday Bowl in San Diego. But it was that stifling loss against the other team from Colorado that did the most damage to the 1994 season.

Chapter 44
Coaching Philosophy

A little bit of Bo and a little bit of Mo. Even before Lloyd Carr was named permanent head coach on November 13, 1995, Falk liked the make-up of his longtime friend.

"There were little pieces of both former coaches mixed into him," Falk observed.

Carr accepted the observation as the highest compliment. Upon being named interim head coach before the start of the 1995 season, Carr leaned on all the lessons he had learned from Bo and Mo. Fifteen seasons after making the most of his opportunity of being hired as a Michigan assistant, Michigan fans were grateful for Carr's selection.

"Lloyd was a student of the game," Falk said. "He paid attention to everything that went on around him. He was good with details and very concerned with each player on the team. A wise man is smart enough to take advantage of the education he receives."

There is no single formula for becoming a successful major college football coach. Borrowing lessons from the best, however, is an advantage only a fool would refuse. And who were better teachers than Bo and Mo?

As did his two mentors, Carr embraced the traditions of the program. He had a tireless work ethic. He was a relentless recruiter and used the whole country to fill his rosters. And once he brought the kids to campus, each one was treated the same.

The game itself was undergoing change. The NCAA had reduced football scholarships from the 105 Bo was able to utilize to 85. The reduction in numbers forced a change in practice philosophy.

"Bo believed in hitting almost every day," Falk said. "With 105 scholarship players and a batch of walk-ons, he could work over almost any injury. By the time Lloyd took over, hitting in pads was reduced to Tuesday and Wednesday with only light contact on Thursday."

Nevertheless, all three coaches had a handful of plays they could rely upon to come up with a first down in short-yardage situations. Yet each coach was an individual who added a little more to the program than was there when they started.

"Lloyd was a very conscientious man," Falk said. "He viewed coaching and life with a very wide spectrum. He wasn't restricted by tunnel vision. He viewed everything in a much broader sense.

"Bo looked head-on at the task he wanted to accomplish and how he wanted things done. He really wasn't concerned that much about what other people thought or what happened outside that vision.

"Bo's perspective was simple and clear. The only thing that mattered was the team and the program. He really wasn't concerned with what other people thought or what the media had to say."

Carr pursued the same goals as Bo. Each just had a slightly different path for reaching them. "Just like Bo, Lloyd had a vision for how he wanted his program run," Falk said. "But he was able to look outside of it and gauge how it might affect other people. Lloyd was more open to what people thought and said.

"Like Bo and Mo, Lloyd was a very tough and competitive person. After a loss, he'd sink deeper than a hundred-pound anchor. But after a while, he was able to get out of it and move on."

Each coach, Falk came to realize, is chasing the same rainbow. They just follow different paths to get there. Falk is fortunate to have served four giants.

"That's the way it's supposed to be at the University of Michigan," he said.

Chapter **45**
Lloyd Carr: Falk a Voice

L ong before becoming the head coach of Michigan, Lloyd Carr got an up close look at Falk. Real close.

Carr was hired by Bo as an assistant on March 12, 1980. Until his family was able to join him in June when the kids were out of school, he roomed with Falk at the golf course apartment that Falk called home since his Ann Arbor arrival in 1974. The apartment had a room that was divided into a kitchen and living room. There was one bedroom and a bathroom. So for three months, Carr bunked on the sofa.

"Jon is a character to begin with, plus he was a bachelor at the time," Carr recalled with a laugh. "Let's just say it was quite interesting."

After serving as an assistant until he was named head coach in 1995, Carr had plenty of time to evaluate Falk and his work ethic. And he liked everything about it. "As a coach, you want people in the locker room—those in the center of the storm—to be a positive force," Carr said. "That's the thing about Jon. He's very much involved with the players and always a positive force. Regardless of the circumstances, he's always talking about winning the next game. He's always telling the players that we have to win this one."

Having such a force is a significant asset—and relief—for a head coach who is constantly under pressure in the high stakes of contemporary major college football.

Falk has to walk that fine line between the players and coaches. It's more of a feeling than an acquired technique. He's done it since the first day he reported to Bo and continues to play that delicate role.

"You can't play that role without the complete trust of players and coaches," Carr said. "It's true of every coach he's worked for. Jon didn't tell the coaches everything he knew from the locker room. He just relayed what was important for the benefit of the team.

"He knew when a player was up or down. Maybe there were family problems or academic issues. He might just say that something is bothering a certain player. That's a great asset to be the voice of information that might benefit the team and the players."

Since Carr spent the majority of his college coaching career at Michigan, Falk became the yardstick by which Carr measures the importance of equipment managers.

"I can't imagine anyone better than Jon Falk with all the intangibles he brings to the table," he said.

And Falk continues to make sure that the table is always full.

Chapter 46
1995: A Nobody No More

F alk enjoys his role as a locker room instigator. If there's a way to provoke a player's intensity before a big game, Falk knows which button to push. Sometimes he'll wander through the locker room twisting one of his 17 Big Ten championship rings around his finger. He also has one National Championship ring. "This is what we're playing for, men," he'll say. "This is why you came to Michigan."

Sometimes he uses a slice of history from a classic game. "Everyone remembers that Charles Woodson touchdown punt return in 1997," he'll throw out. "But you should have seen the blocking. Any men here today ready to step up and knock someone silly for the good of the team?"

And sometimes it's a piece of news that has emanated from the enemy's camp. The table had been set for Falk before Ohio State visited Ann Arbor in 1995. Terry Glenn was an outstanding receiver for the Buckeyes. But the words

Any men here today ready to step up and knock someone silly for the good of the team?

—Jon Falk

he used in a newspaper article in Columbus earlier in the week were far too preciously volatile for Falk to leave alone.

"Hey!" Falk began his trek around the locker room. "Did you read what Terry Glenn said in the Columbus paper? He said Michigan is a nobody! He called Michigan a nobody! Are we gonna stand for that? Are we gonna let Terry Glenn call us a nobody?"

Already fired up, the Michigan players started to boil.

Ohio State came into Ann Arbor undefeated and ranked No. 2 in the nation. They were foaming at the mouth with Rose Bowl and national championship aspirations. Michigan was ranked No. 18. But a funny thing happened on the Buckeyes' drive toward a perfect season. They had to play a "nobody" that refused to believe what they had been called.

Michigan led after each quarter and ambushed the Buckeyes with a weapon called Tshimanga Biakabutuka. If the Buckeyes didn't quite know how to pronounce or spell the powerful tailback's name, they got plenty of time to read it while chasing the back of his jersey.

In one of the most electrifying individual performances in the history of The Big House, Biakabutuka carried the ball 37 times for 313 of the 381 yards the Wolverines gained on the ground. Michigan wound up beating the Buckeyes 31–23.

After the game, Falk went into the visitor's locker room that had cleared except for what Falk thought were trainers. He was collecting used towels for the laundry when he heard their voices moaning.

"Man, how could we lose to Michigan?" one of them said. "Why did we do this?"

On the way out of the room, Falk made a passing comment.

"Hey men," he said. "Another great Michigan–Ohio State game. Except we won today."

There was tense silence.

"Yeah, yeah, it wasn't any good," one of them said.

Falk was still upset by the comment made by Glenn earlier in the week.

"Let me tell you guys something," Falk said. "I don't know Terry Glenn from Adam. But for Terry Glenn to say Michigan is a nobody, he better go back and check the records.

"Michigan is a somebody. Notre Dame is a somebody. Ohio State is a some-body. And when you're playing one of those teams, you're playing a somebody every doggone game because each one of them is coming full tilt after you.

"When we play Ohio State, we know Ohio State is bringing their best. But we also know that Ohio State knows we're bringing our best."

One of the three locker room stragglers said the Glenn statement was mis-quoted. Falk wasn't satisfied.

"Even if Terry Glenn thought Michigan is a nobody, he'll have to think about it again," he said. "Michigan is a somebody. Ohio State is a somebody."

Falk was walking out the door when one the three asked if he would come back for a moment. He extended his hand to Falk and said, "I'm Terry Glenn."

Falk shook his hand but was not dissuaded.

"I'll be honest with you, Terry," he said. "I'm not taking back a single word. But I do want to tell you I respect your courage. You didn't have to tell me who you are. You showed me a little courage."

Certainly Glenn discovered who Michigan was that day on the field.

Falk enjoyed that first season under Carr. Even though Carr had been an assistant for Bo and Mo, there were a lot of new responsibilities he had to master as head coach.

"He would ask me a lot of questions pertaining to equipment and practice," Falk said. "He was easy to talk to and understood my personality. He appreci-ated the fact that I like to talk to players. He felt it helped to promote team unity."

Carr's first game in the top job was a memorable nail-biter. Trailing 17–0 to Virginia in The Big House, Michigan rallied to win 18–17 on a touchdown pass from Scott Dreisbach to Mercury Hayes with no time left on the clock.

"That's No. 1," Falk said to Carr walking up The Tunnel. "There's gonna be a lot more."

The Purdue game on November 11 in Ann Arbor was a slush bowl in which the field was so wet and sloppy the players had a tough time just staying on their feet. "It was the worst I ever saw," Falk said. "I cleaned enough mud out of those cleats to build a whole village of mud huts. The big thing, though, was that we managed to win 5–0."

It was also big enough for Athletic Director Joe Roberson to name Carr the permanent head coach two days later.

No victory that year, obviously, was as sweet as the regular-season closer over Ohio State. Michigan was invited to the Alamo Bowl in San Antonio and was nipped by Texas A&M 22–20. The Aggies knew they were playing somebody. Most teams do when they tangle with Michigan.

Chapter *47*
1996: Better Than a Kiss

When it comes to emotion, Falk is a jack-in-the-box on steroids. He's that vital supporting actor who evokes the best from a cast of stars.

"Football is a game of emotion," Falk said. "A lot of times, emotion makes the difference between winning and losing. Most college players are pretty much the same. It gets down to how you attack the game on a certain day. You can always tell if players are gonna have a good game by the way they attack that field.

"That's what makes my job so much fun. I can see it building all week. I can help to build it. Attitude is everything. That's why I go around patting players on the back every day and telling them that they have to bring everything to the table on Saturday."

Falk thrives on his bag full of motivational incentives to prod each player in preparation for the upcoming game. Some incentives are reasonably ordinary. A few are pulled from Falk's own theater of the absurd.

Before the Ohio State game of 1996, Remy Hamilton was the recipient of an unconventional incentive that initially made the reliable place-kicker recoil at the thought. "Remy, let me tell you something," Falk told Hamilton at Tuesday's practice before the game. "If you kick the field goal that beats Ohio State, I'm gonna kiss you."

Hamilton raised his eyebrows. Then he frowned. Finally he smiled and dubiously asked, "That's my incentive?"

It's one thing to make an outstanding play to beat Ohio State. But when the "reward" is a kiss from Falk, it does tend to make a player consider the consequences. Before finally conceding a winning kick over Ohio State would be worth the dubious prize, Hamilton told Falk, "Let me think about that one."

According to the two teams' records and all of the so-called experts around the country, Hamilton wouldn't have to worry about making a Tyrone Wheatley type sprint away from Falk once the score was settled. Many, in fact, thought Michigan would have trouble merely moving the football into field-goal range.

Ohio State was a menace that year with a perfect record and a No. 2 national ranking when Michigan rolled into Columbus. Michigan was ranked No. 21, and the question wasn't whether the Buckeyes would win as much as it was by the number of points.

If bookies had been taking bets on whether Falk would lay a wet one on Hamilton, the odds for it happening would have been off the board.

Making matters even more porous for Michigan, Ohio State had invited all the players who had ever played for the Buckeyes back for the game. The field looked as if it held more people than all those red-jacketed fans in the stands screaming for Michigan blood.

"I have to admit, it did look pretty intimidating out there," Falk said.

The Michigan–Ohio State game, however, is noted for surprises. So maybe the sight of Falk puckering up on the field wasn't totally out of the realm of possibility.

Despite moving the ball against the Wolverines in the first half, the Buckeyes had to settle for three field goals and a 9–0 lead. It was all the room Coach Carr needed to deliver his own brand of incentive during his halftime talk.

"Men, they got close to the end zone three times and had to settle for field goals," he said. "All we need is a touchdown because I think these Ohio State

Keep playing hard, and something good will happen.

—Lloyd Carr

players will start to think about it. We're one touchdown away from turning this game around. Keep playing hard, and something good will happen."

That something happened quickly after the second-half kick. Within the first minute of the third quarter on a second-and-9 from the Michigan 31-yard line, quarterback Brian Griese fired a short slant pass across the middle of the field to wide receiver Tai Streets. Ohio State cornerback Shawn Springs momentarily lost his footing, and that was all the room Streets needed. He streaked down the middle of the field for a 69-yard touchdown completion.

"Looking at the Ohio State players, suddenly you could just feel that they thought Michigan could win," Falk said.

Falk couldn't help himself.

"Whenever one of their players lined up close to our bench, I kept repeating to them, 'Hey man…we're Michigan. Don't ever forget it. We're Michigan. We're coming at you.'"

As time expired in the third quarter, Hamilton boomed a 43-yard field goal into the wind to give Michigan its first lead, 10–9.

Were the odds on Falk puckering up on Hamilton slowly shifting? Hamilton sealed the deal with 1:19 left in the game when he booted a 39-yarder and let the defense do the rest. "I never saw another team or the fans look so depressed," Falk said. "They thought that this was their year. Evidently they didn't think that much about Michigan."

After the game, Falk hugged Hamilton and told him he had a better reward than any old kiss. When the team convened for its meeting on Sunday, Falk presented Hamilton with an imprinted T-shirt that read, "Remy Hamilton— this is your kiss for beating Ohio State."

"Whenever Remy comes back to visit, he always brings that shirt," Falk said. "Some things are priceless…even better than one of my kisses."

Michigan was invited to play in the New Year's Day Outback Bowl against Alabama. Two of the nation's most powerful defensive units went head-to-head with Alabama holding on for a 17–14 victory. Michigan finished the season at 8–4.

But the table had been set for the following season. And that one required no kiss from Falk.

Chapter **48**
1997: "The Team...
The Team...The Team"

Quarterback Brian Griese visited Falk in his office after meeting with coach Lloyd Carr in March 1997. Before every spring practice, the head coach meets with each player on the team to determine his position, define his role, and even to discover if the player is returning for the upcoming season. Griese would earn his degree at the end of the semester but still had one year of football eligibility left.

"Well, Big Jon," Griese said. "I just talked to Coach Carr. I'm coming back for my fifth season." Falk was visibly surprised. He knew Griese would have his degree. The team would not be loaded with seniors, and the preseason prognosis wasn't exactly blinding.

Falk liked Griese as a person. He also liked the idea of having experience at the position. But he was still surprised at the decision. "My God, Brian," Falk said. "You know there are no guarantees that you'll be the starter. You could walk out of here with a degree and four good years in your pocket for life."

Griese was undeterred. He had made his decision. "You know what, Jon?" he said. "I want to go to the Rose Bowl. I want to play in the Rose Bowl."

Falk's eyes twinkled. Any mention of the Rose Bowl makes Falk's eyes double in size and sparkle. "Let me say this," he said. "If you keep that attitude and someone beats you out for starter, then that quarterback will probably take you to the Rose Bowl. That's the attitude you have to keep all year."

The Big Ten championship is the goal of every Michigan team. Before the BCS that debuted the following year, the Rose Bowl was the big prize. "In all my years here, I never really thought we could win a National Championship," Falk said. "The league is too hard. The schedule is too tough to expect to go through undefeated. At the beginning of 1997, no one was thinking about the National Championship. We set our goal on winning the Big Ten."

Before the season started, Carr established a theme that he borrowed from a book he had read dealing with the drive, desire, and dedication it requires to achieve a goal as demanding as climbing Mt. Everest. Written by Jon Krakauer, *Into Thin Air* depicts all the perils of fulfilling the dream when all of the surrounding elements are just daring you to quit.

Carr invited the author to speak to the team during summer practice. He also presented each player and member of the staff a mountain-climbing pick to hold on to the dream. He had a mountain drawn on cardboard with the name of each opponent attached to the point of the mountain where they would meet according to the schedule.

"I have never seen any team buy into the theme as much as that one did," Falk said. "We just had so many leaders on that team. Guys like Brian Griese and Rob Swett and Jon Jansen and so many more. Nobody would let anybody else quit. Not for a minute.

"Eric Mayes was a captain. He got hurt in the first game and had to sit out the season. But he was at every practice pushing the players. I could see those guys developing as a unit right before my eyes. It was a fun team to watch and fun to be around. You could just feel it."

Michigan breezed through its first five games, including a 21–14 victory over Notre Dame. "That game was a tip-off," Falk said. "They were up 14–7 at the half. They had the ball near the goal line four or five times, and we snuffed them out. Wherever the ball went, our guys were on it."

The first real test came against Iowa in Game 6 at Michigan. Late in the second quarter, Tim Dwight returned a punt 61 yards for a touchdown and a 21–7 lead at the half.

Walking up The Tunnel, the Iowa players were flexing their muscles. "It's over, Michigan," they were jabbing. "Your undefeated season is done. No. 5 bites the dust today. It's over."

When the team reached the locker room, Falk scurried around with his own message. He kept patting players on the back as if he were running for governor. "They think it's over?" he kept repeating. "They don't know Michigan. We're coming back. We'll let them know when it's over."

The real message of the day came from Griese who stood up in the middle of the room to confess how poorly he played in the first half. "I didn't play good at all," he said. "I can't do anything about that. But I can do something about the second half. I'm going out and playing my best game, and I ask that you do the same thing." It was enough of a charge to let Griese's teammates realize that the real Michigan team was just about ready to take the field.

Iowa clung to a 24–21 lead with 2:55 left in the game when Griese found tight end Jerame Tuman wide open in the end zone for the deciding touchdown.

"The emotion on the field and in that locker room was amazing," Falk said. "In the backs of their minds, they had to know something special was going on."

The following week at East Lansing, the defense unleashed a suffocating attack that would have squeezed the air out of an elephant. The Wolverines tied a school record by picking off six Michigan State passes in a 23–7 win.

Charles Woodson put his name on the Heisman Trophy ballot with an interception seen 'round the world. ESPN did the rest by running the replay at least as many times as the one of Kirk Gibson hitting his celebrated pinch-hit home run that powered the Los Angeles Dodgers over the Oakland A's in the 1988 World Series.

Leaping in front of the Michigan bench with one arm stretched just slightly lower than the pressbox high above the stands, Woodson made a one-handed grab and somehow willed one foot to land clearly in bounds. The only man who came close to leaping as high as the Heisman-bound cornerback was Coach Carr to celebrate the physics-defying catch.

One of Falk's jobs during a game is to keep the players on the bench away from the sideline. One of the referees approached Falk and told him to keep his players back.

"Wait a minute," Falk responded. "I just saw a 52-year-old man jump 6 feet in the air. It's awful hard for me to tell that guy to get back."

The referee laughed and nodded approval. After the game, the same ref told Falk that was one of the best interceptions he had seen in his entire officiating career.

The nation was starting to believe in the Wolverines. Before the following week's Minnesota game at Michigan, Falk visited Minnesota assistant coach Elliot Uzelac, who had previously served at Michigan.

"Jon, I've been watching your team on film," Uzelac said. "They're good…
they're really good."

Falk tried to brush off the comment.

"Jon, I'm telling you," Uzelac insisted. "This is a special team."

After beating Minnesota 24–3, No. 4 ranked Michigan traveled to No. 3
ranked Penn State on what ESPN billed as "Judgment Day."

Judgment was swift and lethal. Playing before a raucous record crowd of
97,498 fans, Michigan thrashed Penn State 34–8, the worst-ever losing margin
in Joe Paterno's years as head coach.

Keeping with the season-long theme in the locker room after the game,
Carr told his team, "The air is getting thinner…next week we'll probably be
battling snow…we've got to really buckle down."

It was ice cold at Madison, Wisconsin, the following Saturday, but by then
the elements didn't matter. Michigan crushed the Badgers 26–16 to set up the
annual showdown with Ohio State at The Big House.

Michigan took a 13–0 lead into halftime by scoring a pair of touchdowns
within a couple of minutes of each other in the second quarter. The second
came on a 78-yard punt return by Woodson. It was the first of his career and
drove at least one nail into the Buckeyes' coffin.

Andre Weathers returned a pass interception 43 yards in the third quarter
to make the score 20–0. The Wolverines then turned it over to their defense
and held on for a 20–14 victory that clinched a Rose Bowl berth while keeping
their record perfect.

"The air is real thin now, men," Carr said in the locker room. "One more
victory, and we are the national champions."

Falk, of course, went around the room personally congratulating each player.
He stopped at Griese's locker to give the fifth-year senior quarterback a hug.

No kisses had been promised. Griese had just completed a rare father-son
phenomenon. His father, Bob, longtime college football analyst for ABC-TV,
quarterbacked Purdue to a Rose Bowl victory over the University of Southern
California. He then quarterbacked the Miami Dolphins to an undefeated season
and Super Bowl championship. Brian matched the Rose Bowl accomplishment
and led the Wolverines to an undefeated season.

"You said you wanted to play in the Rose Bowl," Falk said. "Now you're going to be the starting quarterback in one. And I'm gonna tell you one thing right now. You're gonna have a helluva game."

Not only did Griese play as superbly as he had all season, he was named the game's Most Valuable Player for setting a Michigan Rose Bowl record with three touchdown passes in a 21–16 victory over Washington State. Tai Streets snagged the first two, and Jerame Tuman caught the third.

Falk will always remember the dramatic moment when Carr called his players to gather around him in the locker room after the game.

"Men...you just won the National Championship," he said emotionally.

"That team was probably the best I've ever been part of," Falk said. "It was a real team. Nobody picked us to do anything like this before the season started. We knew Woodson was good, but nobody dreamed he would win the Heisman Trophy. Griese was a solid quarterback, but nobody knew he would have that kind of year. And who could have guessed the defense would refuse to let anyone move the ball?

"Of all the teams I've been around, I never saw such a tightness between guys as a group. They were like a bunch of guys you put into a cornfield and told them to start picking. And for 12 straight weeks, they picked and picked and picked. They never turned around to see how much they had picked. They put their heads down and just kept picking. They never knew where they were because they were too busy working. Finally at the end, they could turn around and say, 'Hey, we picked a lot of corn.'"

In the hotel bar after the game, the band of former Michigan players, coaches, and loyal fans gathered to celebrate their first National Championship since 1947. Bo, Dan Dierdorf, and Jim Brandstatter were smoking victory cigars long enough to make a third-and-1 first down.

At midnight, the newly passed California ordinance that prohibits smoking in public buildings went into effect. Apparently, Californians were taking the new law seriously. At the stroke of midnight, the manager walked into the celebrating crowd instructing everyone to extinguish all cigars and cigarettes.

"What are you talking about?" Bo responded. "We just won the National Championship."

***You know, coming from Ohio State, I
have to hate Michigan. But I have to
tell you, I do enjoy watching them play.***
—*Eddie George*

Even after pleading his case in his own eloquent fashion, Bo was asked to leave the bar.

Falk was returning from his room where he had spent some time with Cheri and his family. Upon spotting Bo and wife, Cathy, sitting in the lobby, he wondered why they weren't celebrating in the bar.

"Bo-Bo here just managed to get us thrown out," Cathy smiled.

Falk grinned and assured Cathy that no one would know that she'd been asked to leave.

"But Bo, I hate to tell you," Falk said. "You're gonna be in the *USA Today* tomorrow morning."

And sure enough, his picture with the long stogie was prominently displayed.

After the celebration finally began to subside, Falk decided to return to his room. Upon boarding the elevator, he noticed a familiar face that was eyeing the Michigan apparel Falk was wearing.

"Eddie George…Jon Falk, equipment manager for Michigan," Falk said to the Heisman Trophy–winning running back from Ohio State. "I remember you from that 1995 game."

George's face contorted as if having been stung by a bee.

"Oh man, that one," he said. "You know, coming from Ohio State, I have to hate Michigan. But I have to tell you, I do enjoy watching them play."

The 1997 team made it enjoyable for a lot of people. For Falk, the memory lives forever.

Chapter **49**

Brian Griese: Coming Back

Brian Griese knew he was taking a gamble when he decided to return to Michigan as a fifth-year senior. He also figured he had more to gain than he had to lose. "As I told Jon Falk, I wanted the opportunity to start at quarterback and play in the Rose Bowl," Griese said. "Maybe the odds weren't that good, but I didn't want to give away the last chance I'd ever have."

Griese already had his pockets full of opportunities—more than most college graduates walking into the real world. Griese had his Michigan degree. After walking on to the team in 1994, he had won three varsity letters. He had a graduate academic scholarship already approved for George Washington University.

But he had never been a full-time starter and wasn't promised the job for 1997. So why take the gamble? It was Griese's brother, Jeff, who flipped the switch for little brother's decision.

"He told me I had the rest of my life to spend in the real world," Griese explained. "If I decided to leave Michigan, I could never go back to this sort of fantasy world."

With that decision made, Griese immediately made another. "I dedicated myself to give 120 percent to become the starting quarterback," Griese said. "I knew the job wasn't going to be given to me, and no one knows how a season is going to work out. But I also knew I wouldn't walk away without leaving everything I had on the field."

The storybook gamble, of course, had a magnificent ending. Griese led the Wolverines to an undefeated season and a National Championship. He turned himself into becoming a third-round pick of the Denver Broncos in the NFL draft. And for more than a decade, he quarterbacked such teams as the Denver Broncos, Miami Dolphins, Tampa Bay Buccaneers, and Chicago Bears.

"I had never planned on playing in the NFL," Griese said. "I guess winning a National Championship wields a little influence."

His time-consuming career has prohibited him from attending a Michigan game since his departure. When that opportunity arises, however, he knows the first stop on his return will be Falk's office.

"I love talking to Jon," Griese said. "He's a wealth of knowledge about Michigan history. Coming from Miami, I didn't know a whole lot about all the traditions. Jon is such a great conveyor of the past to 25 to 30 fresh faces in the program every year. He's the only man in the building who can do that. That makes him pretty important."

More than his historical expertise, Griese considers Falk to be a true friend.

"He has his peculiarities," Griese said. "But nobody cares more about the team and all the players than he does. It's amazing how much Jon does behind the scenes to lift a player when he needs a little help."

I love talking to Jon. He's a wealth of knowledge about Michigan history.

—Brian Griese

Chapter 50

Falk the Diplomat

Unlike the 37 years he's spent as equipment manager for the University of Michigan, Falk may have lasted only 37 minutes had he chosen politics for a profession. That's the consequence of talking straight and speaking the truth.

He did experience his moment of Washington "diplomacy," however, when the 1997 National Championship team was invited to meet President William Clinton in the White House in April 1998. The event was one of those once-in-a-lifetime opportunities only a handful is privileged to enjoy.

The 1997 team met at Schembechler Hall. The team, all the coaches, and the entire football staff then boarded busses for Detroit's Metropolitan Airport and a flight to Washington, D.C.

The Michigan entourage was treated to a bus tour of various historical sites in the D.C. area. They visited the Museum of Aeronautic History where they lunched with the Washington, D.C. Michigan Alumni Association. Then they stopped at Arlington National Cemetery before heading to the White House for their promised meeting with President Clinton.

"The trip was something that a kid only dreams about," Falk said. "It's one of those special opportunities that going to a university like Michigan provides. How else could a kid from Oxford, Ohio, do something like this?"

Also making the trip was the 1997 University of Nebraska team that finished No. 1 in one poll while Michigan topped the other. "I remember reading something that [Nebraska coach] Tom Osborne said," Falk said. "He said he was sort of glad that Michigan was a co-champion. He said that we deserved it. We went 12–0 and did everything we were asked to do."

Even for both National Championship teams, security was tighter than a James Bond secret assignment. Methodically, each member of both teams was screened and checked for identification.

When the guided tour of the White House was complete, both teams were escorted into a spacious meeting room where President Clinton greeted them. After a few brief remarks about how proud he was of both universities, the president posed for team pictures with each school.

And that's when Falk was called into voluntary diplomatic duty.

A White House aide began to escort all guests from the room as the photographer was finishing his assignment. "Wait a minute, sir," Falk began. "We were told that each person was gonna have the opportunity to meet the president."

The aide tried to employ diplomacy of his own. "I'm awfully sorry, sir," he said, "but you're not going to have the chance to meet him. The president just returned from Cincinnati, and his schedule is completely full today."

Falk, of course, respected the demanding schedule of the president but was dismayed over the misunderstanding. "Sir, even the president said we were going to have a chance to meet him," Falk insisted.

Falk was still grumbling and half of the team had already boarded the busses when the same aide came dashing outside. "President Clinton wants everybody from Michigan back in the White House," he said. "He wants to meet everyone from Michigan and shake their hands."

Though confused, Falk and the entire team were elated.

"I thought you said the president couldn't do this," Falk said.

"Well, he is the president and can do whatever he wants to do," the aide said. Now it was Falk's turn to smile.

"Yeah, we're a large industrial state with a lot of electoral votes," Falk said. "I don't think he wanted us going back to Michigan without the chance to meet him."

The entire contingent was hustled back into the room without stopping for identification. President Clinton slowly shook each person's hand and offered congratulations on a job well done.

"When he shook my hand, he looked straight into my eyes for what seemed like 30 seconds," Falk said. "He made you feel you were the most important person in America. That's the kind of charisma he has."

Although definitely of a different brand, Falk is filled with a charismatic twist of his own. He may never be a diplomat, but he will always relish his day in the White House.

Chapter **51**

Jim Brandstatter: Amazed by Falk

When Bo needed to contact a specific sports celebrity, he usually turned to Falk to set up the call. More often than not, Falk had the number scribbled in his telephone book. If he didn't, he knew someone who did. The typical college football equipment manager doesn't have a list of bona fide celebrity friends that might impress even Paris Hilton.

Of course, few have accused Falk of ever being typical in any fashion.

It's not unusual during any given day for Falk to be in contact with such sports luminaries as Johnny Bench, Tom Seaver, Bobby Knight, Yogi Berra, Ara Parseghian, Alan Trammell, Jack Morris, or Ken Griffey Jr. He knows enough NFL standouts to fill a two-deep All-Star roster on both sides of the ball.

Even the late President Ford became more than a handshake acquaintance.

"I'm always amazed at how many people tell me to remember them to Jon when I travel to different stadiums across the country," said former Michigan standout Jim Brandstatter.

Brandstatter is the longtime voice of Michigan and Detroit Lions radio broadcasts. "Jon is one of the biggest men in the association for equipment managers, and I'm sure Coach Rodriguez was told that when he came from West Virginia."

Even Bo probably didn't realize the total package he was getting when he coaxed Falk out of Oxford, Ohio, for the big stage in Ann Arbor. "Jon Falk is Jon Falk," Brandstatter said. "If he hadn't made it in football, he may have made it on the stage. He's a play waiting to happen. There's nobody else like him. That's all I can say."

People love Jon because they know he always delivers.
—*Jim Brandstatter*

The fame of various notables means little to Falk. Their friendships are what he cherishes. Falk has a sense of humor that would have made Henry Kissinger burst into a belly laugh. And his personality just might be the norm on some planet orbiting at the edge of the universe. Other than that, he's loyal to a fault, more honest than the pope, and more devoted to the University of Michigan than Fielding H. Yost ever could have imagined anyone to be.

"People love Jon because they know he always delivers," Brandstatter said. "If you ask Jon to do something, consider the request done. Nobody works harder or longer than Jon Falk. Bo spotted that before he hired him."

The beautiful part about Falk is that he treats the barber who cuts his hair the same way he treated President Ford. And that carries into the locker room with the Michigan football team. It doesn't matter to Falk if a kid is a walk-on freshman or a three-year All-American. For anyone who needs something in the locker room, Falk is always there.

"Players have to earn his respect," Brandstatter said. "But that's what makes Jon so likable and credible. He can walk up to a starter and tell him he isn't acting properly just as easily as patting a lonely freshman on the back and promise things will improve. Jon isn't concerned with impressing anyone because he's done everything there is to prove."

Amazing to Brandstatter are the physical responsibilities that Falk handles like a juggler day after day. "I get tired just thinking about it," he said. "Just imagine how many uniforms and how many different pieces of equipment and how much laundry is involved for 125 players day after day.

"Sometimes a kid might develop a blister from a certain shoe. Jon always comes up with another pair. He refuses to let a blister be the cause of a potential loss."

It's the enthusiasm Falk has for Michigan football, however, that amazes Brandstatter the most. "After a big win or a disappointing loss, Jon is already looking forward to the next game," Brandstatter said. "He knows how to take the job seriously without taking himself seriously. That's the big difference between Jon and so many other people in the game."

Brandstatter is among the countless former players who always stop at the locker room when visiting Ann Arbor. "They visit the head coach first and their position coach second," Brandstatter said. "But they never leave the building without saying hello to Jon. He's had an impact on every kid he's touched, and it's a powerfully positive impact."

With most of those coaches now gone from Michigan, players still drop by to visit Falk and swap old stories. And as he did when they were players before becoming valuable members of the community, Falk always finds time for each one.

Chapter **52**

1998: Only the Moment Counts

O ne of the festivities before the Alamo Bowl in San Antonio in 1995 featured world-class rodeo riders, including the world champion bull rider.
He was a wiry, fierce competitor who looked like a free safety who never wore
a face mask and specialized in decapitation.

The Michigan players were fascinated by the champion's confidence and
wanted to know how someone got to be the bull riding champion of the world.
The champ made his approach to success sound so simple.

"You have to understand one thing," he began. "I ride a different bull all the
time. I don't know that bull, and he doesn't have any idea about anything I did
before. He doesn't know I'm the champion. The only thing that counts is what I
do when I'm riding him. That's the only thing that matters to him and the only
thing that matters to me."

Lloyd Carr loved to tell that story because it's the essence of what athletics
is about.

"Athletics don't care what you did before," Falk said. "They only care about
what you do today. What you did in the past may have been nice. But what you
do today is how it's gonna look tomorrow. That's the only thing that matters."

Michigan ran into a couple of ornery bulls the first two games of the 1998
season. And neither of them cared they were playing the defending National
Champion. In the season opener at South Bend, Michigan allowed five unan-
swered scoring drives and was outscored by 23 points in the second half in a
36–20 loss to Notre Dame.

In the home opener the following Saturday, quarterback Donovan McNabb
led Syracuse to a relatively easy 38–28 victory. Michigan scored 21 points in the
fourth quarter after falling behind 38–7.

"That was the best quarterback play I had ever seen at Michigan," Falk said.
"McNabb was a magician. I have to give him credit."

After an undefeated record the previous season…after being crowned
National Champion…after meeting the president in the White House…the
1998 team really didn't care.

Falk is always mindful of the two responsibilities that Bo imposed when he hired him in 1974. Falk is responsible for all matters pertaining to equipment, and he's also charged with doing everything possible to help the team win.

It was time to exercise that latter charge through a little conversation with team captain Jon Jansen. "We've got to tell all the kids to forget about 1997," Falk told Jansen. "That was all nice and dandy, but it's old news. It's a thing of the past. This is 1998. This is our team. And we better do something about it right now."

Jansen admired Falk's experience and quickly called for a players' meeting. In simple and blunt terms, he told all the players to put the past where it belonged and start doing something about the present.

"If you talk about a captain as a true leader and somebody concerned with every person on that team, that's Jon Jansen," Falk said. "He's nice, but he can get serious when necessary. He embodies what a real captain is."

If you talk about a captain as a true leader and somebody concerned with every person on that team, that's Jon Jansen.

—*Jon Falk*

Talk can be cheap, but apparently Jansen's speech was worth the listening. Michigan crushed Eastern Michigan 59–20, and then the Wolverines won their 17th straight Big Ten opener 29–17 over Michigan State.

Michigan moved its record to 3–2 the following week at Iowa in a hard-fought 12–9 victory over the Hawkeyes. Although Anthony Thomas gained only 68 yards, he was emerging as an explosive runner. "You never want to say who the best back at Michigan was because we've had so many great ones," Falk said. "But Anthony was special. He was a tough, tough guy. You never had to worry about giving the ball to Anthony. He was gonna get you some yards.

"I absolutely love Anthony Thomas. He was such a quiet kid and always so nice. I used to tease him—'You don't say much, but when you get the ball, you really run hard.'

"Anthony would just smile and say, 'I run Jon…I love to run.'"

The following week, Michigan got tangled in another low-scoring game and outlasted Northwestern 12–6 at Evanston.

"That was probably the worst rain game of my life," Falk said. "Rain was rolling down the stairways onto the field like a waterfall. Every player had mud up to their ankles.

"Conditions like that put a lot of pressure on everyone. I had to worry about shoes. We kept changing jerseys and pants. Players get short-tempered in conditions like that. You have to understand never to get into a confrontation with a player. Everyone is on edge, and it's too easy to lose your concentration."

During the downpour, Carr yelled at Falk that he was having trouble hearing anything but crackling static through the headset. "Let me tell you something, Lloyd," Falk said. "If I go lift up that trunk top to look at the wiring, you're gonna get water in your ear." Carr laughed and said to leave it alone.

Michigan followed with a 21–10 victory over Indiana and then needed five fourth-quarter points to nip Minnesota 15–10 in Minneapolis.

The following week in Ann Arbor, the Michigan offense and defense meshed for a 27–0 blanking of Penn State. It was Penn State's first shutout in 130 games. "You could see Tom Brady taking command," Falk said. "Everybody on the team looked up to him. He was always even-tempered. He always had control of the team."

Michigan grabbed sole possession of first place in the conference the following week by ending Wisconsin's bid for an undefeated season with a 27–10 victory at Madison.

The worst Michigan could do was finish in a tie for the Big Ten title regardless of the outcome of the annual showdown with Ohio State. As always, however, Columbus served as the stage for the totally absurd.

Falk was slapped with a three-prong attack before, during, and after the game. Not only did Ohio State hand Michigan a 31–16 defeat, Falk was only a few moments away from being thrown into jail before the game and came within an eyelash of being hospitalized afterward.

After preparing the locker room for the arrival of the team Saturday morning, Falk headed for his usual stop in the pressbox to set up the phone lines for the coaches to communicate.

Only one problem—he was denied access.

Upon reaching the elevator and dressed in full Michigan coaching gear, Falk was asked to present a press credential for admission. He explained to the operator that he was not a member of the media. He was merely addressing his usual pregame assignment of setting up the phone lines.

"No pass, no entry," the operator said.

Falk again explained his regular game-day assignment and assured her that she would never see him again once he got the phone lines working.

"You're still not going up there," she said.

Rather than lose time in a fruitless argument, Falk decided to wind his way through the bleachers and attempt entry to the elevator from another level.

"I told you, you're not going up there," she said.

Concerned now that he was losing time, Falk stepped into the elevator and pressed the button for the pressbox. Falk was busy making sure that each phone was properly connected when a couple of his counterparts from Ohio State warned him that the elevator operator had contacted the police.

"You're kidding," Falk said.

Before they could answer, two sheriff's deputies arrived on the scene.

"Sir, if you don't have a press pass, we're gonna take you downtown for breaking and entering," one deputy said.

Falk calmly pleaded his case and received the same response he had gotten from the elevator operator. Fortunately for Falk, the Ohio State Intramural Director, a longtime friend of Falk, arrived. He questioned the deputies about the misunderstanding.

"Officers, this is Jon Falk," he said. "I know him, and I'll stand right here until he finishes his job hooking up the phones. Then I'll walk him down, and everyone will be happy."

The two deputies stared at each other for a moment before one conceded, "He's in your custody."

With that roadblock out of the way, neither Falk nor anyone in the Michigan contingent could prevent the 31–16 shellacking that happened in the game. Any loss to Ohio State is painful. The fiasco that followed this one, however, was nothing less than frightening.

Because Michigan had defeated Ohio State the previous three years, Ohio fans swarmed the field like bees buzzing around a honey-soaked hive. As Michigan players, coaches, and staff headed toward the locker room, fans kept charging onto the field, trampling anything that happened to get in their way.

Someone hit Falk in the head, sending his glasses into a snakepit of delirious dashing feet. "As I'm lying on the ground, the only thing I could think of was to find my glasses," Falk said. "Without them, I couldn't even find my way to the locker room."

Falk got to his knees and tried to direct his fingers through all the stomping feet. Just when his fingers reached the glasses, a foot came crashing down on his hand.

"Anybody wearing Michigan gear was getting hit in the head and punched in the side," Falk said. "It was ugly. I decided to just hunker down and protect my body 'til the wave went by."

Fortunately, quarterback coach Stan Parrish and team physician Dr. Dan Hendrickson, accompanied by two Ohio State Troopers, were able to fight their way through the mayhem and lift Falk off the ground to carry him to the locker room.

"I don't know if I was shocked or scared or what," Falk said. "But when I got to the locker room, I didn't know where I was. I sure found out what it's like to be in a panic situation. It's something I'll never forget."

Falk and the rest of the team had time to recover by traveling to Hawaii for a bonus game before playing in the Citrus Bowl. In Honolulu, Michigan unleashed its own lethal attack for a 48–17 victory.

Behind the crisp passing of Brady and the ruthless running of Thomas, the Wolverines pounded Arkansas 45–31 in the Citrus Bowl. After starting the season with two straight losses, Michigan finished with a 10–3 record and the No. 12 ranking in the country for both polls.

"Nobody likes to start the season the way we did," Falk said. "It was embarrassing what Syracuse did to us. But sometimes people forget that players have feelings and emotions, too. Once we got that straightened out, we played the way we expected to play."

Sometimes it takes a little reminder that the bull doesn't care who the rider is.

Chapter **53**

Jon Jansen:
Seize the Moment

Even as a professional in the NFL, Jon Jansen smiled at the thought of Falk after each road game. "Win or lose, whenever we reached the locker room after a game, Big Jon would walk around the room telling us to hurry up and pack your bags so we can 'get outta this hellhole,'" the All-American tackle said. "Thinking about it always brings back a lot of good memories."

Of course, Jansen carries a truckload of treasured memories from Michigan and Falk.

The players, Lloyd Carr, and his assistant coaches rightfully drew the head-lines for the National Championship season of 1997. Looking back, however, Jansen will always be appreciative for Falk's pivotal role behind the scenes.

Anyone familiar with the program knows that no one loves Michigan football more than Big Jonny.
—Jon Jansen

"He knew what we were capable of doing," said Jansen, who became as dominant in the NFL as he was at Michigan. "Every day in his own way, he kept reminding us not to let this opportunity slip away. Very few teams get the opportunity we had. Whichever way it would go, he kept telling us that it was going to live with us for the rest of our lives. He made sure we knew how hurt we'd feel if we had let it slip away."

Even the good teams sometimes slip from mental mistakes rather than a lack of physical talent.

"In the locker room during the week…before and after practices…he kept reminding us not to make stupid mistakes," Jansen said. "He helped to keep us focused. He had seen everything before. He wanted to share his experiences so we could capitalize on everything we had right in front of us."

Jansen, along with every player who puts on that winged helmet, learned to embrace all the intangibles that only Falk brings to the program. "Anyone familiar with the program knows that no one loves Michigan football more than Big Jonny," Jansen said. "If someone says something bad about the program, he gets right in their face. He's always fired up and full of energy. You don't expect that much from an equipment manager. He's actually become part of the fabric of the program.

"He's seen so much—the good times and the rough times—that he's a walking piece of history. And he loves sharing that with each player. When you're young, you really didn't take time to notice everything he does for Michigan. Then one day you realize just how important he is to the team."

Jansen particularly appreciated the way Falk took time to brief players about the peculiarities of different stadiums and some of the memorable Michigan moments that live in each one. "He's got the pulse of the team in his back pocket," Jansen said. "If anyone ever wants to know what's really going on with the team, they can just ask Big Jonny."

There's no question in Jansen's mind that Falk remains an integral part of each Michigan team. "He's more than that," Jansen said. "He's part of the Michigan tradition."

Chapter **54**

Tom Brady: Always "The Next One"

Tom Brady contributed a lot to the tradition of Michigan football. In return, he was rewarded with valuable life lessons that only athletics provide. One he cherishes dearly came directly from Falk.

After the Hall of Fame–bound quarterback had just won his third Super Bowl championship ring for the New England Patriots, he was asked by a reporter which of the three meant the most to him. Without taking time to contrive an answer, he spoke straight from his heart.

"The next one," he said. "I learned that lesson a long time ago from Jon Falk, our equipment manager at Michigan."

Brady then explained that with Michigan, Falk had won enough Big Ten championship and bowl rings to decorate all the arms of at least three octopi.

"Whenever a player asked him which one means the most, he always answered 'The next one,'" Brady said. "I stole the answer from Big Jon and use it all the time. He taught me it's the only way to play the game. Nobody cares what happened last year. All people care about is what's happening now. Jon taught me always to set my mind on the next challenge. The one you finished will never come again."

Like so many other Michigan players over nearly the last four decades, Brady formed a lasting relationship with Falk, whose passion for Michigan—sprinkled with just the right amount of eccentricities—provided a pillar upon which to lean, especially when times were tough.

It never mattered to Falk whether a player was a standout destined for NFL stardom or a walk-on freshman afraid to tie his cleats. Falk always took it upon himself to make time for any individual who might eventually do something big for the team.

"Big Jon is not someone who just makes sure the helmet fits right or that you have the proper pair of shoes on," Brady said. "He's a counselor you can trust and also the most passionate Michigan person you will ever meet."

Brady said there were countless times when things weren't going right that he would spend time in Falk's office. "I can't count the times after a practice or on Sundays after a loss that I went in to see Big Jon just to talk," Brady said.

Brady knew their conversations would never leave the office. "He's got more experience than all the football history books and is always generous with his time," Brady said. "He helped me to appreciate the fact that Michigan is all about the team. Individuals make up the team, but the whole team is needed to win a championship.

**Jon taught me always to set my mind
on the next challenge. The one you
finished will never come again.**

—Tom Brady

"Big Jon is always positive and enthusiastic. He shares all that with everyone he touches. If we happened to lose a game, he never let it destroy what the team was trying to accomplish. He always set his sights on the next game."

Brady also admires Falk's appreciation for the tradition that Michigan football enjoys. "He gave all of us a tremendous perspective on rivalries," Brady said. "Games like Ohio State and Michigan State and Notre Dame hold a special meaning. Jon has a great memory and would go over players and certain plays that stand out in the history of Michigan."

Brady particularly enjoys the fact that Falk is as pretentious as a sweat-filled, game-worn jersey. "The most beautiful part about Jon is that he's such an authentic person," Brady said. "What you see is what you get."

That comes from experience and all the great leaders under whom Falk has served.

"No question about it," Brady said. "Jon Falk is a true Michigan Man."

Chapter **55**

1999: Small Talk, Big Results

Sometimes a man picks his spot, and sometimes the spot is picked for him. Tom Brady picked his spot with Falk, and Falk was wise enough to seize the moment.

Brady and Drew Henson were splitting time at quarterback. Naturally, each wished to claim the job as his. Both had enough talent to start on any team in the country. And each had the right kind of confidence to make a heart surgeon envious. After the younger Henson got the call to start a game, Brady suddenly felt alone in the middle of 110,000 people.

Brady needed someone to confide in. He needed someone he could trust. His choice was simple—Jon Falk. "Sometimes it's easier to talk to the equipment manager than it is to one of the coaches," Falk explained. "Players don't want to talk to coaches a lot.

"I have a unique position. I can be a player, and I can be a coach. That's the neat part about the job. The equipment manager is around the players more than the coaches. He's with them every day of the year."

Falk is keenly aware of the fact that players are different in the locker room than when sitting with a coach. He's learned to laugh with the players and make them laugh. When a situation begins to affect the team, an equipment manager has the opportunity to add some time-earned perspective.

Brady understood the dynamics. Above all, he trusted Falk. "Just look at all the experience Big Jon has had through the years," Brady said. "He's seen everything. He's worked with all the greats that have passed through Michigan. He's helped more players than anyone knows. I'm proud to be his friend."

He's helped more players than anyone knows. I'm proud to be his friend.
—Tom Brady

Falk explained to Brady that the battle for the position was a good thing for the team. Henson was brimming with talent, and the coaches were looking to get him some experience.

"I know this thing is eating at you," Falk told Brady. "But you have to understand one thing. You're the leader of this team. And the leader of the team is the one guy that everybody looks up to. If you show any signs that you're upset with the way things are going, then it's going to filter down to the other players. As long as you keep your nose to the grindstone and don't complain, everything will work out."

Brady obviously listened. His dedication allowed him to add his name to the long list of celebrated Michigan quarterbacks.

"Tom Brady is an amazing leader and a good person," Falk said. "Everybody looked up to him. They still do in the NFL. It takes a leader to accept the suggestions of someone who has been down the road and use them to his advantage. I wish more young men would listen to people who have experienced all these situations. Brady was one guy wise enough at that young age to listen."

Falk understands the parameters of his position and is careful never to step across the line. "It does feel good when you talk to a player who listens," he said.

In 1999 as a fifth-year senior, Brady put together another solid season to become perhaps the most successful sixth-round selection in NFL draft history.

In the season opener against Notre Dame, Brady completed 17-of-24 passes in a 26–22 victory. Jeff Del Verne was a kicker who entertained all the coaches and players with impressions of everyone on the team. On that particular day, Del Verne provided a startling imitation of legendary kicker Lou Groza. The fifth-year senior connected on four field goals and two extra points in a game where the lead changed hands six times. Late in the fourth quarter, Anthony Thomas' second touchdown put Michigan up by three points. Del Verne's second PAT cemented the lead.

"Del Verne made everyone laugh during practices and before team meetings," Falk said. "He had his impression of Lloyd Carr down pat."

He did an impression of Falk that forced a belly laugh from Falk every time he heard it.

At practice during overcast afternoons, Falk walks around with a weather radio tuned in for upcoming pattern changes. When a storm unloads over Jackson, about 45 minutes west of Ann Arbor, Falk walks up and down the sidelines announcing, "Storm over Jackson…storm over Jackson…45

minutes to rain in Ann Arbor...45 minutes to rain in Ann Arbor." Coaches immediately know how much time is left to cram in repetitions for the rest of the day.

Michigan was riding a five-game winning streak and ranked No. 3 in the nation when the team was upset 34–31 in East Lansing. Brady led a furious three-touchdown fourth-quarter rally that fell just short. For the day, Brady completed 30-of-41 passes for 285 yards.

The following week in Ann Arbor, the Illinois phone lines failed during the game. A few years prior, the Michigan lines had broken at Illinois, and equipment manager Andy Dixon helped get them repaired.

Falk was busy trying to return the favor when an Illinois coach yelled, "Get these [expletive] phones fixed." Falk turned around and told him that if he yelled one more time, there would be no phones for the rest of the game. Illinois went on to score three fourth-quarter touchdowns for a 35–29 victory.

"Maybe I should have just let the phones die," Falk joked.

Michigan rebounded with a 34–31 victory over Indiana in Bloomington when Falk witnessed an off-the-field phenomenon he had never seen before. Soon after the busses dropped off the players for the game, a couple of locals showed up in a pickup truck at the locker room door. They were carrying two large containers.

"We don't know what's in these, but we thought you might need them for the game," one of the men told Falk. "We saw them fall from one of the busses."

Falk immediately recognized the containers that carried all of the trainers' equipment. Without the honesty displayed by the two visitors, a few Michigan players may have had to play with untaped ankles.

"Indiana people are really down to earth," Falk said. "I love playing there. They're always hospitable. Can you imagine what would have happened to those containers if it had been a couple of other cities?"

Michigan crushed Northwestern 37–3 the following week to set up a classic confrontation at State College against No. 6 Penn State. Trailing 27–17 with 3:26 remaining in the fourth quarter, Brady scored on a 5-yard touchdown run to cut the lead to three points. After forcing Penn State to punt following the kickoff, Brady engineered a 35-yard drive with an 11-yard touchdown pass to Marcus Knight with 1:46 left to seal the 31–27 victory.

"It was one of the best college games I'd ever seen," Falk said. "Penn State is a good place to play. The people are good. The fans are good. They respect good football and how you play. After the game, some fans came up and said, 'Good game Michigan.' You don't get that kind of treatment in most places on the road."

Brady's roll did not stop there. In fact, he turned in one of his most brilliant performances in his final game at The Big House by leading Michigan back to a 24–17 victory over Ohio State.

Trailing most of the game before a record-setting Michigan Stadium crowd, Brady demonstrated his leadership by throwing a pair of clutch touchdown strikes. The first was an eight-yard toss to Shawn Thompson to tie the score with 37 seconds left in the third quarter. The winner was a 10-yard strike to Marquis Walker with 5:01 left in the game.

The victory earned Michigan a spot in the Orange Bowl against Alabama. And once again, Brady provided a flash of things to come in the NFL. He finished his Michigan career with a record-setting performance, completing 34-of-46 passing attempts for 369 yards and four touchdowns.

It took a bizarre finish in Michigan's first-ever overtime game, however, for the Wolverines to seal a 35–34 victory. Michigan scored on its first overtime possession when Brady hit Thompson over the middle for a 25-yard touchdown. Reliable Hayden Epstein kicked the extra point.

Alabama responded with a 21-yard touchdown pass from Andrew Zow to Antonio Carter. The try for the extra point, however, sailed wide right.

"Everything seemed to happen in slow motion," Falk said. "When he kicked the ball, it appeared to be sailing right. In my mind I said, 'This thing is over.' I nudged Lloyd and he looked up, and then we all started dancing."

There was plenty to celebrate. Michigan finished 10–2, good for fifth place in both national rankings. And the mid-season meeting Falk had with Brady is one both men remember.

Section 5

2000s

Chapter **56**
2000: Ring That One Up

Each day of the week prior to the 2000 Ohio State game, Falk walked around the locker room, sliding one of his many championship rings up and down his finger. Once in a while, he stopped in front of a particular player to make sure he was watching. A few times, he took the ring off and let the player stare.

A couple of players said, "Hey Big Jon, give me that ring, man...give me that ring."

That was the phrase Falk was waiting to hear.

"Sorry, men," he said. "I'd love to give you this ring, but I can't. This is one of those rings no one can give away. The only way you can get one is by going down to Columbus and beating Ohio State. Then you'll have your ring. And it'll mean something special for the rest of your life...because you earned it."

Also during the week, Falk called quarterback Drew Henson aside. "Do you realize that every Michigan fan all over the country always remembers what a quarterback did against Ohio State?" he asked.

"I know," was Henson's simple answer.

And then Henson proceeded to play the best game of his career.

Henson flashed all the magic that everyone expected of him since he first stepped onto the campus. He passed. He ran. He led the team as if he had created the position himself.

"Drew Henson was one of those special athletes who could excel at any-thing he did," Falk said. "On top of that, he was a good kid. He didn't fool around too much. He was always polite and always got down to business. They don't come much better than that."

Henson led the 38–26 demolition of Ohio State after the Buckeyes had jumped to a 9–0 lead on their first two possessions. He connected on 14-of-25 passes for 303 yards and three touchdowns. The first came on a third-and-10 screen pass to Anthony Thomas, who weaved his way behind a wall of blockers on a 70-yard jaunt. Henson fired touchdown strikes of 21 and 32 yards to David Terrell. The first covered approximately 60 yards of air space as Henson rolled to the right sideline and then fired to an all-alone Terrell in the left corner of the end zone. Henson capped the victory with a 1-yard quarterback keep touchdown.

As soon as the game ended, Michigan players ran around the field with arms held high and one hand imitating putting a ring on the finger of the other hand. "That was a wonderful sight," Falk said. "I guess they got the message I was trying to get across."

The message was almost derailed before anyone set foot on the field for the start of the season. Henson suffered a stress fracture in his foot and couldn't play until midway though Game 4 at Illinois.

In the season-opening 42–7 rout of Bowling Green, redshirt freshman quarterback John Navarre made an auspicious debut by tying a Michigan record with four touchdown passes in a 15-for-19 265-yard performance. He followed that game with a 10-for-15 performance in a 38–7 rout over Rice.

Michigan suffered a disappointing 23–20 loss at UCLA before the start of the Big Ten season at Illinois. It took just one half for Henson to provide a pic-ture of things to come.

Making his season debut late in the first half, Henson led a 28-point second-half explosion to defeat Illinois 35–31. Henson connected on 8-of-17 passes for 141 yards and a touchdown. He also ran four times for 23 yards and a touchdown. Anthony Thomas led the offense by lugging the ball 35 times for 228 yards.

After defeating Wisconsin 13–10, No. 6 Michigan was nipped 32–31 on a field goal with four seconds to play at Purdue. Back-to-back shutouts over

Indiana and Michigan State preceded one of the most disappointing losses that Falk and the team had ever endured.

In a shootout at Northwestern, Michigan fell 54–51 on an 11-yard touchdown pass by Zak Kustok with 20 seconds to play. On a second-down run in an effort to let time expire, Thomas had the ball stripped from his hands while trying to kill the clock. Northwestern recovered to set up the dramatic game-winning touchdown.

"It was the most devastating game I had ever been in," Falk said. "Everybody in that locker room was crushed. I went around to pat each man on the back, but you have to be careful what you say after a game like that."

A victory over Penn State the following Saturday set the stage for Michigan's shot at the Big Ten Championship at Ohio State. And Henson made sure the job got done.

Michigan never trailed in the Citrus Bowl against Auburn. Led by the passing of Henson and the relentless running of Thomas, the Wolverines held on for a 31–28 victory. Henson completed 15-of-20 passes for 294 yards and two touchdowns. Thomas ran for 182 yards on 32 carries. The Wolverines finished No. 10 in two polls and No. 11 in a third.

* * * *

Except for the principle characters involved, one of Falk's fondest memories from the 2000 season had nothing at all to do with football. Instead, it involved driving a Los Angeles Freeway in the teeth of rush-hour traffic with an irate Bo Schembechler sitting at his side.

Bo decided to travel with the team for the game against UCLA. On Friday after the team walkthrough of the stadium, Falk told Bo and radio broadcaster Jim Brandstatter that he had made dinner reservations for three at Lawry's The Prime Rib. He told them he would pick them up at their hotel after getting the locker room ready for Saturday's game.

Falk was waiting for them when they walked out the door. Unfortunately, the freeway traffic was also waiting and flashing a devilish smile. L.A. rush-hour traffic has its own way of gobbling up anyone daring to test it.

"I can still hear Bo grumbling even today," Falk smiled. "I felt like a referee who had called a penalty on Michigan."

"We're never gonna eat," Bo started. "I'm hungry, and we're never gonna get to Lawry's. This dumb S.O.B. driving doesn't even know where he's going."

Between chuckles in the back seat, Brandstatter told Bo to calm down.

"How am I supposed to calm down when we aren't moving?" Bo grumbled. "When we finally get there, the line will be a thousand people deep. We're probably gonna have to eat at some hamburger shop because this guy screwed it up and can't get us to the restaurant."

When Falk finally managed to reach the restaurant, about 50 people were standing in line.

"I told you we weren't gonna eat," Bo ranted. "There's a hundred people standing in line in front of us."

After parking the car, Falk maneuvered his two passengers through the line to the maître d's podium. "Reservations for Jon Falk," Falk said to the nattily dressed attendant.

"Oh yes, Mr. Falk," he replied. "We've been waiting for you."

The trio was led to a table set in the middle of the restaurant. Once seated, no one spoke for a few moments. Finally, Brandstatter couldn't wait to verbally jab Bo. "Well, Bo, what do you think of Big Jon now?" he said. "No hamburger shop tonight."

Bo looked around the room sheepishly and finally cracked a smile.

"Pretty impressive, Falk," he smiled. "Pretty impressive."

Some memories are keepers even when they don't happen on the field.

Chapter 57
James Hall:
Learning Tradition Early

James Hall got his first taste of Falk's passion for the University of Michigan at a meeting for incoming freshmen in late summer of 1995. Coach Lloyd Carr always scheduled Falk to speak to the new class to outline various practice and game procedures, along with sharing some of the fire that burns within him for Michigan.

"Look at this kid sitting in the front row," Falk began.

Hall didn't know Falk was referring to him until Falk pointed at the T-shirt Hall was wearing. The T-shirt featured the Indianapolis Pacers of the NBA. Hall wasn't even sure which T-shirt he was wearing at the time.

"If you're wearing a T-shirt around here, it better say something about the University of Michigan on the front," Falk said. "We are Michigan. And you are part of it."

Coming from New Orleans, Hall was unfamiliar with many of the traditions that only Michigan enjoys. In fact, he wasn't very familiar with the Big Ten at all. "I thought Indiana was a basketball school and that was it," Hall said. "Jon spent a lot of time every day explaining all the Michigan traditions. He taught us about the Little Brown Jug and the Paul Bunyan Trophy and just how big the game with Ohio State is. He'd play the Michigan fight song in the locker room and tell us how privileged we were to play for the University of Michigan."

Hall discovered it was an easy sell for Falk because he believes in everything he was pushing. "The beautiful part about Jon is that he lives those traditions," he said. "That's what makes him tick. That's the reason he's still there no matter who the coach is."

Hall came to appreciate Falk's in-your-face honesty. No one ever wonders what Falk means after he has stated his case.

"You either got with the program, or you got in Jon's doghouse," Hall said. "And that was never the right place to be. If he liked you and thought you needed a gentle reminder, he'd pull you aside and talk to you privately. But if you got on his bad side, he'd call you out in front of the whole team."

Hall also appreciates a lesson from Falk that he has carried into the real world after graduation. "'There are creeps everywhere in this world,' Falk used to tell the players. 'You have to watch out for them and always do the right thing,'" Hall said.

You either got with the program or you got in Jon's doghouse. And that was never the right place to be.
—James Hall

Visiting Falk after graduation, Hall thanked his mentor. "I finally understand what you once taught us about creeps in the world," Hall said.

When Hall arrived in Ann Arbor for the 1995 season, Michigan hadn't won the Big Ten championship for two years. They went two more years without one before going all the way in 1997. Not only did the Wolverines win the conference title, they went to the Rose Bowl and beat Washington State for a National Championship. Hall was a starting rush linebacker on that memorable team.

"Jon loved walking through the locker room before big games showing one of his many Big Ten Championship rings to all the players," Hall said. "He kept pounding into our heads that this was what we played for. He didn't have enough fingers to wear all the ones from the teams he had been on."

The message hit its target. Hall will always remember his Michigan experience. And he's grateful for the lifelong friendship he made with Falk.

Chapter **58**

2001: When Football Matters Less

Falk remembers the silence. So hauntingly different than anything he had experienced before. Hundreds of times since arriving in 1974, he stood in silence as the American flag was raised to the playing of the National Anthem before the opening kickoff.

This time it was different. He, along with 110,000 people, could actually hear how silence sounds. It was a mournful, lonely emptiness. It was felt as much as it was heard. The date was September 22, 2001. It had been 11 days since the inconceivable bombing of New York's Twin Towers. The wounds of a nation were still raw and bleeding.

In the blink of an eye, four U.S. Air Force fighter jets buzzed The Big House at the precise moment the Anthem finished. And as their roar faded into the sky, tears that had trickled down cheeks began to pour like a leaky faucet.

"The tears were flowing," Falk said. "I cried like a baby. Every player and coach on that team cried. It was one of those experiences that everyone there will never forget."

A stadium packed with people, frozen in time, stood in disbelief that such deep silence could be shared by so many. The game against Western Michigan had been scheduled for the previous Saturday. Because of the tragedy of September 11, of course, the game was postponed a week.

When the catastrophe struck, Falk was working in his office. A call from his wife let him know that the unthinkable had just occurred. All the coaches were upstairs gathered around a television set, sickened by what they were watching. Lloyd Carr called a team meeting for that evening, during which it was determined that no one desired to play the regularly scheduled game.

"We had two practices and then took the next weekend off," Falk said. "Just like throughout America, there was an uneasy feeling all around the football building."

Before that ill-fated Monday, Michigan had split its first two games. The Wolverines hammered Miami of Ohio 31–13 and dropped a 23–18 decision at Washington.

The team was still trying to establish its own identity following a spring surprise that cost its senior quarterback. "I remember the day in spring practice when I asked [quarterback coach] Stan Parrish how things were going," Falk said. "He said he had a superb senior quarterback who was playing hard, and it could be a great year."

Obviously, the coach had forgotten football's 24-hour unwritten rule of how much things can change in one simple day. The following day, Drew Henson announced that he had signed a multi-year, multi-million-dollar contract to play baseball for his childhood dream team—the New York Yankees.

A few years later, Henson visited Falk during a trip to Ann Arbor.

"Drew told me he didn't totally regret the decision he made," Falk said. "At the same time, he said the most fun he ever had in athletics was playing quarterback for Michigan. He said the best time he ever had was throwing that touchdown pass and running one in to beat Ohio State.

"Now think about that. Here's a young man who played on the biggest stages in sports. He played for the New York Yankees. Later he played for the Dallas Cowboys and then the Detroit Lions. And then he says the most fun he ever had was playing for Michigan. So many players come back and say the same thing even after they had great professional careers.

"We have a feeling of family here. Everybody cares for everyone else. That's not the way it is in the pros—someone is always coming after your job.

"Nobody begrudged Drew for what he did. He always wanted to play for the Yankees, and you have to do what's best for you. At the same time, we were disappointed because we could have had a great year."

Despite Henson's departure, Michigan still managed to have a respectable year. And as Falk maintains about any player who leaves, "They come and they go, Hobbs, they come and they go."

The one who came in this case was John Navarre. In his three years as a starter, Navarre passed his way into the Michigan record books and proved to be a strong leader.

I love John Navarre.... All the players loved him. He was a leader in the true sense of the word.
—Jon Falk

"I love John Navarre," Falk said. "He took a lot of unwarranted criticism from the fans. He and I spent a lot of time talking in my office. But he never said a word in public about the criticism he had to endure. All the players loved him. He was a leader in the true sense of the word."

Starting with Western Michigan, the Wolverines ran off a five-game winning streak, including a 20–0 shutout at Penn State. It was Joe Paterno's first shutout at home in his 36 years as head coach.

Then came the "unofficially extended" game at Michigan State that ended in a controversial 26–24 Spartan victory. Michigan took a 24–20 lead with 4:44 left in the game on a 20-yard pass from Navarre to backup quarterback Jermaine Gonzales. Suddenly, everything seemed to spin out of control.

Following a Michigan State punt, Michigan also had to punt the ball away. Herb Haygood returned it to the Michigan 44-yard line. After quarterback Jeff Smoker was sacked and tossed two incomplete passes, a 15-yard face-mask penalty was called on Michigan to keep the drive alive.

Smoker completed a 17-yard third-down pass to Haygood then was sacked again. He was rescued by an illegal participation penalty called against Michigan. After three straight missed passes, Smoker hit T.J. Duckett with an eight-yard first-down pass to the Michigan 3-yard line.

With 17 seconds left, Smoker tried to run the ball but was stopped on the 1-yard line. After the Spartans scrambled to set formation, the clock ticked to 1 second when the referee set the ball. Smoker proceeded to spike the ball when it looked to many that time had expired.

"When I looked up and saw 2 seconds and the ball still not snapped, I pulled down my cap and started to run across the field," Falk said. "I was happy to get out of there with the win. Then I noticed that no one was leaving. How the clock stopped with 1 second is way beyond me."

On fourth down, Smoker hit Duckett in the end zone for the touchdown.

"To this day, I don't know how it happened," Falk said. "There were a lot of innuendoes that circulated after that call. Since then, I studied a lot of spiked balls, and each one of them takes two seconds to execute. But that was the call, and you have to live with it."

The following week, Michigan bounced back at The Big House to whip Minnesota 31–10. At Wisconsin the next Saturday, Michigan rallied late for a 20–17 victory. Tied at 17-all, Michigan was forced to punt with less than 30 seconds to play.

"Camp Randall is such a tough place to play," Falk said. "The fans go absolutely wild. They start jumping up and down in the bleachers so hard that the pressbox actually shakes. I asked someone standing next to me what a team has to do to win here."

And suddenly came the answer.

Hayden Epstein booted a 40-yard punt that bounced sideways and brushed the back of returner Brett Bell on the 13-yard line. Brandon Williams alertly noticed the touch and grabbed the football. On the ensuing play, Epstein kicked a 31-yard field goal for the victory.

"So that's all you gotta do to win here," Falk said.

At Ohio State, the Wolverines fell behind 23–0 at the half. Michigan held the Buckeyes to a fourth-quarter field goal and scored 20 points in the second half in a 26–20 loss.

In the Citrus Bowl, Michigan was dismantled by Tennessee 45–17 to finish the season 8–4, good for No. 20 in all three polls.

It was a year to remember and a year to forget.

Chapter **59**

2002: Fielding Yost Sat Here

The Michigan football contingent that traveled to Columbus for the 2002 game with Ohio State had the security accorded to touring rock stars. The Buckeyes were undefeated and ranked No. 2 in the country. A victory—

or loss—against Michigan had the potential to trigger another ugly postgame fiasco, and Lloyd Carr was taking no chances.

"Lloyd made a big deal about the 1998 incident," Falk said. "He didn't want anyone getting hurt again. He demanded tighter security on the sidelines and increased crowd control for after the game."

After the 1998 episode, Falk could certainly identify with the situation.

Ohio State complied. Uniformed police officers lined the field after the game. So many clustered behind the sidelines during the game it was almost impossible not to bump into someone anytime a person moved.

Falk was squished near a member of the down-marking crew when the man asked Falk, "You've been with Michigan a long time, haven't you?"

"Yes sir, I have," Falk answered.

"Were you here with Gary Moeller?" he asked.

"Yes sir," Falk said.

"Did you work for Bo?" he asked.

"Yes sir," Falk said. "He hired me back in 1974."

Falk heard the man talking to his partner.

"This guy goes all the way back to Bo," he said to his partner. "He's worked for Bo, then Mo, and now Lloyd. He must be alright."

That's the respect the real Ohio State fans have for Michigan.

In the game, Michigan scrambled to the doorstep of upsetting the Buckeyes before falling 14–9. Michigan took a 9–7 lead into the third quarter but finished the game without scoring at least one touchdown for the first time all season. Kicker Adam Finley provided all the Michigan scoring with three field goals.

The Wolverines topped the Buckeyes in total yardage 368–264. They also kept possession of the ball for 34:36. They just couldn't push the ball into the end zone.

At home against Wisconsin the previous week, Michigan scored a third-quarter game-winning touchdown in a 21–14 decision. Some of the real fireworks, however, exploded after the game.

The boiler providing hot water into the visitor's locker room broke, forcing players and coaches to endure cold showers after suffering a heart-breaking loss.

Upon hearing of the situation, Falk immediately contacted Athletic Director Bill Martin to accompany him to apologize to coach Barry Alvarez. As Martin was speaking to Alvarez, Falk personally apologized to all the Wisconsin players. "Look at those toilets over there," Alvarez began. "Do you realize Fielding Yost must have sat there? I know he was there. And not to have hot water… what the hell is going on here?"

After venting his frustration, Alvarez finally smiled. "I want to thank you guys for coming over here," he said. "I never had anyone come over in a situation like this and hear someone apologize. Your apologies are accepted."

One of the biggest victories of 2002 came at The Big House against Michigan State. There was no controversy over time as there had been the previous season at East Lansing. And there certainly was no debate over which school had the better team.

Scoring two touchdowns in each quarter except the third when the Wolverines were held to one, Michigan thundered to an overwhelming 49–3 decision.

"We were still stinging from the previous year," Falk admitted. "But I guarantee Lloyd did not purposely run up the score. He was sending in replacements almost the entire second half. You can't tell your guys to simply lie down."

Michigan played Florida in the Outback Bowl and matched the Gators punch for punch in a 38–30 shootout victory.

"Seems like every time a Midwestern school plays one from Florida, people think that Midwestern team is gonna be treated just like fodder," Falk said. "Well, we just happened to have a pretty good ball club. And John Navarre was turning himself into a pretty good quarterback."

Michigan finished the season at 10–3, good for No. 9 in both final polls.

Chapter **60**

John Navarre: Learning the Right Way

J ohn Navarre loved to listen to the stories only Falk can tell.

He particularly liked hearing about former Michigan quarterbacks such as Rick Leach and Jim Harbaugh and Elvis Grbac and Brian Griese and Tom Brady. Quarterbacks have etched a special place in Michigan folklore. They all share a significant trait. All had to learn to deal with some of the unforgiving scrutiny that goes with the privilege of playing the position for Michigan.

Navarre persisted through relentless scrutiny and criticism to become one of the most prolific quarterbacks in the history of the celebrated program. And to this day, he attributes much of his determination to the support from his friend.

"There were times when I'd go into Jon's office two or three times a day," Navarre said. "We would just talk. It wasn't necessarily about one play or one game. It was mostly about character and how Jon never wanted to see anyone quit."

Navarre certainly got the message as he carved his spot on the all-time record lists for Michigan quarterbacks. He may not have been the most graceful performer, but he always got the job done.

"Jon never tried to patronize anyone," Navarre said. "He was blunt. He always told the truth."

From the first day of a player's freshman season, Falk is up front with what is expected of every Michigan player. And he's unafraid to approach a player when the time is right.

"Time after time after a tough game, he would seek out a player to deliver a word of encouragement," Navarre said. "He always seemed to know when someone needed a pat on the back or a kick in the behind."

Because of his lengthy experience, Falk always takes time to explain to players what to expect in certain games at stadiums that are historically challenging to first-time visitors.

"The University of Michigan is a special place with special people," Navarre said. "They have a tremendous influence on your life. Jon has left his mark on so many players over the years. His contribution to the program is impossible to measure. He's way more than just an equipment manager. He's been a key figure in my life. Not just as a quarterback, but also in becoming a man."

Jon has left his mark on so many players over the years. His contribution to the program is impossible to measure.

—John Navarre

That doesn't show up on the job description. For Falk, though, it's the best part of the job.

Chapter **61**
2003: Perry Made Bo Smile

C hris Perry was one of those friendly guys who liked to jabber. Rarely were they long conversations, but in the locker room and on the sidelines, Perry simply liked to talk. After the game at Spartan Stadium in 2003, the likable senior was walking off the field when he said, "I think Coach Schembechler is happy with this one."

Perry knew that Bo was watching the game at home on TV. He also knew the way Michigan ground out a 27–20 victory was sure to make Saturday evening a whole lot happier for Bo as he settled down to watch the late games on TV.

Perry set a Michigan record by carrying the ball 51 times. He totaled 219 yards, scored a touchdown, and personally accounted for most of the 39:19 that Michigan possessed the ball. It was, in fact, a dominating performance that returned Michigan fans to the 1970s. And Bo did, indeed, savor every moment Perry lugged the ball.

Riding the equipment truck home, Falk made the customary call to Bo that he placed after each game—win or lose, home or road. "He always liked going over some of the things that I saw from the field and some of the things he noticed on TV," Falk said. "I loved those calls. They're some of my favorite memories."

Falk knew what to expect from his former boss after Perry's personal march through East Lansing. "Michigan showed we can run the ball," Bo said. "That line was mean. They made holes, and the kid didn't waste them. When you can run the football, you can win a championship."

A few years later, Falk made a point to call Bo every night, especially when Cathy was out of town. "What the hell are you doing calling me every night?" Bo barked into the phone. "You're checking on me, Falk. I know exactly what you're doing. You're checking on me."

On the final play of that Michigan State game, the Spartans had a chance to win or at least send the game into overtime, but Jeff Smoker's desperation toss from midfield into the end zone was intercepted by linebacker Scott McClintock.

After the game, Falk witnessed one of the most moving talks by a player in his career. Standing on a chair in the middle of the locker room, with tears dripping down his cheeks, quarterback John Navarre pleaded with his teammates.

"I'm asking all of you," he started. "We need to play together for two more games. We have to go to Northwestern and then play Ohio State at home. I'm asking each one of you guys to play your best. I want this championship. I want that ring. I want this for the team. I want this for Michigan."

The Wolverines complied with their field general by pulverizing North-western 41–10 to set up the 100th meeting between Michigan and Ohio State. And Perry and his teammates saved the best for last.

Michigan had invited all former players to attend the game. They formed two long lines feeding from the mouth of The Tunnel to the center of the field through which the current players charged into daylight.

"It's always a thrill to come out of that tunnel," Falk said. "Especially against Ohio State. But that day the goosebumps were the size of baseballs. There were so many familiar faces that I had worked with. Their hearts always stayed at Michigan."

The emotion on the field electrified the NCAA record crowd of 112,118. And the Wolverines used that emotion to jump to a 21–7 lead by the half.

Trailing 28–14 after three quarters, Ohio State scored a touchdown early in the fourth quarter to cut the deficit to just one touchdown. Perry settled the matter with 7:55 left when he broke through the middle and went nearly untouched into the end zone for the final score of the 35–21 Michigan victory.

Perry finished with 154 yards rushing, while the Michigan defense held Buckeye runners to merely 54 yards. Perry ran for two touchdowns and Steve Breaston one. The Navarre–Braylon Edwards connection was as precise as a GPS. Edwards snagged seven passes, including two for touchdowns.

The victory gave Michigan the outright Big Ten championship for the first time since 1997. The Wolverines lost 28–14 to USC in the Rose Bowl but still finished the season at 10–3, good for No. 6 and No. 7 in the two final polls.

It was a special season for Navarre, Perry, and all the seniors. Victories over Ohio State, Notre Dame, and Michigan State always make the highlight film more lively. The 38–0 shutout over Notre Dame was the first over the Irish since 1902.

"It was a fun team to work with," Falk said. "All good young men. Navarre dealt with a lot of undue criticism without saying word. He was one of the best. And we had another good one on the way."

Chapter **62**

Mike Hart: The Shoe Collection

Nobody sets the Michigan career rushing record of 5,040 yards gained without a lot of help from a whole lot of friends. That's around three-and-a-half miles of hard-earned football real estate running through and around extremely dangerous roadblocks wearing uniforms belonging to Ohio

State, Notre Dame, Michigan State, Penn State, Florida, Texas, and a host of other headhunters.

Even the record-setting Mike Hart needed plenty of help from his big bully friends on the line all the way down to the water boy who helped to keep him refreshed. Hart heaps plenty of gratitude on Falk, who kept coming up with something new throughout Hart's four dynamic seasons as the most productive ground-gainer in Michigan's storied history.

When you play football for Michigan, you never really leave. It will always be part of your home.

—Mike Hart

"Big Jon would have four or five different shoes on the sidelines for me every game," Hart said. "If the field was high, he'd tell me to put on a certain shoe. If the field got wet, he'd switch me to another. There were different shoes for high grass, short grass, and all other conditions. He watched me during a game, and if he spotted something where the field changed, he'd have me switch shoes before the next possession."

Falk was always looking for that one tiny opening where he could make a positive difference in the game for Michigan. Along with the shoes, Falk tried about four to five different thigh pads a week on Hart. He kept looking for the one that might help Hart gain maybe just a couple of extra yards.

For Hart, there was a lot more to Falk than the man who only administered the equipment. "All week before a game, Big Jon would walk around the locker room and say little things to get the team fired up for Saturday," Hart said. "He knew how to keep a player's confidence high. He did the same thing during a game. He would never get into a player's face to get him upset. He always gave us a word of encouragement to keep playing hard because something good could happen."

Normally on Thursdays, Falk came up with a story to share with the players. It usually involved a previous game with the team Michigan was preparing to play on Saturday.

"He always amazed me," Hart said. "He knew all the games and all the key plays that happened for every game since he came to Michigan. He would put some catchy saying on the door to his office to remind us how important the upcoming game was."

Hart particularly appreciated the opportunity to talk to Falk when something didn't feel right. "Any player could go into his office and talk to him about anything," Hart said. "And that player didn't have to worry about the story going any further. It never left his office."

Hart also appreciates the fact that whenever a former player returns to Michigan for workouts or any other matter, that player can visit Falk and feel like he had never left.

"He's the one guy who has been through it all," Hart said. "He can tell stories going all the way back to Bo. That's a good feeling for a former player. That's what Michigan is all about. When you play football for Michigan, you never really leave. It will always be part of your home."

Especially with a housekeeper like Falk.

Chapter 63
Stanley Edwards: Words for a Lifetime

During his celebrated football career at the University of Michigan, running back Stanley Edwards chose friends wisely. "I could laugh with Jon," Edwards said. "I could confide in him. We could talk about football, classes, or simply life in general. I knew I could trust him."

A quarter of a century later, Edwards asked Falk for another session. Not with himself, but rather his son, Braylon. Following Braylon's junior season, talk swirled around Ann Arbor and throughout the college football world that the brilliant wide receiver might forego his senior season by making himself eligible for the NFL draft. Braylon was on his way toward setting every conceivable Michigan receiving record. He was a certain first-round selection.

"Jon sat my son down and explained the importance of being a Michigan Man," Stanley said. "He made him consider how important it was for him to play all four seasons and leave at the top. He would have plenty of time to prove himself professionally. Once he left Michigan, he would never have the opportunity to wear that winged helmet again."

Whether Falk's discourse had any significant impact on Braylon, no one knows for sure. But Braylon did return for his senior season and wound up as the NFL's third selection in the draft by the Cleveland Browns.

All the players know how long Jon has been part of Michigan. They know how much he's seen and how valuable he is.
—Stanley Edwards

Stanley maintains that those college years comprise a young man's biggest transition in life. "From 17 to 22 years old, there's a lot of personal growth going on," he said. "A coach or anyone in an advisory position has to get players to buy into a system. It requires a lot of tough love."

And that's where Stanley believes Falk's role is so critical. "He's way more important than just an equipment manager," Stanley said. "Jon has more exposure to the players than any of the coaches. He's around them nearly every day of the year.

"There are times when a player needs someone other than a coach to confide in. Maybe something is going on in a player's personal life. Maybe the player feels a coach is riding him too hard. All the players know how long Jon has been part of Michigan. They know how much he's seen and how valuable he is."

Stanley marvels at the litany of All-Americans who consider Falk a friend.

"Rick Leach, Desmond Howard, Charles Woodson, Tom Brady," Stanley said. "The list goes on and on. Jon has had the privilege of working with so many players who have wound up in the NFL or the College Football Hall of Fame. They all talked to Jon at some point. We'll never know how many guys he's helped to stay in Ann Arbor when things were tough and they were thinking about leaving. They come in as starry-eyed boys and go out as men— Michigan Men."

One of the reasons Stanley considers Falk to be part of his family is Bo. "I worshipped Bo Schembechler," Stanley said. "I absolutely worshipped him. Because of that, I trusted all the people around him."

One of those people is Lloyd Carr, who arrived at Michigan as an assistant coach in 1980 when Stanley was a junior. Carr successfully recruited Braylon, who re-wrote the records books for receivers. Another is Falk, who preceded Carr to Michigan and was handpicked by Bo.

"When someone is as close to Bo as Jon was, you know you can trust him," Stanley said. "He'll always be my friend."

With only Falk still on the staff from when Bo coached, Stanley never fails to visit his friend when in Ann Arbor. "Therapeutic reminiscences," Stanley joked. "Those will never end."

Chapter 64
2004: No Freshman Jitters

The whole week before the 2004 game with Ohio State, Falk wondered what kind of nightmare he would have to face after arriving in Columbus. He had already encountered the loss of water in his hotel room, the theft of five helmets, an accident with the equipment truck, a near arrest by the county sheriff, and a frightening postgame incident in which he was trampled by celebrating fans.

But he never expected the Feds to get involved.

"It never fails," Falk said. "You can always count on something that throws you out of whack when you go to Columbus."

But the Feds?

You can always count on something that throws you out of whack when you go to Columbus.

—Jon Falk

The trip started quite normally with Falk, his assistants, and the equipment truck arriving early Friday morning to unload and set up the locker room. The veteran team worked like a machine, leaving only extra equipment such as rain capes, helmets, jerseys, and a smattering of shoes on the truck.

At 7:00 AM Saturday, the equipment team was about to unload the rest of the truck when out of nowhere three Homeland Security agents and a dog suddenly made their presence emphatically felt.

"You're not taking anything into that locker room," one of the agents said.

Falk, of course, was dumbfounded and perhaps for the first time in his life somewhat tongue-tied.

"We want you to unload every piece of equipment you have on that truck so that we can inspect your gear," the agent said.

Falk was not yet boiling, but his frustration was beginning to simmer. "Now wait a minute, sir," he tried to reason. "We're not gonna bring out all our Michigan gear and lay it out on the parking lot in front of all these Ohio State fans and people walking by."

The agent was persistent. "Well if you don't, that stuff is not coming off the truck," he said.

Falk's simmer was rising quickly. "Sir, now let's be reasonable," he said. "Nobody told me we were gonna have to do this on Saturday morning. If I had been told yesterday, I could have brought all this stuff in on Friday."

The agent refused to budge. "I'm just telling you right now that if you don't take all that stuff off, you're going to have to move the truck."

Falk's simmer was now starting to boil. "Now look," he said. "That truck is parked here, and that's how we get stuff off the field and out of the locker room after the game. We're not moving that truck."

The agent had become belligerent. "You will if I tell you," he said.

Besides getting angry, Falk was now concerned that he and his assistants were falling behind schedule. "Sir, let's come to some sort of compromise," he said. "I understand your position. Please try to understand mine. Is there any way we can get around this without unloading all of our gear in the parking lot?"

Fortunately, one of the other agents did in fact understand Falk's position and proposed a solution. "We could take our dog into your truck to smell all of the equipment," he said. "That would work just as well as unloading the truck."

Falk was ready to comply before the first agent interjected.

"That truck is gonna be unloaded," he said.

Falk turned to the agent who was at least willing to reason.

"I understand this man's point," he said. "He can't have all his Michigan gear all over the parking lot. Let's take the dog into the truck. I'll approve that."

The gear passed the sniff test and was unloaded into the locker room by Falk's crew. Although disruptive, at least everything was settled before the coaches and players arrived. At least that's what Falk figured.

When the team busses arrived at 10:30, Falk, as usual, was there to meet Lloyd Carr. Again Falk was surprised when the same three agents and their dog appeared. They ordered that no one was allowed into the locker room until everyone put their carry bags on the ground for the dog to sniff.

One of the agents grabbed Carr's arm and said, "You can't go in there 'til we see your briefcase."

"Give me your briefcase and I'll take care of this," Falk quickly interjected to Carr. "I'll explain everything later. You go in and get dressed."

Of course, there was a lot of heated discussion as every player had to drop his bag and wait until the dog was finished sniffing.

"When you go into a game—especially a big game like that one—you just don't want a disruptive incident like that to occur," Falk said. "When coaches and players arrive, there's a strict time schedule for everything to happen. Players have a mindset. They are going straight to their lockers to prepare for the game."

After hearing all the details of the incident, Carr was furious. Ohio State administration officials said that Homeland Security conducted such a search with every team that played at Ohio Stadium that year.

The following week, Falk contacted friends at all of the schools that had played at Ohio State that season. Each team was subject to a search but had been informed it would occur at the hotel before the teams boarded their busses on Saturday.

"It was really confusing before the game," Falk said. "That wasn't the reason we lost, but it sure didn't help matters, either."

Falk informed Bo about the incident during his phone call home while riding on the team truck. Needless to say, Bo exploded.

"In retrospect, I think Ohio State was upset that something like that had occurred," Falk said. "Bo trained all of us to treat Ohio State with respect. He insisted that we give them everything they needed. That's how much respect he had for them."

On the bus ride home, the team learned that Iowa had beaten Wisconsin. That victory gave Michigan and Iowa a share of the Big Ten title. Because Michigan had beaten Iowa 30–17, Michigan received a berth in the Rose Bowl. That was small consolation for the players at the time but an honor well deserved for a conference record of 7–1.

The 2004 season was also the beginning of another era that was dominated primarily by quarterback Chad Henne and tailback Mike Hart. Henne became Michigan's first four-year starting quarterback since Rick Leach. He set the school career record of 9,715 yards through the air. Hart also started all four years and set the school career record of 5,040 yards rushing.

"Henne had a demeanor about him that set him apart from other freshmen," Falk said. "He never showed an ego but had all the confidence in the world. He was able to make all of the upperclassmen believe in him without going around acting like a big shot.

"When a freshman quarterback plays in this league, the chances of winning are pretty slim. But he took us to the Rose Bowl. He was no ordinary freshman quarterback."

Hart also beat all the odds.

"Everybody said he was too small to take the punishment of the Big Ten," Falk said. "Inside, though, he's a warrior."

Falk enjoyed talking to Bo at two-a-day practices in the fall of 2004. "Take a look at this little Mike Hart," Falk told him.

Bo had already scouted him and said, "He's too small, Jon…he's too small."

Now that Bo wasn't coaching, it was easy to say a lot more to him than before. "Bo, I'm telling you, he's gonna be a good back here at Michigan," Falk said.

Before the end of fall practice, Bo delivered one of his patented pokes to Falk's chest. "You know what, Jon?" Bo said. "This little Hart kid is gonna be pretty good. Do you know that?"

Despite diverse personalities, the pair of freshman prodigies connected both on and off the field. "Henne rarely spoke," Falk said. "He just went out and played. He had a way of keeping all the players calm. He had a command of the game and the players without sounding like a dictator.

"Linemen loved to protect him. Football players are like hunting dogs. You have to train them to hunt. They have to want to hunt for you. If you berate them, all of a sudden those dogs don't want to hunt for you.

"It's the same with the players. If you get them where they are hunting for you and you happen to be the quarterback, you're gonna have a pretty good team."

Hart was an outspoken character. He always had something to say. "He laughed a lot, and I loved to tease him," Falk said. "He was the kind of guy [who] made everyone around him feel good."

After crushing Miami of Ohio 43–10 in the season opener, Michigan traveled to South Bend. Notre Dame has a natural-grass field that can cause trouble for unsuspecting opponents. Falk checked the field on Friday and saw one of his buddies mowing the grass.

"Pretty high out there," Falk said. "Are those blades turning, or are you just rolling it down for the day?

"You gotta remember, Jon," he said. "I've got my orders, too."

Long grass invariably slows down every team. Cleats are unable to dig deep for traction. It wasn't the grass, however, that caused Michigan to allow three fourth-quarter touchdowns in a 28–20 defeat.

Michigan won the next eight games before the loss to Ohio State.

In a Rose Bowl classic, Texas nipped Michigan 38–37 on a Dusty Mangum field goal as time expired. Henne connected on 18-of-34 passes for 227 yards. Hart rushed 21 times for 83 yards. Senior Braylon Edwards capped his career with 10 receptions for 109 yards and three touchdowns.

Michigan finished at 9–3, good for No. 12 and No. 14 in the final polls.

"Not bad for a freshman quarterback and freshman runner," Falk said. "That's something you won't see again for a long time."

Chapter **65**

2005: The String Is Snapped

I t wasn't exactly a crack heard 'round the world, but it certainly made a lot of noise throughout the world of college football. It occurred on October 22, 2005. Falk will always remember the date, the time, and the play that could have ended his football career.

About four minutes into the game at Iowa, Chad Henne threw a sideline pass only yards from Falk. Iowa defender Abdul Hodge was trying to contain the play. He hit the ground and started to roll and couldn't stop until he crashed into Falk's legs. What looked like an incidental sideline takedown turned into a career-threatening nightmare for Falk.

Falk was sent sailing into one of the members of the yard-marker team and wound up sitting on one of the coaches' sideline phones. Rick Brandt, one of Falk's assistants, came running to tell him he had to move.

"You hit the switch, and the coaches can't communicate," Brandt shouted. "You have to move."

"I started to get up, and my left leg angled to the right," Falk said. "I knew right then my leg was broken."

Almost immediately, trainer Paul Schmidt reached Falk to find out what had happened.

"I broke my leg, Paul," Falk said.

"You don't know that," Schmidt said.

Falk already knew. You don't tell a pregnant woman she's not ready to deliver when she's already started contractions.

"Suddenly, I fainted," Falk said. "I realized I was done. When you break your leg in my business, you're done. You have to be able to move around in this job, and I couldn't even stand."

Paramedics finally lifted Falk onto a stretcher that was then placed on a golf cart for the trip to the locker room. Assistant Athletic Director for Football Scott Draper quickly went into the stands to gather Falk's wife, Cheri, and daughter, Katie. The family was in town visiting Falk's sister, Ann, who lives in Iowa. All were transported to the hospital where Falk was examined.

"You have a pretty significant break here," the doctor told Falk. "When you get back to Ann Arbor, you'll have to see your doctors."

Falk wanted a more immediate prognosis.

"Sometimes it requires surgery, and sometimes it doesn't," the doctor said.

Falk wanted to know the odds.

"You've been in this business a long time, Doc," he said. "What's the percentages of me having surgery?"

The doctor paused. "Oh, about 98 percent," he said.

A brace was placed on Falk's left leg, and he was sent back to the locker room. The fans were screaming wildly before Michigan scored to send the game into overtime. Lying on the trainer's table, Falk was thinking that if Michigan loses the game, no one would care about his broken leg.

He didn't have to worry. After Iowa kicked a field goal on the first overtime possession, Michigan came back to win 23–20 on a 1-yard Jerome Jackson touchdown run. As soon as the players returned to the locker room, everyone crammed into the training room to visit Falk. Lloyd Carr was the first to enter.

"You know, Lloyd, if I can't make that trip next week to Northwestern, it'll be the first game I've missed after 384 straight," Falk said, choking back tears.

Carr arranged to have Cheri and Katie fly home on the team plane. Athletic Director Bill Martin arranged to have a van transport Falk to the airport. While in the van, Falk called Bo.

"I broke my leg, Bo," Falk said as soon as Bo had said hello.

"You just get back to Ann Arbor, and we'll take care of you," Bo said. "I told Cathy when I saw you go down that Jon's done. He's not gonna make the rest of the season."

At the airport, three players lifted Falk and carried him to the stairway of the plane. He had to take each step slowly as if he were walking at the edge of a mountain. He was wearing only a pair of baggy rain pants that slipped down his hips with each step. Someone from behind kept lifting his pants after each step.

"The pain was almost paralyzing, and I couldn't look back to see who was helping me with my pants," Falk said.

When he reached the top step, he was finally able to turn around to see who it was. "It was Lloyd Carr," Falk said. "That just goes to show you the kind of guy he is. Here was the head coach of the University of Michigan football team helping me to keep my pants up."

The trip to Ann Arbor was excruciatingly painful. Upon reaching his home, he settled into a chair and remained awake all night counting every second. He finally fell into a fitful sleep when a litany of phone calls started at 9:00 AM. The first, of course, came from Bo. Next in line was Rick Leach.

"Those calls meant a lot to me," Falk said. "There were so many. Carr and Martin also called that morning."

Falk was taken to St. Joseph Hospital. After the examination, Dr. Sean Adelman explained that if the nerve running down over the knee to the foot was severed, there was nothing he could do. Falk would suffer from "drop foot" for the rest of his life. Surgery was scheduled for Monday morning.

After surgery, Falk was told the good news and the bad. The nerve was nicked but not severed. The bad news was that the surgeon discovered a hole as big as a fist in the tibia. He cleaned it out and filled it with cadaver bones to heal.

Because of an abrasion on the knee, the surgeon had to cut around the wound. The extraordinarily long incision would add extra time to rehabilitation. Falk had suffered the abrasion when falling on the field in celebration of the previous Saturday's victory over Penn State when Mario Manningham caught a touchdown pass from Chad Henne with no time left on the clock.

About 10:30 that evening, Falk was visited by Bo, Cathy, and Jim Brandstatter.

"Brandy kept talking about how everything was going to be alright when Bo finally told him to shut up," Falk said.

"The man's in pain," Bo said. "Just let him rest."

Throughout his 10-day hospital stay, Falk kept busy with phone calls from former players and coaches in football and baseball from around the country. Iowa head coach Kirk Ferentz called, as did TV commentators Bob Griese and Lynn Swann.

"I got a call from Keith Jackson," Falk said. "I couldn't believe it. I had to make him prove it was really him."

On the day after surgery, Falk was surprised about a call he didn't get. He had been expecting one from Michigan State equipment manager and long-time friend Bob Knickerbocker. Almost as soon as Falk mentioned the fact to Cheri, Knickerbocker walked through the door and Falk's eyes filled with tears. "He said he took off from practice because it was more important to him to visit his friend," Falk smiled. "He said they would have to play without him."

President Bush was busy running the country at the time so he couldn't visit. But he did send a letter of encouragement, which Falk will keep forever.

Falk watched the Michigan victory over Northwestern on TV from his hospital bed. On Monday, team captain Pat Massey visited the hospital to give him the game ball.

After being released from the hospital, Falk returned to the practice field in a wheelchair on Thursday before the game with Indiana. He was asked by Carr to speak to the team.

"I want to tell you two things," Falk said. "First, I want to thank you for all of your support. Second, go out and beat Indiana and send a message to Ohio State that Michigan football is still here."

Falk watched both games—the victory over Indiana and the loss to Ohio State—on TV in the recruiting lounge of the stadium.

"That was tougher for me than all the rehab I had in store," Falk said. "Especially the Ohio State loss. We were up 21–19 and then let them score with 24 seconds left."

The final score was 25–21.

After having his office rearranged so that he could move around safely, Falk returned to work in December. The team was preparing to play Nebraska in the Alamo Bowl. Falk accompanied the team to San Antonio and watched the disappointing 32–28 loss from the pressbox. Michigan finished the season unranked with a 7–5 record.

For Falk, the physical therapy was scheduled to kick into high gear. But it didn't come without a struggle. "There were times when I thought I was through…that I'd never be able to do my job again," he admitted. "There were nights I thought I'd never sleep. Some mornings I thought I'd never get out of bed. Then all of a sudden, something hits you and you know you just have to get with the program."

He began to attack his rehabilitation with the same vigor he had always attacked his job. It didn't go unnoticed.

"I knew you were a warrior," Carr told Falk. "But the determination I saw from you every day was amazing. Walking in the pool…exercising…trying to get yourself back to walking right. It was a pleasure to watch."

Finally in March, Falk felt as if he had returned.

In 2006, Penn State coach Joe Paterno suffered a broken leg in a similar accident at Wisconsin. Falk called Tom Venterino, a friend who worked for Penn State, and told him to tell Paterno there are three things he must understand—walkers, wheelchairs, and urinal bottles.

Venterino said Paterno wouldn't use any of those.

"He will," Falk laughed. "He just doesn't know it yet."

Before the 2007 Penn State game at Michigan, Falk visited the coach to exchange "war stories."

I'll tell you the most important thing. We came back.

—Joe Paterno

"I guess your injury was a little worse than mine," Paterno said. "But I'll tell you this."

Paterno poked his index finger into Falk's chest and kept repeating, "I'll tell you this…I'll tell you this."

Falk expected Paterno to say that the older one gets, the harder it is to return. "No, no, no," the coach insisted. "I'll tell you the most important thing. We came back."

The message sticks with Falk. He tries to share it with those who need it most.

"I have more empathy for injured players now," he said. "When I see them in the training room, I usually go in and pat them on the back.

"When a player gets injured, there are still all those other players on the team. The train is still rolling, and it's hard for them to understand how it keeps going without them. They need that encouragement to get back on board."

Falk knows. He's still riding today.

Chapter **66**

2006: A Season to Remember and Forget

Before the start of the 2006 football season, Bo told Falk that he was going to accompany Cathy and himself to a Tigers game at Comerica Park. Falk was going to drive and—by the way—arrange for tickets.

Since Bo's departure from the Tigers in 1992, he and Falk had been to only one game when Alan Trammell managed the team. This time Jim Leyland was the manager, and Falk took Bo to his office before the game.

The three were swapping stories and laughing, as only longtime sportsmen can, when Bo mentioned to Leyland that he had initiated the modernization of all Tigers minor league operations.

Leyland, of course, was familiar with the history and added that he and the Tigers "will always be indebted for what you did for the organization."

Bo smiled and said he was merely doing his job. "Now I'm back at Michigan, and a lot of people are gone," he said. "I've still got Falk to take me around. Look how much things have changed. Now it's Falk getting me tickets for a game."

It became obvious to Falk that Bo was beginning to feel poorly that summer. Bo never complained, but the actions of his body were as honest as his character. It was impossible for him to hide all the physical turmoil boiling inside.

Early in the season, Bo told Falk that he had fallen down the steps to the parking lot at Schembechler Hall. "Damn papers I was carrying flew all over the place," he said.

That's when Falk made it a habit to call him every night.

"Why the hell are you calling me all the time?" he barked at Falk. "I'm fine."

"Just want to hear you say so, coach," Falk said. Often the conversation was as brief as that.

Soon after the incident, Falk mentioned to Lloyd Carr, "It's really gonna be tough around here when Bo leaves."

"It'll be a cold day in hell," Carr said.

Bo was particularly enthusiastic about the 2006 team. He loved the way everyone blocked and tackled. The team had spirit, and it was fun watching them play. Bo enjoyed going to the pressbox with Cathy, confident in the effort he expected from the team.

Starting the season ranked No. 14 in the nation, Michigan scored in each quarter to handily defeat Vanderbilt 27–7 in the opener at The Big House. After dismantling Central Michigan 41–17, the Wolverines faced their biggest test by going to South Bend for the battle against No. 2 Notre Dame.

The game was a mismatch. Michigan scored 20 points in the first quarter and rolled to a 47–21 victory. Mike Hart ran for 124 yards on 31 carries. Chad Henne completed 13-of-22 passes for 220 yards and three touchdowns.

After the game, Carr told a photographer to take a picture of himself and Falk in the victorious locker room. "I started to get a little sense of something going on," Falk said. "I wasn't really sure what it was, but I was suspicious."

Michigan dumped Wisconsin 27–13 before heading to Minnesota to reclaim the Little Brown Jug. Carr told Falk before the game that if Michigan won, he wanted Falk to be in the middle of the team walking arm in arm across the field to take the prize.

"What a tribute that was," Falk said. "I felt really proud to accept that Jug and give it to the players."

Michigan was definitely rolling. After going to East Lansing and defeating Michigan State 31–13 for the fifth straight victory in the series, the Wolverines traveled to Penn State and won their eighth straight against the Nittany Lions, 17–10.

Before their next game against Iowa at The Big House, the Wolverines had moved to the No. 2 spot in the rankings. Michigan had no trouble holding on to the position by disposing of Iowa, 20–6; Northwestern, 17–3; and Ball State, 34–26 before heading to Columbus for the dream match-up of No. 1 against No. 2.

I felt really proud to accept that Jug and give it to the players.

—Jon Falk

ABC-TV had hit the big lotto numbers. To the winner went a ticket to the National Championship Game. To the loser went a ticket to the Rose Bowl, along with inevitable thoughts of what could have been.

On the Saturday of the Ball State game, Bo was hospitalized to have a pacemaker placed into his chest. It was arranged to have a big screen TV put in his room for Bo to watch the Wolverines in their final tune-up for the Buckeyes.

After the game, Falk spent three hours watching an evening game with Bo.

"When I was leaving, he put his arm around me," Falk said. "I can't explain it, but there was a special feeling I'll always remember."

The showdown in Columbus was an instant classic with Ohio State holding on for a 42–39 victory. Any loss to Ohio State tastes like melted chocolate ice cream topped with a half bottle of vinegar.

But it didn't seem to matter. In fact, nothing about football mattered at the time. About 24 hours before the first kickoff, Bo died in Michigan—and nothing felt the same.

Chapter **67**

The Greatest Loss

The week before the Ohio State game was always the most precious time of the year for Bo. So many things to do. So many people depending on him. And so little time to get everything done.

He never thought about compromising such obligations. Not even in 2006 when probably only he understood the fatal implications of the moment. Only in hindsight do all the pieces fit together. But earlier in that week, a handful of incidents arose that concerned Falk even more than usual about the fragility of his longtime friend's health.

On that Monday, Falk was called by Bo's secretary, Mary Passink. She said Bo was feeling weak and asked him to drive Bo home. During the drive, they reminisced about old games, old plays, old players, and some good old-fashioned times they had shared. After pulling into the driveway of the condo, Falk jumped from the car and went to the passenger side to help Bo out.

"What are you doing to me?" Bo demanded.

"I'm helping you get into the house," Falk said.

"Get out of my way," Bo barked. "I can walk, you know. I have two legs."

Bo took one step, and his legs began to quiver. He looked at Falk with one of those "oh no" grimaces, then let Falk hold one arm as they walked through the garage. Once inside the kitchen, Bo turned around and started poking Falk in the ribs.

For the moment, Bo may have felt slightly challenged physically. But nothing could dent his sense of humor. "I know what you're doing to me, Falk," he teased. "I know exactly what you're doing to me."

Falk was puzzled. "What are you talking about, Bo?" he asked.

Bo resumed poking Falk's ribs. "If something happens to me tonight, you'll tell every S.O.B. tomorrow, 'Hey, I got him into the house. It wasn't my fault. He was okay when I left.'"

The two smiled, and then Falk left.

For Wednesday's practice, Falk provided a stool upon which Bo could rest. Falk and Bo were joined by Athletic Director Bill Martin and Administrator Ted Spencer. The three were spellbound by the stories Bo spun about his "10-year war" with the legendary Woody Hayes.

"Bo kept talking about Woody dying," Falk said.

Falk even returned to his office for a moment to print Woody's bio off the Internet. The bio contained a picture of Woody's gravestone.

Falk received a bigger jolt on Thursday when Bo arrived to give his customary talk to the team before the Ohio State game. The event took place in the team meeting room in Schembechler Hall. As soon as Bo walked through the door, Falk felt shivers throughout his body.

"Oh my God," Falk whispered to himself. "That's Woody. That is Woody Hayes."

Falk was convinced Bo looked just like Woody had the last time they had seen him in 1987. The affair at which Bo and Falk saw Woody was a dinner to honor Bo in Dayton, Ohio. Bo asked Falk to drive him, along with Bill Gunlock, who had also worked for Woody when he was young.

Woody's health was failing, and those closest to him knew his time to live was short. Nevertheless, the old coach forced himself out of bed. He dressed appropriately to bestow an honor upon his former student and long-time friend.

For him to come over and speak on my behalf is something I'll always remember.

—Bo Schembechler

Woody couldn't hide his condition. His voice was weak, and it was painful to watch such a dynamic personality struggle. On the drive back to Ann Arbor, Bo, Gunlock, and Falk shared concern over what they had seen.

"The Old Man didn't look good tonight," Gunlock said.

Bo was silent, deep in his own thoughts.

"My heart feels heavy for him tonight," Bo finally spoke. "For him to come over and speak on my behalf is something I'll always remember. I told him not to do it. I told him to stay home. He's given enough speeches for one man. But the son of a gun is stubborn. He was gonna do it anyway. Once he puts his mind to something, nothing is gonna change it."

Falk smiled and glanced at Bo.

"Sounds like someone I know," Falk said.

Three days after the event, Woody died. The loss was devastating to Ohio State, Bo, and the whole world of college football. Coaches like Woody come only once in any school's history.

So Falk was deeply concerned when Bo entered the room to address the team on Thursday. Bo had to dig deep, but his talk captured every person privileged to be in the room.

Weighing heavily on his mind was the passing of Tom Slade only two days before. Slade had been a Michigan quarterback and one of the toughest competitors ever to wear the winged helmet. Bo visited him each day to comfort Slade in his battle with cancer.

Bo told the team about how Slade and he discussed Saturday's Ohio State game. He told the players how much Slade was pulling for them. He reminded them of the great privilege it is to attend the university and have the opportunity to play in such an important game.

"Before Tom died, all he talked about was the University of Michigan and how important the football program was to him," Bo said. "That's how important it is to everyone. And I expect it to be that important to you."

Even to his final speech, Bo remained the master of motivation. He had the power to nudge a good team to greatness. His will could transform underachievers into champions.

Fittingly, the master saved his best for last.

After the meeting, Bo returned to his office. Strength coach Mike Gittleson and Falk visited him before leaving.

"Coach, that was your greatest speech," they both said. "There's nothing left to say."

Bo had a look of disbelief on his face.

"Are you two telling me the truth?" he asked.

"Bo, that was your greatest," they repeated.

On Friday morning as Falk and his crew were setting up the locker room in Columbus, Falk received a call from Mary Passink to tell him that Bo had fainted in the studio where he was preparing to tape his weekly TV show. Shortly afterward, she called back to say Bo had died.

Falk knew the first person he had to call was Joe Hayden, who had been Bo's roommate at Miami of Ohio and subsequently a good friend of Falk's. The three had traveled together, and Hayden attended each Michigan home game. At the time, he was in Florida.

"You just told me my brother died," Hayden said to Falk. "I'll be up there in a day."

It was difficult to make sense out of everything going on. The University of Michigan had just lost the foundation upon which the football program had been based for almost four decades. The state of Michigan had just lost one of its iconic personalities who actually transcended the world of sports. And Falk had just lost not only his former boss but also his best friend.

Falk had seen the end coming but certainly not the impact that shook the whole state.

News about Bo's passing circulated quickly in Ohio. Although Bo had coached hated Michigan, even Buckeye loyalists admired his honesty and loyalty that never wavered. Similar to their feelings for Woody, they simply thought Bo would always be around.

Falk still had to prepare for the big game because that's the way Bo would want it. Fans walking by the gate as Falk was unpacking equipment stopped to say, "We're sorry for your loss today."

"That goes to show you how much respect Michigan and Ohio State have for each other," Falk said. "Not one of them said anything bad."

After practice, a Detroit TV sportscaster was interviewing Falk near the gate where Ohio State fans were chanting for the Buckeyes and laughing about how Michigan was going to lose.

"You know, when I came to Michigan, I really wasn't convinced about making the move," Falk told the sportscaster. "At four o'clock in the morning, my mother woke me up and told me that I had to take the Michigan job. She said, 'I know that Coach Schembechler and the University of Michigan will take care of you.'"

That's when Falk lost his composure and had to step away from the microphone to dry his eyes.

Suddenly, a silence came from the taunting Ohio State fans from outside of the fence. They had been listening to what Falk was saying and somehow felt his loss. "Everybody realized how important and how big an event they were witnessing," Falk said.

A couple of years later, Falk read an article on Michigan State basketball coach Tom Izzo, who said he cried upon hearing of Bo's death. "He said he often watches a tape of the 10-year war between Woody and Bo," Falk said. "The respect he had for Bo is unbelievable. He admires a guy who came to Michigan and got a bunch of people to work together for a common goal of making Michigan even more successful than it already was. To gain such respect from men like that is unbelievable."

Bobby Knight was another basketball coach who cried upon hearing of Bo's death. "I called Bobby that Sunday morning," Falk said. "He told me he was going to write a speech that he wanted read at the tribute they were going to have for Bo in the stadium on Tuesday."

Knight said he would fax the speech to Falk as soon as he finished writing it.

"I want you to read it," Knight insisted.

Falk was hesitant to promise because the program was being organized by the athletic department. "You tell them you are reading this for me," Knight said. "That's it. If you don't read it, it doesn't get read at all."

Needless to say, Falk read the speech. Isn't it strange how coaches such as Bo, Woody, and Knight somehow always manage to get their points across?

Everyone still talks about Bo. He had risen to a level that even the finality of death fails to silence. Each succeeding coach has his own personality. But each carried on the tradition set by Bo.

"Brady Hoke will be the same way," Falk said. "He has a lot of Bo in him. He's a tough guy and is all business. Just give him a little time, and you'll see great things at Michigan. He's a good coach and a good man. And just like Bo, nothing matters more than the team."

Chapter **68**
Knight's Message to God

egendary basketball coach Bobby Knight was a longtime admirer and
friend of Bo. He still regards Falk as one of his best friends and insisted
that Falk read the following tribute at the public memorial held for Bo at The
Big House:

> During those last moments before eternal peace came to him, I'm
> sure Bo was thinking of all the people, family, and friends who
> had been close to him during his lifetime.
>
> Most of all, I'd bet he was thinking of Cathy who, for the last
> 13 years, has exposed him to places that he didn't even know
> existed. Yet during those last moments, I also believe he looked
> the Grim Reaper right in the eye and said, 'You son of a bitch,
> you've been trying to get me since that first operation in 1970 and
> I've beaten your ass for 36 years!'"
>
> I know that every player who has ever played for Bo, if asked
> what teacher in his educational experience had taught him the
> most about success in life…the answer, without exception, would
> be Bo.
>
> Now, I'd like to take just a moment to address the Almighty
> God.
>
> I don't know if You've met and talked to Bo yet or not, but I'm
> sure that in the short time he's been with You he has found that
> in some areas your people up there are throwing too many passes
> and not running enough, while in other places, there is some
> sloppy blocking and tackling going on. Now my advice, God,
> would be that You immediately put him in charge of heavenly
> organization and discipline. He's made things far better every-
> where he's been, and I know he'll do the same for You.
>
> One other thing now, God—don't even ask him a question
> that you don't want an honest answer to. He might seem a little

opinionated at first…just keep in mind that he's right one hell of a lot more than he's ever wrong.

Well, God, that's about it. We've sent You the best we've ever had. Listen to him, trust him completely, and don't try to change him. I've never seen a coach of any sport who was better than Bo. Nor have I ever had a friend that I cherished more.

Bobby Knight

Chapter 69
2007: A Fitting Farewell

O n New Year's Day 2008, the Citrus Bowl was merely moments away from its surprise ending. Falk was busy walking up and down the sideline telling players what they had to do. "When this is over, you guys pick up Coach Carr and carry him off the field," he instructed.

Michigan defeated seemingly invincible Florida 41–35 in an emotional upset that boldly painted a picture of a season that could have been. It was Carr's last game as the Michigan head coach, so it came to an accommodating end.

"We were proud for Michigan and proud for Lloyd to go out the way he should have gone out," Falk said. "He was a winner here. He was a good coach."

Carr finished his 13-year head coaching career with a 122–40 record and six bowl victories in 13 appearances.

Not long after the loss to Ohio State in November, Carr publicly announced his retirement. He confidentially confided in Falk immediately after the Ohio State game. The following week, Carr assembled the assistant coaches and entire staff to inform them of his decision.

"Lloyd cried," Falk said. "We all cried. It was reminiscent of when Bo stepped down. You think of all the good times that happened during all those years. Nobody knows their status when a head coach bows out."

Everyone sensed, however, that it was the end of an era—an era started by Bo and passed carefully to Gary Moeller then Lloyd Carr. "We knew an abrupt change was coming," Falk said. "It had to happen. It happens to everyone. Every school has to go through it."

So the upset of Florida was a fitting kiss good-bye. Before the game on the field, some of the Florida players started to taunt Michigan about getting ready for a blowout. A few shoves and pokes were used to emphasize their inflated confidence.

When Michigan returned to the locker room just before the game, Falk went around to each player to express precisely how he felt. "They have no respect for Michigan football," Falk kept repeating. "No respect at all. Let's go out and show them what Michigan football is all about. Let's see what they have to say after the game."

Florida got a taste of what Falk was saying. When the game was over, only Michigan was left to talk.

Chad Henne bade good-bye to his record-setting four-year tenure as the Michigan quarterback. He completed 25-of-39 passes for 373 yards and three touchdowns. His primary target was Adrian Arrington, who had career highs of nine receptions and 153 yards. He tied his personal high of two touchdown receptions. Florida Heisman Trophy winner Tim Tebow was held to 17 completions in 33 attempts for 154 yards. Mike Hart capped his four-year run by adding 129 rushing yards to his Michigan all-time leading total.

Florida's final attempt to win the game ended on its 23-yard line after four straight pass incompletions. Michigan was content to kill the remaining time.

"Injuries happen to all teams," Falk said. "But you couldn't help but wonder what might have been without Henne and Hart hurt for so much of the season."

As impressive as they looked in their final game, the Wolverines looked almost as lethargic in their season opener. No Division I team had ever lost to Appalachian State—at least not 'til the Mountaineers visited The Big House on that history-making Saturday.

Michigan didn't take a second-half lead 'til Hart electrified the crowd with a 54-yard touchdown run with 4:36 left. The Mountaineers re-claimed the lead on a 24-yard field goal with only 26 seconds left. Michigan drove to Appalachian State's 20-yard line, but Jason Gingell's game-winning field-goal attempt was blocked as time expired.

On Friday before their walk-through of the field, Falk went into the visitor's locker room to show the coaches around. After finishing, head coach Jerry Moore asked Falk if he could have a Michigan hat.

"Sure, Coach," Falk said. "I'll go get you one right now."

As Falk was leaving, Coach Moore asked if he could have a Michigan shirt.

"Yes sir, Coach," Falk said. "I'll get you one of those, too."

Walking into the visitor's locker room after the game, Falk was spotted by Coach Moore. He shook Falk's hand. "I want to thank you for the kindness you have shown me," Moore said. "I will never forget my experience at Michigan and the first-class treatment you gave to me and my team."

Falk understood the situation. Even though serving successfully as head coach for several years, playing in The Big House was a moment to remember—not only for the players but for every person in the Appalachian State program.

While the whole college football world treated the upset with the shock attached to Hurricane Katrina, Falk appeared to take the loss in proper perspective. "Was it heartbreaking?" he asked. "Yes. But most people never realized how many great athletes were on that Appalachian State team—disciplined and very quick."

Nonetheless, the loss to Appalachian State was embarrassing. The 39–7 dismantling by Oregon the following week was absolutely suffocating. A performance like that was not to be expected of a senior team.

Henne had to leave the Oregon game with a shoulder injury that lingered throughout the season. Against Notre Dame the following week, Ryan Mallett replaced him at quarterback, but it was a smothering defense that stifled the Irish 38–0. Notre Dame was limited to 79 yards of offense, while Michigan totaled 379.

With Henne and Mallett sharing time, Michigan followed with victories over Penn State, Northwestern, Eastern Michigan, and Purdue. They headed to Illinois at 5–2 for what Falk calls "the most gutsy quarterback play I have seen in my life."

"After the Purdue win, I said to Scott Draper standing next to me that I think we've finally gotten things straightened out," Falk said.

"Don't get too excited," Draper said. "Hart just hobbled off the field."

Hart was out for the Illinois game, and Henne was operating with his throwing shoulder hanging by a thread to go along with rib injuries. Henne had to go to the locker room for treatment during the second quarter.

When he returned in the third, he had trouble even raising his right arm on the sidelines. Arrington threw a touchdown pass to Mario Manningham in the fourth quarter on a trick play to break a 17–17 tie. K.C. Lopata added a 39-yard field goal for the 27–17 victory.

"Most courageous football game I have ever seen," Falk said, referring to Henne. "He was just like Rick Leach. That was another one."

Henne and Hart were out for the Minnesota game that Michigan won 34–10. Both returned for the game at Michigan State. Henne passed for four touchdowns, and Hart rushed 110 yards on just 15 carries. The winning score came on a Henne to Mario Manningham touchdown with 2:28 to play in a 28–24 victory.

As the final seconds ticked away, Falk approached Carr on the sidelines. "This is a great win for you today," Falk said.

"No, Jon," Carr responded. "This is a great win for Michigan."

After the locker room had cleared, Carr called Falk into his office before boarding the bus. He told Falk to have one of his "young boys" take a picture of the two together.

"I began to realize that this was probably gonna be Lloyd's last year," Falk said.

The game had been a classic.

"I don't think you can give enough accolades to Henne for what he did in four years," Falk said. "We always say that quarterbacks are judged on what they do against Ohio State. Did he beat Ohio State? No. But as far as I'm concerned, Chad Henne is one of the best quarterbacks ever to play for Michigan. No one will know how much he was hurting against Illinois and Michigan State."

Henne and Hart played at Wisconsin, but both were too hurt to perform as expected. "When I saw Henne's first pass, I said to myself, 'Oh no…he can't throw,'" Falk said. Wisconsin snapped Michigan's eight-game winning streak, 37–21.

After the 14–3 loss to Ohio State, Falk went to the visitor's locker room to congratulate coach Jim Tressel. "Is Lloyd retiring?" was the first thing Tressel asked Falk.

Falk knew the decision but was loyal to Carr. "You know what, Jim?" Falk said. "I'd rather have Lloyd tell you than me."

Tressel reflected for a moment. "People always ask me about Lloyd Carr," he said. "He's been the head football coach at Michigan for 13 years. Very successful for 13 years. Any man [who] can coach a team at the level of Michigan for 13 years…I take my hat off to him."

**Ten years at this level is
an eternity.**

—Jim Tressel

Falk smiled and shared a story with him that involved Bo. "Bo and I argued about coaches all the time," Falk said. "I told him there will never be another coach like you. There will never be another coach who can stay at this level for 20 years. Not with all the harpoons and criticism and degradation that happens at this level."

Tressel smiled. "You're right, Jon," he said. "Ten years at this level is an eternity."

Soon there would be another coach to make his mark at Michigan.

Chapter **70**
Butch Woolfolk:
Like Father, Like Son

Butch Woolfolk vividly recalls his first meeting with Falk upon arriving at Michigan from his home in Westfield, New Jersey, in 1978. Woolfolk asked for jersey No. 40, the number he had worn in high school.

"Nice number, son," Falk replied. "Here's No. 24. Now take it, and get outta here."

Woolfolk stands as Michigan's fifth all-time leading rusher with 3,861 yards. He came to appreciate the number he was assigned and values the lesson he learned. Within the Michigan football program—as in life—respect is earned, not merely handed out like another pair of socks.

He's a whole lot more like having an extra coach.

—Butch Woolfolk

"I didn't realize it at the time, but Jon was doing me a favor," Woolfolk said.

For that and countless other lessons he feels privileged to have learned, Woolfolk is ecstatic that his son, Troy, is now enjoying his own Michigan experience under the same equipment manager as did his father.

Falk is the only man left in the program since Woolfolk starred in The Big House. And echoing the sentiments of so many other former players, Woolfolk maintains that Falk far transcends his title of equipment manager. "He's a whole lot more like having an extra coach," Woolfolk said. "Because of [Falk's] enthusiasm and the way he interacts with the players, coaches think he's a player. He's able to walk that fine line between coaches and players that always must be maintained. More than anything, though, he's a friend."

Over the years, Woolfolk believes Falk has mellowed while still being able to maintain his passion for Michigan football. "He'll always be the person [who] coaches and players feel they're able to talk to," Woolfolk said. "He's serious about every game, every practice. But he knows how to make a person laugh. He wants the players to have some fun."

As a starting defensive back for the Wolverines, Troy is having the time of his life playing on the same field that his father dominated under Bo. Of course, with that situation, Woolfolk now appreciates some of the feelings that his parents experienced thirty years ago.

"As a defensive back, Troy is on the last line of defense," Woolfolk said. "I worry about a big play being made in his direction. And I always worry about him getting hurt. Every parent has to deal with that."

The first year Woolfolk arrived at Michigan, Falk nicknamed him "Pitchfork."

Although neither Woolfolk nor Falk can now explain the basis for the name, it certainly made the one Falk concocted for Troy easy. He's now known to Falk simply as "Young Pitchfork." Woolfolk admits he feels a sense of security in the fact that he and his son can share experiences with Falk.

When Troy arrived at Michigan, he told Falk he wore No. 10 in high school.

"Nice number, son," Falk said. "Here's No. 29. Now take it, and get outta here."

Some things never change.

Chapter **71**
Husband...Father...Friend

"**F**alk...I need Falk!" the unmistakable voice growled into the phone. Married to Jon since 1987, Cheri was as familiar with Bo's voice as she was with her son's or two daughters'. Phone calls at any hour, day or night, were as common as the Michigan Band playing "The Victors."

This time, though, the voice was filled with anxiety.

"Usually he would start with: 'Bo here, Cheri...I need to talk to Jon,'" she said.

No time for small talk on this occasion.

Bo and Cathy were relaxing on the patio behind their condo as a spring evening slipped into darkness. Deciding to go inside, Bo had trouble opening the sliding glass door. He yanked so hard that the golf club he used in the door's runner for security fell into the track to ensure there would be no entry.

Big problem and who else to call but Big Jon Falk.

Bo went to a neighbor's house to place the call. Falk kept a garage door opener for Bo and Cathy's home. He used it to collect mail and check the house when the Schembechlers were out of town. Living in Chelsea, about 15 miles west of Ann Arbor, Falk jumped into his car and was inside the house within a half-hour.

"Hey Bo," Falk taunted him from inside the living room. "What are you doing out there?"

As relieved as he was to see Falk's face, he was in no mood for joking. "Save the wisecracks and open this goddamn door," Bo barked. "When I get in there I'm gonna kill you."

When all three were inside, it was time to laugh.

"You always did have trouble with that nine iron," Falk cracked.

Cathy and Falk still smile at the memory.

On one occasion when Falk was picking up Bo at the airport, the flight was delayed for a couple of hours. Not so unusual except it was the evening Cheri and Jon were celebrating their anniversary.

"Jon told me he would be home about 6:00 PM," Cheri said. "He called around 8:00 and said he would be a little late."

Cheri now smiles at some of the comedy after coming to understand the peculiarities and responsibilities of her husband's position. "Especially with Bo," she said. "Jon was so close to him. It was more like a father-son relationship. They got even closer after Bo retired from coaching."

Cathy confirms the observation. "Jon was so loyal to Bo and me," she said. "He was our 'go to guy.' Whenever we needed something, we could always rely on him. He misses Bo as much as I do."

Mary Passink was also hired by Bo and kept his schedule orderly while also serving as the recruiting secretary. "Jon absolutely loved Bo," she said. "And Bo loved him. Jon is such a loyal person who can't say no to anyone. Without a doubt, he's my dearest friend."

Cheri's abrupt change in lifestyle, however, did require a few years of serious adjustment because despite having been born in Ann Arbor, she had never attended a Michigan football game. "I never cared for football," Cheri smiled. "When Jon and I met, and he told me what he did for a living, I told him that was nice, but I wasn't impressed by that."

Of course, now she goes to most of the games and enjoys the complete atmosphere. "It's one way to at least see Jon for a few hours once the season begins," she said.

During her first marriage, Cheri lived a traditional family lifestyle. The family ate dinner together, vacationed together, and did all the conventional things an average family does. Not once during his time on earth, however, has Falk been accused of being conventional.

"No one can truly appreciate the hours Jon puts into his job or all the responsibilities he has," Cheri said. "When something goes wrong, Jon's the man everyone calls on to fix it. He's an inherently generous person. He likes to take care of people. He may not know how to do everything, but he knows who to call. He always has a name of somebody who can do something. He's very resourceful."

Along with being resourceful, Falk has a sense for spontaneity. "Jon really has no hobbies," Cheri said. "We enjoy going up north to our cottage in Lewiston, Michigan, in the summer. He loves putting so much time into his job. Once the season is over, though, he's a very spontaneous person. If I suggest going somewhere, he's in the car before I'm out the door."

Cheri loves to dabble in antiques. When going to various shows, Jon wanders around the displays examining all of the items.

"He also loves to window shop at grocery stores," Cheri said. "He walks up and down all the aisles and gets to know all of the girls who work at the store."

Falk's adjustment to married life also has been rewarding. He accepted his role as stepfather to Cheri's son, Joe Winkle, daughter, Nicki—recently married to Kurt Pfefferle—and grandson, Joey. Katie was born in 1989 to the Falks and is a student at Eastern Michigan University.

Having a man like Falk around the house is as conventional as a tuna and jelly sandwich. But she's adjusted and smiles at the thought of never knowing what to expect beyond the loyalty to her, the family, and, of course, Michigan football.

"Jon's loyalty to the football program and the University of Michigan is the same as Bo's," Cathy Schembechler said.

What more can be said?

Chapter **72**
What Size Would You Like?

I
f only the items weren't all black, look basically the same, and didn't have cleats on the soles, imagine the thrill just one slice of Falk's job would be for any fashion-conscious female. How many women wouldn't leap at the chance, for just once in their lives, to order 2,000 pairs of shoes in a single sitting?

That's the normal off-season average Falk orders to equip about 125 players, along with the coaching staff, trainers, management, and student managers who work in equipment.

Every size from 8 to 17 is carefully stored and immediately available for quick switches during practice or a game when weather and field conditions dictate. Along with a pair of practice shoes, each player is provided one pair of shoes with a seven-stud cleat, one with a rubber sole, and another with a flat rubber sole for sticky field conditions.

"We have somewhere between 1,200 and 1,500 pairs of shoes always available," Falk said.

And that's just one aspect to Falk's role as haberdasher of the gridiron. There are helmets, shoulder pads, thigh boards, jerseys, pants, gloves, underclothing, socks, jocks, and a variety of incidentals that must be accounted for.

"We are definitely full service," Falk jokes. "Anything that a football player could possibly need."

Helmets and shoulder pads are of particular concern to each player. "No piece of equipment is as personal to a player as a helmet," Falk said. "He practices in it. He plays games in it. He's got to feel comfortable in it because it becomes part of him."

Only a handful of helmet companies exist in the country. Obviously, the famous winged design adorns the exterior, but each player is allowed to select the style of helmet he prefers.

"Whatever feels best," Falk said.

About 250 helmets of various sizes and styles are kept in stock. Each spring, Falk sends his supply of helmets to a pair of companies that apply the Michigan maize and blue colors to the yellow base. With the wing masked, navy is applied. With the navy masked, the maize is applied to the wing.

"It takes three maskings to make it right," Falk said.

During the season, after Thursday's practice, each helmet is collected for polishing with Future Floor Wax. "The standard joke is, 'Who's gonna give those helmets their future today?'" Falk said.

Leading the polish patrol early Saturday morning for home games is Herbie Fredericks. He has volunteered his time to Michigan football for 56 years. He also cleans helmets after practice on Thursdays before road games. Those helmets "get their future" from the student assistants early on Saturdays on the road.

Nicks and scratches are touched up with paint from assistant equipment manager Bob Bland.

"They have to look brand new for each home and road game," Falk said.

Bland is also the leader of the "wash patrol." After each practice, about 10 loads are fed into three commercial washers and dryers located in the equipment room of Schembechler Hall. Numbered underclothes are placed into loops that are returned fresh to each player the next day.

Uniforms are washed immediately after each home game. For road games, uniforms are gathered for packing into the belly of the plane and washed upon the team's return. Falk and his crew check each helmet on Sunday to repair or replace any damaged facemasks and to tighten each screw.

"The most fun I have with players is after a practice," Falk said. "That's when you really get to know the guys and get a chance to maybe help them a little."

Often he puts his arm around their shoulders in search of a flaw in the pads. He scours their faces for scratches or abrasions that perhaps he can prevent with adjustment to the helmet or chinstrap. He looks to ankles and feet to see if they are twisted or red—perhaps a different pair of shoes can help.

The best feeling in the world is when they feel better the day after you fixed a little problem.

—Jon Falk

"The best feeling in the world is when they feel better the day after you fixed a little problem," Falk said.

But it's not just the players that are Falk's responsibility. In addition to all of the uniforms and equipment, he is responsible for all of the coaching gear and apparel mandatory for each home and road game.

Every coach and working staff member of the team must wear a pair of Adidas shoes to be on the field. Coaches are dressed in Adidas slacks, shirts, jackets, and baseball hats. Adidas is the exclusive supplier for Michigan, and it's Falk's responsibility to see that exclusivity is enforced.

The head coach and Falk collaborate on design each September for the apparel that will be used the following September. "That's what makes it tough when ordering jerseys and pants," Falk said. "Especially for an incoming freshman class that isn't even determined."

To ensure a properly attired team, Falk has enlisted the services of seamstress Laura Sartori for the last 30 years. "About 60 guys on the team have personalized jerseys that fit them so there's no loose cloth around the shoulder pads," Falk explained. "We don't want them grabbed and taken down from the back."

Falk maintains a list of sizes for every member on the team. "I keep a list of sizes and a list of every piece of equipment that might be needed for any situation," he said. "You couldn't function today without a list for everything you do.

"I never envisioned this would get so big when I first started. It's grown so much. Much more corporate. Every game is televised, at least to some parts of the country. There's a lot of pressure to make sure all the uniforms are proper. I've gotten some calls on that. You have to make sure the decisions you make are politically correct for the company, for the university, and for the football team. You have to accommodate the players most of all."

It's all part of the job for Falk. Once a season begins, he's already planning for the next.

And wouldn't you like to make that shoe order just once?

Chapter **73**

Loaded Up and Ready to Go

Home or on the road, preparations for Saturday's game start Thursday evening for Falk and his crew. Bags are packed. Helmets are cleaned. Equipment is moved. Lists are checked. Then checked again. And once more, just to be sure. Before the team bus arrives at whichever stadium on Saturday, Falk's top priority must be complete.

"The locker room must be in order," Falk insists. "Everything there and everything ready. Nothing out of place. Each player and coach must feel confident when he walks up to his locker, there's nothing to think about except the game to be played."

It sounds so simple. But with all of the uniforms, equipment, and special needs of players, putting all the pieces together is like solving a jigsaw puzzle with mittens on your hands. "There's a flow to the locker room that must never be disrupted," Falk said. "Everyone should be concentrating solely on that game. Misplaced equipment is like fumbling away the ball."

Over the years, Falk has perfected the process. He humbly admits it doesn't require a genius. But having an equipment manager who is totally unforgiving with himself and the most passionate of Michigan faithful certainly helps.

As players enter the Schembechler Hall locker room after Thursday practice, they deposit helmets and shoulder pads into oversized rolling hampers for cleaning and adjustment. Falk then paces the aisles of the locker room, barking familiar commands that the upperclassmen have jokingly come to parrot.

"Black bag day, men, black bag day," he shouts when the upcoming game is at home. "Don't forget to pack your black bags. We're going to The Big House."

The bags, identified by a player's number, are black-laced net sacks in which players pack their thigh pads, knee pads, and any miscellaneous items they want in their locker for Saturday's game. The bags are placed into a hamper and rolled on to the truck that is filled with the rest of the equipment. After all equipment is loaded, the truck makes the short trip to Michigan Stadium where Falk and his crew prepare each locker for Saturday's game.

Spit-shined game shoes, collected after each game, also await each player in his locker. "If a player wants to wear his practice shoes for a game, that's fine," Falk said. "We discourage it, though. We like to have a few days to clean and polish all of them properly."

For a noon home game, Falk and his crew arrive at The Big House at 6:00 AM. So many things to do, and each assignment must be complete before the team steps off the bus.

"Nobody wants a problem on Saturday," Falk said. "We want the athletes to go to the locker room, put on their gear, and go out and play a football game. We want their minds clear. We want them to know they came to the stadium to win a football game."

Of course, there is one particular item that must rank high on Falk's list of priorities—the football. In fact, many footballs.

Falk has 12 game balls checked by the officiating team before each game. He also keeps 15 in a bag in the event of wet weather. After each game, the equipment crew collects the balls to prepare them for the following week.

"Once you break in a game ball, quarterbacks don't like to switch," Falk said. "They get a feel for them. Some balls make it through the whole season. Some don't. In a rain game, you lose most of them because you lose the tack on the balls. You have to start all over."

In addition to the game balls, there are 36 balls used only for pregame warm-ups. "At $43 a ball, that gets pretty expensive," Falk said.

It takes about an hour for the players to clear the locker room after the game. Players are required to turn in their helmets, shoulder pads, shoes, and laundry loops that contain all of their underclothing. After the truck is packed, assistants Bob Bland and Rick Brandt drive it back to Schembechler Hall where they and the student assistants unload.

Bland immediately soaks the uniforms to remove stains and sweat. After about an hour, he starts the washing and drying process. Sometime after 7:30, Falk and his crew are finally able to leave. They return by 9:00 AM Sunday to wash the laundry loops and put all of the uniforms in order.

The process for road games is similar but warrants a different starting command after Thursday's practice.

"Getaway day, men, getaway day," Falk shouts through the locker room. And again, the upperclassmen echo the command they have heard for a few years.

For road games, players pack their numbered travel bags with helmets, shoulder pads, thigh pads, knee pads, and various other necessities they wish to have waiting for them in their lockers when they arrive at the visiting locker room on Saturday.

The travel bags and road uniforms, along with all of the equipment and coaching uniforms, is somehow squeezed into the back of a semi that is appropriately painted in maize and blue, complete with logos.

The amount and variety of material that must be transported and returned for each road game is enough to supply a small village. Travel teams are comprised of 70 players and a full staff of coaches and various other team officials.

"When you play a road game, you have to be prepared for every situation, just like you are at home," Falk said. "That means warm-weather gear, cool-weather gear, jackets, capes, gloves, heaters, phones, tools, kicking net, practice balls, rain gear, extra shoes, jerseys, pants, pads…everything but the kitchen sink."

A must for every home and road game is an assortment of tights for players to wear under their pants to keep their legs warm in cold weather.

"Years ago, the joke around here before tights came on the scene was the Big Mama panty hose we used to buy at K-Mart," Falk said. "We used to buy about seven dozen for the boys. Nobody was laughing, though, when the temperature kept falling."

The equipment truck departs soon after it is packed on Thursday evening with Falk, Brandt, and three student assistants on board. Bland and a student assistant fly on the team plane Friday morning. By the time the team arrives, the locker room has been set up.

It better be.

The entire equipment staff returns to Ann Arbor on the team plane after the game. Laundry loops and uniforms are loaded into the belly of the plane and are washed immediately upon return. When the truck arrives at about 9:30 AM on Sunday, the rest of the postgame process resumes, and preparation for next Saturday's game begins.

"People don't understand the massive undertaking of game preparation and transportation," Falk said. "They show up for a game or turn it on TV, and everything looks like it did the previous week. And that's the way it should be.

"But it's so much bigger today. So much more corporate. It's a big business. I never envisioned all this when I first started. If it wasn't for the lists we keep, it would be impossible to function."

Following are lists used for each road game:

EQUIPMENT PACKED FOR GAMES

Hampers Packed

	HAMPER #1		HAMPER #3 & 4			HAMPER #6
1	HAMPER #1		HAMPER #3 & 4	1	Gloves
2	Cutter Gloves		Sideline Capes	2	Muff Pockets
3	Lineman Gloves		QB Coats	3	Hot Packs
	adidas gloves		Phone tarps	4	Head Gators
	scorch comp				HAMPER #7
4	reggie		Long Game Socks	1	Tights Each Player
	Assigned Gloves	1	Maxit Socks	2	Extra Tights
		2	Extra Maxit Socks	3	Gray Sweat Pants
	HAMPER #2	3	Game Socks		HAMPER #8
	Friday Sweats			1	White C/W tops
					Extra Sleeveless Under Jerseys

Shoe Trunks Packed

SHOE TRUNK #1	SHOE TRUNK #2	SHOE TRUNK #3
Game Shoes	Extra Grass Shoes	Detachables

Phones Packed

	PHONES		PRESS BOX PHONE AMP	2	FIELD PHONE AMP BOX
1	Phones Field Trunk	2	1). Ring Down Phone		Wireless Belt Packs (10)
	1). Cord Belt Packs		2). U.P.S.		Frequency Card
	2). Waist Belts		3). Belt Pack		
	3). Batteries "AA" 120		4). Switches		
	4). Field Cord		5). R.J. 14 Wires	3	PRESS PHONE HEADSETS
	5). U.P.S.		6). Extension Cords		1). Coaches Headsets
	6). Phone Lines		7). Amp cords		2). 4 binoculars
	7). Ring Down		8). 4 sets binoculars	4	EXTRA AMPS (1)
	8). R.J. 14 Wires				
	9). R.J. 14 X Wires			5	RING DOWN PHONES TRUNK
	10). Headsets				

	FIELD CART TRUNK #1		FIELD CART TRUNK #2		
1	Helmets	1	Sh. Pads	6	Cleat Cleaners
2	QB Hats	2	sideline boards	7	Hot packs
3	Tool kit	3	gloves	8	tape
		4	QB towels	9	pant pads
		5	Pant pads	10	tees
				11	Bench letters/diagram

EXTRA EQUIPMENT

1). Video Equipment	9). Wireless Phones	17). 2 power plates
2). Box of Footballs	10). 6 Fans-Hose & Pump Truck	18). 3 bikes
3). Kicking Net	11). Equipment Belt	19). 2 generators
4). Game Balls (8)	12). 2 Chalkboards	20). 1 weight room bag
5). Hotel Balls (3)	13). 4 Hampers	a. 2 extension cords
6). 12 Extra Game Balls	14). 6 Laundry barrels	b. Bands
7). 46 Practice Balls	15). 4 Big Hampers	c. Tarp
8). 8 Warm-Up Balls	16). 2 Red Flags	

10/19/2008

EQUIPMENT PACKED FOR GAMES

Equipment Trunks Packed

BOOK TRUNK #1		FLAT TRUNK #4		TRUNK #7
Drawer 1	1	Air Pump		70 Game Laundry Loops
Extra Kicking Tees L-R	2	Drill/Extra Bits		Travel Team
Red and Black wristbands	3	Cleats		**TRUNK #8 "M"**
Duct Tape - Double Tape	4	Helmet Tape		Extra Game Jerseys
Grease Board Pens and Sharpies	5	Wrenches /Tools		(1# of Each Travel Player)
Yellow Tape		a. screw driver (flat/phillips)		**SMALL TRUNK #9 - Extra Helmets**
Web Belts		b. wire cutter	1	VSR 4 M, L, XL
QB wristbands		c. channel locks	2	Pro Air II M, L
Pad locks and chains		d. t nut holders	3	Advantage M, L, XL
Drawer 2		e. scissors	4	IQ M, L, XL
Supporters with Cups		f. hole punch	5	XP M, L
Pant Laces		g. poker	6	DNA M, L, XL
Pad Laces	6	Lexol	7	Revo M, L, XL
Shoe Laces	7	Scrubbing Bubbles		
Skull Caps	8	Helmet stickers		
Drawer 3	9	Shoulder Pad Strapping		
Chin Strap	10	Ball Gauges		
Chin Strap Covers	11	Shoe Paint		
Shoulder pad tape	12	Helmet Paint/Brushes		
Drawer 4	13	Future Wax (Cleaner Dish)		**TRAVEL BAG**
	14	Steel Wool		70 Individual Travel Bags
Extra Hip Pads	15	Helmet Cleaner		GA/Support Staff Bags
Extra Thigh Pads	16	Helmet Pumps		
Extra Knee Pads	17	Ball Brushers		
Drawer 5	18	Dry Hands		**COACHES TRUNK #1**
Rib Pads	19	Belt Threaders	1	Shoes
Extra Face Mask	20	Riddell Quick Release Tool	2	Game Whites
ROPO DW, RJOP DW	21	Riddell Valve Pusher	3	Game Shirts
RJOP DW UB, ROPO DW UB	22	Belt Pullers	4	Game Slacks
EGOP	23	Riddell Backs, IQ Liners	5	Go Blue Sign
Revo G2BDR, G2BR, G2EGR, G3BI	24	AHI Backs/Fronts	6	Game Hats
DNA ROPO DW, RJOP DW	25	Adv. crowns, back, side, front	7	Dirty Laundry Bags (2)
	26	Revo Parts E, F, reg crown	8	Clip Boards
INNERSOLES	27	Chin Strap Buckles	9	Extra White
1 **BOOK TRUNK #2**	28	Hardware	10	Pens, Pencils, Markers
2 Gray Girdles	29	Riddell Valves	11	Clock
3 Jocks	30	Riddell Fronts (a,b, & c and pockets)		
4 Girdle L, XL, XXL	31	Chin Straps		**COACHES TRUNK #2**
5 Navy Mesh Shorts	32	Jaw Pads	1	Sweat Shirt
6 Adibody T-Shirts: XL & XXL	33	Extra bench letters	2	Extra Pants
7 Gray Shorts	34	Bottom is for extra misc.	3	Friday Sweats
8 Tight T-Shirts: XL & XXL	35	and extra kicking shoes	4	Pullovers
Full T-Shirts	36	velcro		
	37			**COACHES TRUNK #3**
		TRUNK #5	1	Cold Weather Gear
1 **TRUNK #3 (Big Flat Trunk)**	1	Extra Game Pants	2	Thermals
2 Wristbands		2 each size	3	Head Gators
3 Hand Towels			4	Cold Weather Masks
4 4 Dozen Socks		**TRUNK #6**		
5 2 Dozen Sanitary Hose		70 Travel Uniforms		**COACHES TRUNK #4**
6 4 Dozen Jocks		White Jerseys and Pants	1	Rain Suits
48 M - Armsleeves				

Left Side

Chapter **74**
So Many to Thank

Falk vividly remembers his drive home to Oxford, Ohio, after his first meeting with Bo in January 1974. He was riding with Bud Middaugh, the Miami of Ohio baseball coach, who later filled the same position for Michigan a few years later.

"You know, Jon," Middaugh advised the young Falk, "if you take the job at Michigan, you'll probably have it for the rest of your life."

Falk responded with a skeptical laugh. Thirty-eight years and five head football coaches later, Falk now smiles gratefully for having made the wisest career choice of his life. "I truly am the luckiest man ever to serve the University of Michigan," he still maintains today. "I always tell people, the name 'Michigan' will get you through a lot of doors. The secret is how you conduct yourself once you make it inside."

Obviously, Falk has done a masterful job. So many things continue to change, but Falk and his operation roll on and on.

"What helps is the love and support from Cheri, our kids, Joe, Nicki, Katie, and grandson Joey," Falk said. "When you work in a sports job like mine, the hours are long. There is no clock. That comes with the territory, and I appreciate their support.

"When we first met, Cheri knew nothing about Michigan football. She said she loves me for who I am, not for what I do."

Bo always preached that if a player or team only maintains its level of performance without moving forward, then the individual or team has failed. The same principle is applicable to every walk of life. And Falk certainly has never forgotten that valuable lesson instilled into him by his most trusted friend.

Since Falk's arrival in Ann Arbor while Bo was busy reshaping the essence of Michigan football, the game has undergone incredible change. The rules are still the same. So are the goals and purpose.

But major college football has morphed into the arena of major sports business. Media involvement has swelled exponentially. Sports marketing has expanded into an industry of its own. The stakes of each game have been raised to the limit of do-or-die Saturdays beginning with the first kickoff of the season.

With such monstrous financial commitments and often unrealistic fan expectations, the responsibilities surrounding the position of equipment manager are more staggering than the Sunday punch of Mike Tyson at the pinnacle of his career.

Wisely, Falk has maintained his footing in this tsunami of change that has reshaped the entire face of all professional and collegiate sports. And again Falk continues to employ one of Bo's basic tenets. "The team…the team…the team," Bo always explained his formula for excellence.

Simple as it sounds, it's the identical road map Falk uses to maintain the standards that he established when he arrived in Ann Arbor 38 years ago. When Falk arrived, he received the generous insight of full-timers Bob Hurst and Irv Arnold and part-timers Jim and son Denny Morgan. Herb Frederick, who dates back to Tom Harmon, still polishes the helmets today.

For all the assistants and volunteers who have served during the last four decades, Falk feels truly blessed. These include Ed Whited, Brian Hagens, Mark Payne, Ron Dunn, Danny Siermine, Lee Taggart, and John Daggett.

As the responsibilities continued to grow, so did the position of full-time assistants. Falk feels particularly proud of the three that now serve. Bob Bland joined the staff in 1987 after serving as equipment manager at Otterbein. The two met the night before the Ohio State game in Columbus in 1986. Falk asked if Bland was interested in the position, and neither regret the decision each made.

"Bob is what you call a real pro," Falk said. "I never worry about any assignment given to him."

Rick Brandt came to Michigan in 1997 after serving as an assistant at Illinois. Falk received a strong endorsement of Brandt from Illinois equipment manager Andy Dixon, one of Falk's longtime friends. "I flew Rick up and offered him the job," Falk said. "He immediately accepted, and that was it. Interviews are short around here."

Brett McGiness was looking for a job after serving as a student assistant at Central Michigan. Falk arranged to land him a graduate assistant position at Michigan. Three years later, he was able to convince Lloyd Carr that a third full-time assistant was needed, and McGiness got the job.

Student assistants are called the "young boys," and that staff has grown to eight. They get paid hourly for doing everything from laundry to serving as ball boys on Saturdays. But the experience they gain can't be measured in dollars and cents.

"It really is gratifying to watch these 'young boys' grow into their careers," Falk said. "Over the years, we've had so many good ones. Half of them go on to become doctors and lawyers."

Some of the kids ask to return for a day. "They want to be a 'young boy' one more time," Falk smiled. "They want to be on the sidelines for just one more game."

Over the years, Falk has engendered immeasurable support from the entire football staff. All the coaches, trainers, staff, and secretaries have made Falk's job easier. From Don Canham through all the athletic directors to Dave Brandon, Falk has established mutual respect.

"I have to deal closely with the trainers," Falk said. "Lindsey McLean, Russ Miller, and now Paul Schmidt were the best in the business," Falk said. "The same for Jay Colville and Ken Wolfert of Miami of Ohio."

Of particular pride for Falk is his history with the Athletic Equipment Managers Association (AEMA). With a handful of managers in 1973, Falk was one of the founders of the organization that established credibility and stature for the position. The organization has grown to more than 900 members. In 1986, Falk was named executive director and just this year stepped down from the position. In 2001, he won the Equipment Manager of the Year Award.

AEMA has demonstrated to all in sports that equipment managers are far more instrumental in the success of their teams than simply distributing equipment and collecting dirty towels.

"The organization has helped to enhance relationships throughout the country," he said. "I can pick up the phone and talk to an equipment manager at any school and know we are on the same page. We help each other before every game. Win or lose, a game only lasts 3½ hours. Friends last a lifetime."

Falk never forgets the support of family and friends early in life that was the cornerstone of the success he enjoys today. Among the many are mother Jean, grandmother Rosella Land, grandfather John Land, and sister Ann, who also graduated from Miami of Ohio and was part of the cheerleading squad. Ironically, Ann is married to Mike Bell, who served as a "young boy" student assistant to the football team at Miami of Ohio.

Win or lose, a game only lasts 3½ hours. Friends last a lifetime.
—Jon Falk

Cheri has come to understand that there is no clock for a job in major college football. The hours are long and unforgiving. In turn, Cheri's support stands without measure.

The training and support he received from all of the coaches, staff, and teachers at Talawanda High School laid the foundation for Falk's endless run at Michigan.

The string of coaches and athletic administrators from whom Falk learned will always be appreciated. They include Connie Inman, Gary Stewart, Bob Denari, Clark Froning, Dick Schrider, Wayne Gibson, Darrell Hedric, and Tates Locke.

"So many have contributed to help me succeed in life," Falk said.

As Falk looks back at the last four decades, he can't help but reflect on his baptism into his profession. He remembers the spontaneous guidance he received from Talawanda High School football coach Marvin Wilhelm.

Falk lived across the street from the school. As a freshman, he watched the football team practicing. He managed enough courage to approach Coach Wilhelm and say he didn't want to play football, but wanted to help by serving as a manager.

"What does the manager do, coach?" Falk asked.

The coach eyed him carefully.

"He does what the head coach tells him to do," Wilhelm said.

Falk said he could handle that.

"Things haven't changed in the last 41 years," Falk smiled. "You still do what the head coach says."

Falk just does it with a flair that's impossible to match—the way it should be for the University of Michigan.

Chapter **75**
Bowling with Falk

The Rose Bowl has long been referred to as the "Granddaddy of all bowl games."

And Falk enjoys the same distinction for Michigan men who have been privileged to participate. Among the 34 bowl games in which he has served Michigan, 14 have been played on New Year's Day in Pasadena.

"When I was a kid I thought the greatest thing in the world was going to one Rose Bowl," Falk said. "I never take for granted how fortunate I've been."

In those 14 games, Michigan has a 4–10 record. The last victory was particularly special since the 21–16 victory over Washington State capped the national championship for the 1997 season.

Falk has been to 20 other bowl games with Michigan, and his teams have an overall record of 14–20. While serving at Miami of Ohio, Miami defeated Florida in the 1973 Tangerine Bowl.

The Michigan "bowlometer" reads:

Orange	1976, 00	1–1
Rose	1977, 78, 79, 81, 83, 87, 89, 90, 92, 93, 98, 04, 05, 07	4–10
Gator	1979, 91, 10	1–2
Bluebonnet	1981	1–0
Sugar	1984	0–1

Holiday	1984, 94	1–1
Fiesta	1986	1–0
Hall of Fame/Outback	1988, 94, 97, 03	3–1
Alamo	1995, 05	0–2
Citrus	1999, 01, 02, 08	3–1

Jon and Cheri Falk.

Epilogue: Damon Would Have Loved Him

One day the time will come when Jon Falk won't be in the Michigan locker room barking orders, spinning yarns, solving a problem no one else can handle, or simply making a player or coach smile when it's needed most.

When that day arrives, the transition will be seamless, and the program will continue to be successful, because as Falk has learned so well...no coach, no player, no staff member is bigger than the team.

No one, though, in the Michigan football program wants to think about that day.

Each major college football team employs a valuable equipment manager. But only Michigan enjoys a character who seems to have stepped out of a Damon Runyon classic. Runyon was the post-Prohibition era sports writer turned novelist who carved his niche into American literature. His creation of mischievous misfits, such as those who appear in *Guys and Dolls*, reshaped the face of Broadway. Always a couple of steps outside the mainstream, Runyon's characters are street smart and hopelessly generous. They bring smiles to each person they touch.

The meretricious exteriors of Runyon scoundrels are designed to mask the kindness, concern, and honesty that lie beneath the surface. They make sense out of a complicated world by relying on common sense, intuition, honesty, and above all commitment to loyalty.

That's Jon Falk.

There's nothing romantic about laundering and distributing enough socks, jocks, towels, and T-shirts to serve a whole fleet of sailors for almost 40 years. It's the magic Falk brings beyond the job description that Runyon would have loved.

259

To players and coaches, he can be Dr. Phil or Father Flanagan. He can spin a story like legendary Oklahoma humorist Will Rogers, and he's an incurable cheerleader during good times and bad.

Need a piece of vital player equipment fixed before the next play...call Jon Falk. Need a telephone line from a coach's field phone to the pressbox repaired before the next series of downs...call Jon Falk. Need to phone a high profile celebrity in any sport...call Jon Falk. If he doesn't already have the number in his book, odds are he knows someone who does.

He's the classic jack of all trades and Bo always insisted that "having Jon Falk as equipment manager is like having an extra coach."

In the one game of football Falk played in his life, the tip of his nose protruded into his earlobe following an errant step by an opponent. That one misstep convinced Falk he had a whole lot more to contribute from outside the chalk lines.

The Xs and Os of football never meant much to Falk. He taught himself to appreciate the composition of coaches and the intricacies of players competing at the highest level. Falk calls himself an "intuitionist." He studies, reads, and interprets even the simplest actions of those surrounding him. And his conclusions are almost always dead-eye perfect.

It's a gift that has rewarded him with friends and confidantes across the country. There was no greater confidante than Falk for Bo, who trusted Falk with almost every professional and personal secret.

"When I first came to Michigan, Bo said my job was simple," Falk says. "Take care of all the equipment and do everything in your power to help Michigan win championships." Falk made Bo proud. And he keeps on doing it with the same vigor he displayed during his first day in Ann Arbor.

"M Men" are proud of their tradition. They're proud of the teams they played for and the institution they represent. Although Falk never played for the team or took a step into a Michigan classroom, those "M Men" honored their friend by making Falk an honorary "M Man."

It's the most treasured professional honor that Falk has ever received. The friendships he has made and the stories he has accumulated are enough to fill two lifetimes. Thanks, Jon, for sharing some with us.

— *Dan Ewald*